Fantastic Fit for Every Body

Fantastic Fit for Every Body

How to Alter Patterns to Flatter Any Figure

GALE GRIGG HAZEN

Rodale Press, Inc.
Emmaus, Pennsylvania

To all of the sewers who understand that I would much rather talk than write but who have nagged, begged, and otherwise insisted that I put my fit method in book form.

OUR PURPOSE

"We inspire and enable people to improve their lives and the world around them."

Library of Congress Cataloging-in-Publication Data

Hazen, Gale Grigg.
    Fantastic fit for every body : how to alter patterns to flatter any figure / Gale Grigg Hazen.
        p.   cm.
    Includes bibliographical references (p.   ) and index.
    ISBN 0–87596–792–2 (hardcover : alk. paper)
    1. Dressmaking—Pattern design.   2. Clothing and dress measurements.   I. Title.
TT520.H3 1998
646.4'08—dc21   97-33932

Distributed in the book trade by St. Martin's Press

2 4 6 8 10 9 7 5 3 1   hardcover

Editor: Marya Kissinger Amig
Cover and Interior Book Designer:
  Marta Mitchell Strait
Layout Designer: Susan P. Eugster
Interior Illustrators: Glee Barre, Mary Smith
Interior Photographers: John Hamel, except
  for pp. vi and vii by Kurt Wilson
Cover Photographers: John Hamel,
  Kurt Wilson
Photographer's Assistant: John Grivas
Hair and Makeup: Gena Alvernaz
Photography Editor: James A. Gallucci
Copy Editors: Nancy N. Bailey, Patricia Sinnott
Manufacturing Coordinator: Patrick T. Smith
Digital Imaging Manager: Francis Moninghoff
Indexer: Nan N. Badgett
Editorial Assistance: Nancy E. Fawley,
  Jodi Guiducci, Lissette Santana, Lori Schaffer

RODALE HOME AND GARDEN BOOKS
Vice President and Editorial Director:
  Margaret J. Lydic
Managing Editor, Sewing Books:
  Cheryl Winters-Tetreau
Director of Design and Production: Michael Ward
Associate Art Director: Patricia Field
Production Manager: Robert V. Anderson Jr.
Studio Manager: Leslie M. Keefe
Copy Director: Dolores Plikaitis
Book Manufacturing Director: Helen Clogston
Office Manager: Karen Earl-Braymer

We're happy to hear from you.

For questions or comments concerning the editorial content of this book, please write to:

  Rodale Press, Inc.
  Book Readers' Service
  33 East Minor Street
  Emmaus, PA 18098

For more information about Rodale Press and the books and magazines we publish, visit our World Wide Web site at:
      http://www.rodalepress.com

Contents

Author Profile

Gale Grigg Hazen, who has the heart of a teacher and the soul of a stand-up comedienne, is a nationally known sewing, fitting, and machine expert. She knows what it's like to sew for a less-than-perfect figure, as she is not very tall and has a full bust and torso and thin legs. She is 5 feet 4 inches tall and wears a size 24—definitely above the industry's average—yet her clothes fit and she feels and looks great in them.

Gale lectures to numerous sewing conventions and groups across the country. She also gives speeches on motivation, positive assertiveness, and entrepreneurial skills for women's groups. Each year her appearances, which are entertaining as well as educational, draw standing-room-only crowds.

Gale is the author of *Sew Sane* and *Owner's Guide to Sewing Machines, Sergers, and Knitting Machines* and has contributed to several other books, including *The ABCs of Serging*. She also has had numerous articles published in *Threads* and *Sew News* magazines.

A Certified Color and Image Consultant, Gale started her career in the sewing industry by working at a sewing machine dealership, teaching classes and selling and repairing machines. She opened her sewing school—The Sewing Place—over a decade ago. In January 1995 Gale noticed a decline in the availability of good-quality fashion fabric for the home sewer. She and her partner, Dale Cunningham, decided to expand The Sewing Place to include unique, quality fashion fabric, buttons, and sewing supplies. The store has a World Wide Web site at http://www.thesewingplace.com.

Gale has produced her own line of patterns under the label Patterns for EveryBODY. The patterns are The Perfect Knit Top, The Loretta Coat, and The Gored and Tiered Skirt. She is currently working on a vest pattern and plans to continue expanding the line.

Introduction

As a sewer, you want to make great clothing that fits your body perfectly. So why do you have so much trouble getting a commercial pattern to fit you?

Each of us is a unique individual with a uniquely shaped body, and you must learn how you are built before you can make changes to your patterns that will actually work.

This is not an average book on fitting. I give you the tools you need to figure out what will work on your body shape. I don't give you rules that sound great but rarely work.

I teach classes every week, and my students have found consistent success using this fitting process. You will learn how to evaluate all of the variables that go into creating a garment—patterns, fabrics, and ease.

I will lead you through the process of evaluating your body shape and learning how that shape affects garments you make. Plus, you'll get additional tips and techniques for making decisions that will lead to greater satisfaction when sewing.

Part of the focus of this book is a celebration of women's bodies and spirits. The women pictured in this book are real women like you and me. They are my students, not models, and they are not professional seamstresses.

Each of these women has had problems getting her garments to fit. For the chapter "Make It Fit," they agreed to make two garments of the same fabric—one according to the pattern's instructions and one specially altered to fit their body using my methods. They learned and used my methods and have been extremely satisfied with their results. I'm sure you will agree that these women did a fabulous job.

I also asked them to help me describe and illustrate the various shapes and sizes of the human form by having their photographs taken while they were wearing leotards. Again, they all agreed to help me.

Each has a unique body form, and although they are all different, they are all spectacular, marvelous, wonderful, and perfect just as they are. Size, weight, age—none of these should be a value judgment of who you are as a human being.

I hope with time and effort you, too, will be able to appreciate your own body. The women in this book were willing to share themselves and their sewing so that you will be able make well-fitting clothing that flatters your unique body shape.

If you are looking for a book that will give you a single explanation on how to alter your garments, this is not the book for you. My method takes a bit of time to learn, but in the long run you will become a more successful and confident sewer, and the clothes you sew will fit and flatter you.

Happy sewing!

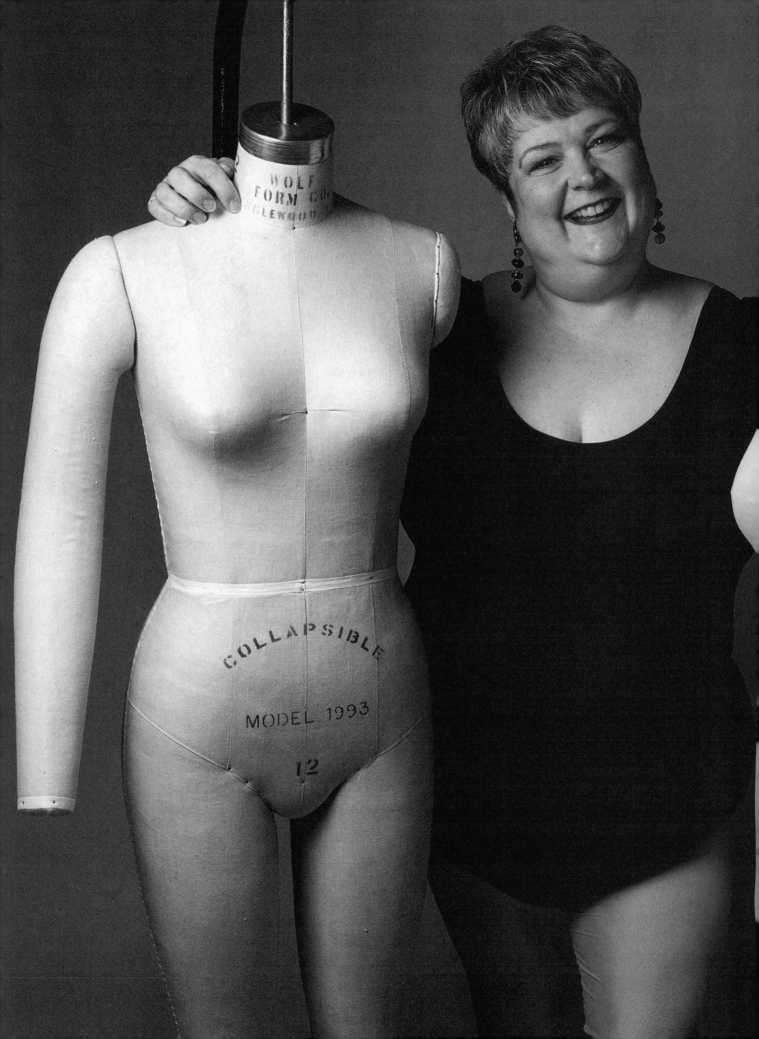

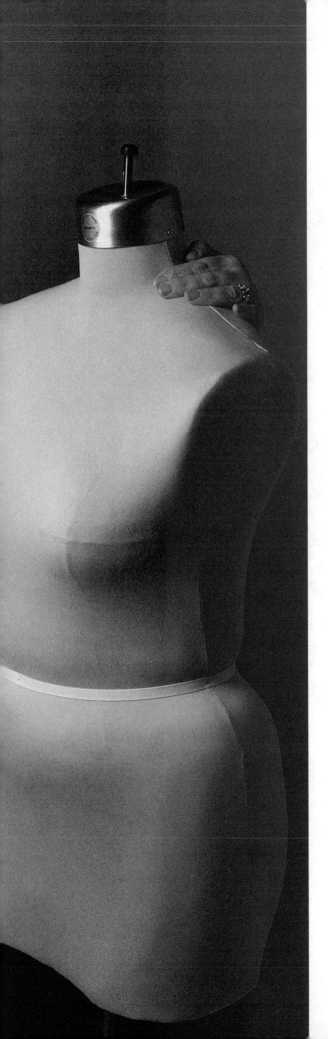

Fit Defined

Do you have trouble finding patterns to fit your body? Perhaps you don't look like what the pattern makers consider "normal." The dress forms on either side of me are both size 12. The pattern makers use the Wolf dress form, on the left, as their standard for sizing even though independent research has found that most women size 12 are shaped like the Gold dress form on the right. But whether you are shaped more like the Wolf form or the Gold form, my fitting method will allow you to make great clothing that fits every time.

Dorothy *has a small bust, a shallow upper chest, and very small arms.*

Cheryle, *my computer guru, has a body that is as deep as it is wide.*

Beverly *has a small upper chest but a very broad back.*

Cindy *is small through the torso but wears a DD-cup bra and is long-waisted.*

Because **Mary Ellen's** *upper torso is longer in the back than the front, her blouses slide down her back and hike up in the front.*

Peggy *has a shallow upper chest and small shoulders.*

Look Your Best

You are about to embark on a journey toward understanding your body, which will allow you to create garments that fit you the way you want every time.

Because her fanny is shallow and flat, *Karlene* has to remove the excess fabric in that area.

Millie is 5 feet, 1 inch tall, and the bust and waist areas on commercial patterns do not line up on her body.

Cynthia is 6 feet tall, and commercial patterns are too short for her body.

Dale, at 5 feet tall, has a small tummy and hip fluff.

You can see by their self-confidence that these women love themselves and the way they look.

A garment that fits is a garment that looks great. It hangs correctly on your body, isn't too tight or too loose, stays in place as you wear it, and always feels and looks great.

Fit is a combination of preference, comfort, and figure enhancement. What the individual is accustomed to wearing frequently plays a larger part in her fit preferences than what actually flatters her body.

Perhaps you have been shopping with a friend, and she tried on an outfit that skimmed over a part of her body that was not well proportioned. You recognized that it looked better on her than

"Create clothing that allows you to radiate a positive attitude."

most of her own clothes. It was more flattering and hung better, but she felt the outfit was too big. In pant classes, I have discovered that a student who consistently wears Levi's or tight-fitting stretch pants will be uncomfortable in a pair of flowing trousers even though the trousers actually look marvelous.

You may like a traditional, close-fitting garment, you may like to have a little room to move inside your clothing, or you may prefer a very loose, full garment. No matter what you like, I want to help you create clothing that is comfortable as well as flattering, that suits your lifestyle, and that expresses your personality. I want to help you create clothing that allows you to radiate a positive attitude and looks great no matter what your age or size.

Look at Your Body Honestly

The first—and the most important—part of the fitting process is to look at your body thoroughly and honestly. Although you will look at the different parts of your body one at a time, you must also take time to appraise your body as a whole. Much of the information you have read about fit is explained one part of the

body at a time. For example, if you have wide shoulders, do this; if you have narrow hips, do that; if you have wide hips, do this. But if your body combines an exceptionally narrow waist with even slightly wide hips, the problem will seem extreme.

To achieve a great fit, you must see and understand your entire body, and when you do look at your body, speak positively about it. Rather than expressing a negative "I have big hips," say "I have an extra-small waist."

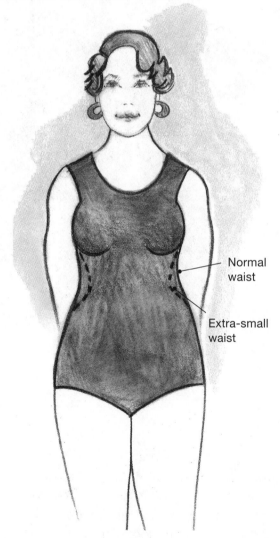

Normal waist

Extra-small waist

If this woman had a smaller waistline, it would make her hips appear larger than they really are.

Looking Good
See the Contours

Our bodies are three-dimensional, and it's this three-dimensional puzzle that creates confusion in the fitting process. We are looking at humans who are round and patterns that are flat. It is almost impossible for us to look at a flat pattern and decide how it is going to fit our bodies. Looking at your own body shape and translating that shape into how your body differs from the flat pattern will help you learn how to make accurate pattern adjustments.

Patterns are similar to maps. When early mapmakers flattened the globe to create a map, they ended up distorting the land masses at the top and the bottom of Earth. In 1923, J. Paul Goode developed his interrupted projection map, which reduces the distortion of the land masses. Although it is a flattened map of Earth, it lets us view the true shape of the nations of the world with no distortion.

A well-fitting garment pattern is like Goode's projection map because it mimics the contours of your body. It has darts and tucks and seams that are used to make the flat fabric conform to the curves of your body. Thus, to create a well-fitting pattern, you must be able to see all of the contours of your body.

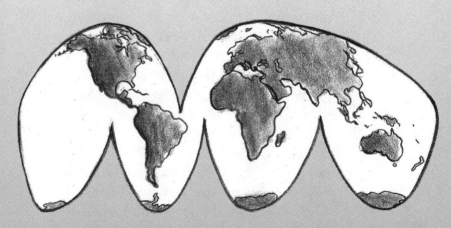

Goode's projection map is really a globe that has been sliced to make it lie flat. To reassemble it, we would have to "stitch together" the "darts" between the sections of the map.

More Tools, Fewer Rules

There are many techniques for adding or subtracting inches when altering a pattern, but they always leave out the individual shape of the human body. Your body is unique, so the changes that you make to any pattern also must be unique.

In the past, you followed the rules for altering patterns and fitting garments but probably failed. Rules are always made to be broken, and that includes the rules of fit.

Wit & Wisdom

Using big flat pattern pieces on a round human body is about as useful as trying to wallpaper a beach ball. All the edges of the paper will hang out at odd angles. These edges of the paper are like the wrinkles and folds of excess fabric on a garment that is not fitted properly to your body shape.

I believe you can build anything—including an incredible, well-fitting wardrobe—if you are given the right tools. Consequently, *Fantastic Fit for Every Body* will give you lots of tools and very few rules.

However, to succeed in creating a garment that fits you the way you want it to fit, you must take the time to work your way through each chapter of this book. Try all the processes and give yourself permission to experiment. You will learn where your body needs more or less fabric so that your garments hang correctly and complement your figure and style. You will learn why fabric type makes a big difference in the fit of a garment. You will learn innovative solutions to many typical fitting problems, and then you will begin to make clothes that you love.

Individual sewers describe fit in a variety of ways. A sewer's fitting goal can be as simple as hoping that her jacket goes around her body and does not cut off her circulation, or it can be a very specific and precise goal of creating a form-fitting garment that has no wrinkles.

The Pattern Standard versus Reality

When I lecture on fit, I ask the members of the audience to look at the person sitting on their left and their right. I then ask the audience to tell me which person's body the pattern companies should use as a guide when drafting patterns. Of course, the audience members always say, "But patterns should be made for me, not them."

Fit is an individual preference, and there is no way the pattern companies can meet the needs of every person. Instead, pattern manufacturers adhere to a set of industry standards that dictate the "average" measurements for a particular size. But you are more than just the measurements at your bust, waist, hips, and back length. You are contours and shapes. You will be most successful in your garment fitting if you know how your body differs from the commercial pattern industry standards.

Are Patterns Made for You...or Me?

Your sister-in-law is 8 inches taller than you and very long through the torso. Your best friend is short and bouncy with a very full bust and an almost equally full tummy. Your close friend has a very tiny upper torso, very small shoulders, and a very small waist and yet blossoms into full hips and a bottom. You can line up a row of women with identical measurements and yet they would look completely different, as shown.

All of these women need clothing that fits and flatters their figures, but not a single pattern or even a single pattern company could give each person exactly what she needs.

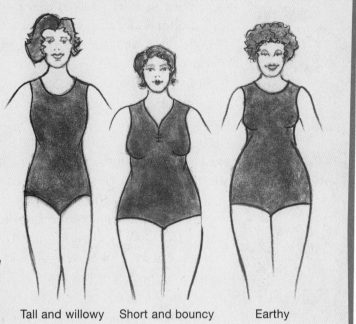

Tall and willowy   Short and bouncy   Earthy

Don't Sew Blindfolded

Most sewers begin working on a garment with optimism and hope. They assume their creation will resemble the pattern company's fantasy fashion illustration or photo, and they try to work their way through the construction process. Actually, they are sewing blindfolded.

About three-quarters of the way through the stitching process, it is time to try on the garment. That's when sewers take off the blindfolds and the bubble bursts. Then they begin the tedious job of trying to make the garment fit.

I like to call these garments "wadders" because you wad them up and put them in a bag in the closet until you are ready to give them to Goodwill. Instead of creating wadders, we're going to look at your actual body shape and how it goes in, out, and around. We'll compare your body shape with what the pattern company uses as *its* ideal body and how *it* goes in, out, and around. Once we develop a clearer idea of where your body differs from the industry standard, we can determine where you will need more length and/or width on a pattern to create a good fit.

Many sewers assume the garment they are making will resemble the photo or fashion illustration on the pattern envelope, but, actually, they are sewing blindfolded.

All Women Are Not Created a Size 12

Clothing manufacturers traditionally use a standard size 12 Wolf dress form as their model. But none of us is built like each other or like the perfect body form. That's why we can't just walk into a store, pick up a garment in our typical size, and purchase it without trying it on.

The same is true for patterns. When you select a pattern, you try to decide how a particular design is going to fit your body. In your mind, you picture the way you want the finished garment to look. But that is complicated by the designer's idea of how it should look and hang on his or her fit model. Most

Have you ever wondered why you just can't walk into a store, pick up a garment in your typical size, and purchase it without trying it on? It's because none of us is built just like the perfect Wolf dress form.

often your body shape and the fit model's body shape are not the same. Meanwhile, you may have already selected a fabric, which creates additional complications, which I address in the chapter "From Fabric to Fit" on page 60.

The size pattern you select will be influenced by all of these factors. Plus, you may choose to use different sizes, depending on the combination of garment style and fabric type. This is one of the reasons that multisize patterns are so useful, since most of us are not just one size.

Also, you do not remain one size all of your life. As you grow from a child to a teenager to an adult, you grow taller. You live many years, and then you get shorter late in life. Our bodies also change when we have children, when we change jobs or lifestyles, and with the onset of menopause. That is why it is important to retake your measurements and complete the other fitting exercises in this book every few years.

FIT AND STYLE

Part of the process of getting a good fit is choosing the correct styles for you as an individual. Good styles are clothes that you want to wear, are comfortable, fit your lifestyle, and have opportunities for fit so that they hang correctly on your body.

You also must take into consideration your fabric preferences, whether or not you want to dry-clean or launder garments,

what kind of upkeep your lifestyle requires, what kind of clothing you require at home and/or on the job, and what outside interests you have.

All of these factors in combination with how you discover your body shape will help you make accurate pattern, fabric, and alteration choices for great clothes that will fit the way you want them to fit.

Child   Teen   Adult   Senior

Our bodies start changing when we are children, and that change continues throughout our life. That is why I would like you to retake your measurements and complete the other fitting exercises in this book every few years.

Each item of clothing you make is a prototype. The combination of your figure, the pattern, and the fabric is different each time you begin a project, and every time you begin a new garment, you have to solve the many layers of the fitting puzzle. If you work through the process of assessing your body and determining how it differs from pattern industry standards, you will sew accurately and successfully every time.

Individual Fit

A garment that fits well creates an illusion that your body is symmetrical and well proportioned—you can just grab a jacket, a coat, a blouse, or a pair of pants, throw it on, and it fits. If your arms are longer or shorter, if you're taller, thinner, wider, or straight up and down, if you have more bust or less bust than the traditional body form, those changes must be translated into the pattern so that the garment will fit.

Good fit does not require a great body. What you want to do is enhance the body you have. People usually see you from a distance of at least 5 feet. They see your overall body outline and how your clothes hang. It is important for you to see yourself like this—just as others do.

Looking Good

Getting a Custom Fit

The difference between a jacket that costs $75 and one that costs $2,500 depends on whether the jacket is custom-made to fit your body. Most sewers believe the term *couture* means that things have to be done the hard way. In truth, the word translates from French into "made for the individual." Couture garments are custom-made for a person, taking into consideration the person's individual body. If you were a customer of a high-fashion couture house, your custom body form would be stored in the back room. The designers would use that body form in the early stages of fitting a garment for you. Thus, a woman who looks fabulous in her clothes looks that way because the garment has been custom-fit to her individual body shape.

Although this vest may look great on your body, the enlarged back causes wrinkles at the neckline and under the arms when the garment is hung on a clothes hanger.

Hanger Appeal

Manufacturers and designers want to make sure their garments look good on the clothes hanger so the garments look attractive hanging in the store. What's more important to you is that a garment looks good on your body. You must begin to separate "hanger appeal" from body appeal.

There are many things that I'll talk about throughout this book that may go against everything that you have ever learned. When a garment fits your body, it may hang funny when it's placed on a clothes hanger. It may be because you have added more fabric to the back length or because you have added more fabric for a very full upper shoulder. Hanger appeal is important to the ready-to-wear market, but it is not important for those of us with less-than-perfect figures.

Every human being has a different body. No body is right or wrong, or good or bad. It's simply that we are all different. Prior to the 1930s, women didn't judge themselves as harshly as they do now. A woman would go to a dressmaker, whose job it was to make clothing that fit her. The dressmaker's skill and talent created a dress that enhanced a woman's body.

With ready-to-wear came the "average" size. Garment manufacturers measured a random group of people, added the numbers together, and calculated an average. We all know that no one is really average, yet when we have difficulty fitting, we don't realize that it is just that we are built differently from that imaginary person.

The further our bodies are away from the average, the fewer things fit correctly, and this is the real problem. Although we categorize our bodies by saying "I'm just too big here or too little there," the truth is we're just different from what is expected. It's not a value judgment—it's simply how we're built.

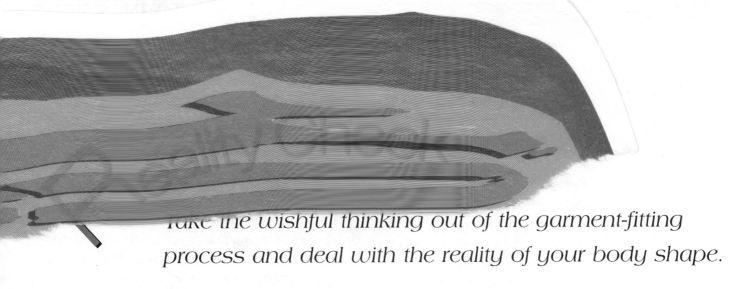

Take the wishful thinking out of the garment-fitting process and deal with the reality of your body shape.

The illustration in a pattern book may lead you to think the garment will make you look small through the middle. But you will only get that look if you're already small through the middle.

Fit is how you believe the final version of a garment will hang and feel on your body. However, there is too much make-believe, too much picturing and visualization rather than objective observing that goes on when most women choose a design, a pattern, and a size. Unfortunately, you will not get a new body with the garment when you make it, so sometimes the picture you have in your mind is not accurate.

For instance, if you happen to be thick through the middle and a fitted design in the pattern book makes the imaginary body look really small through the middle, you may assume that garment will make you look small through the middle. The reality is that only if you're already small through the middle will you get that look.

So what you have to do is take the wishful thinking out of the process and instead deal with reality. You must see how you actually look and determine what designs flatter you the most.

Be realistic when you choose patterns. No matter what you do to a pattern, a garment with a very fitted torso will not make this body look narrow through the middle.

Finding the "Real" You

There are ways to find out how you really look—the "real" you—without guessing or making subjective assumptions.

One way is to look at yourself not in your imagination but in reality, and the best way to do this is by looking at a photograph. Take some photographs of the way you look right now wearing your favorite clothes, ones that you made or purchased. Make sure you have several views—front, side, and back. Look at these photographs of yourself and see how things fit and hang, how you look. Do this in a loving, gentle way.

Now take a few pictures of yourself in garments that you wear but that don't make you feel quite so attractive. Compare the two sets of pictures. This will help you begin to see what works on your body.

Another way to "see" the real you is to create a wrapped body form. A body form is an exact replica of the individual sewer. The My Twin Bodyforms that are pictured on page 28 are made by having a friend wrap you with tape or plaster casting material to create a shell. After the taping is complete, the shell is cut off of your body, put back together, and dried. It is then filled with foam to form a solid shape; it's put on a stand and covered. Carol Stith Zahn, owner of CSZ Enterprises, sells a supply kit and how-to video for creating the My Twin Bodyform. (See "Resources" on page 241.)

It's a great learning experience to be able to actually get outside of your body, move around it, and touch and feel it. This is also an excellent method for those of you who do not have anyone who can help you fit garments.

Looking Your Best

Overall balance and proportion is the key to a good fit. Fit really is creating an overall look that enhances your particular body shape. As I told you earlier, you must realize that as someone walks up to you, you actually see the person from a distance of about 5 feet. A first impression occurs in about the first five seconds that you meet someone.

The idea that you want to create with the clothing you wear is that your garments fit you well and create a pleasing outline. It's clothes that don't fit—that are too tight, too loose, too overwhelming, or too stiff—that make you look less appealing.

Being a short, round person myself, I don't look upon this as a problem, but as a challenge. Over the years I have developed clothing that fits my body shape. By fit, I

mean that it doesn't pull, clothes just skim my body too tight, too sloppy, or too people meet me, the first th aware of is not necessarily my size fact that, overall, things look good on

I am going to spend a lot of time in th book defining exactly how you like things to fit and how you are built. You will know how much fabric you need in a garment in inches and where those inches must be distributed on your body. You can throw away that blindfold and be confident that you will make winners instead of wadders every time you sew.

Fantastic Fit for Every Body will be a journey into understanding your body, and you must go through all of the stages for the process to work well. Please take the time to complete it. You are worth the effort. Don't put it off. Start *now!*

PETITE DOES NOT MEAN SMALL

Fashion industry terms sometimes can be confusing. One of these is the word "petite." Petite does not mean small, and it does not necessarily mean someone who is thin and tiny. What petite actually refers to is the height of a person.

When a woman is only 5 feet 2 inches and the fit of a garment is meant to be for a woman who is 5 feet 7 inches, then the garment isn't going to fit the shorter woman in the appropriate places.

One of your jobs in investigating your body will be to see where you are longer or shorter so that you know where you need to improve the fit of your garments.

If your clothes are always too snug at the waistline, it may be because your waistline is higher than the waistline on the pattern. To solve this problem, you will have to shorten the pattern so the waistlines match.

Create a Croquis

By creating a silhouette, or croquis (pronounced kro-key), of your own body, you will be able to sketch and test designs on your particular body shape. You'll get a more realistic idea of how the garment will look on your body frame. Plus, you'll avoid expensive mistakes by testing the design before you begin to cut into the fashion fabric. So take time to create your croquis, and you will find it to be a revolutionary sewing tool.

Why You Need a Croquis

Create a croquis of your own body, and you can guarantee sewing success before you lay out the first pattern piece.

By creating a croquis of my own body, I can use it to test designs on my individual body shape.

A croquis, pronounced *kro-key*, is a sketch of the outline of a human body. The body outline that most commercial pattern companies feature in their catalogs and on their pattern envelopes to illustrate garments is one example of a croquis. However, those fashion illustrations are drawn on an idealized body that makes any design look good. That idealized body silhouette is a very tall, very thin, and completely imaginary figure that shows off the garment design well but rarely exists in real life. A style that looks good on this exaggerated fashion illustration will not necessarily look good on your body. To get a design to look good on your body, you must know the shape of your body.

Unfortunately, many women don't want to look at their bodies. In fact, some of them claim the name of their personal silhouette should be spelled *croakie*. These women are too self-critical. When you create your personal silhouette, do it with a kind eye, and you will find the croquis to be a revolutionary sewing tool that will prove extremely useful.

Assemble the Tools

Gather the following tools to create your personal croquis:

✦ *Large white or light-colored background (a wall, a large sheet of paper, or a piece of fabric longer than you are tall and wider than your arm span)*

✦ *Additional piece of white or light-colored paper or fabric for the floor, about 1 square yard (if needed)*

✦ *Tacks or masking tape*

✦ *Black or dark-colored leotard, or very close-fitting, dark-colored clothing*

✦ *Elastic hair bands, headband, or hair clips*

✦ *Chalk or narrow strips of any kind of flexible tape*

✦ *Polaroid or standard camera and film*

✦ *Person to take the photographs*

✦ *Chair*

✦ *Photocopy machine with enlargement capability*

✦ *White correction fluid*

✦ *White 8½-by-11-inch tracing paper*

✦ *Fine-line permanent marking pen*

Prepare the Background

To begin the process of creating a personal silhouette, or croquis, of your body, you must have your photograph taken from several angles.

STEP: Find a white or light-colored wall. If you can't find a suitable area in your home, tack or tape a light background such as a large sheet of paper

"Create your personal silhouette with a kind eye."

or a piece of white or light-colored fabric to a wall, as shown in **Diagram 1**, draping the paper or fabric down the wall and across the floor. (If you can't find a single piece of paper or fabric large enough to cover the wall and the floor, use a separate piece of paper for the floor; see Step 4.) Most sewers have some fabric stashed away, and at least one piece should work.

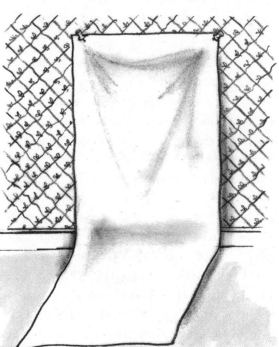

Take your photograph against a white or light-colored surface. If you don't have a wall that will work, dig into your fabric stash, and tape a piece of white or light-colored fabric (or paper) to a wall, allowing it to drape onto the floor.

Diagram 1

17

STEP: Put on the leotard or close-fitting, dark-colored clothing. You will get the best results if you wear a leotard and tights over your everyday undergarments, but any close-fitting knit shirt and pants will work. But don't wear a leotard that squeezes your body and changes your shape. You also can choose to wear only your undergarments, which should be black or another dark color so they provide a strong contrast with the background.

STEP: Move your hair out of the way so you will be able to see your neck and shoulder area clearly in the photograph. Put your hair up in a ponytail, or use a headband or hair clips to push your hair out of the way. The less hair that is in the way, the easier it is to see the overall proportion of your upper body. You can sketch hair onto one of the final tracings if you think that will help balance the proportions of your body on your croquis.

STEP: Stand in front of the white or light-colored background, making sure you are also standing on the same light-colored background. If your background material doesn't extend along the floor and you are standing on an area that is even slightly darker, you will not be able to see your feet as you enlarge the photo and the gray areas turn to black. If necessary, place another piece of white fabric or paper behind and under your feet so they won't disappear during the enlarging and copying process. Also make sure that your background material is wide enough so that you can stand with your arms spread away from your body, as shown in **Diagram 2A** on the opposite page.

TIP: Hang a piece of paper or fabric that is printed with a 1-by-1-inch grid on the wall. Stand with your back as close as possible to the grid when you are photographed. However, the farther away the grid is from the back of your body, the more distorted it becomes. The grid is not precise and can't be used as a measuring device, but it will allow you to see the proportion of one section of your body to another.

Mark Your Body Map

Before taking the photographs, it's important to mark the critical fitting areas of your body. Through the years that I have created croquis, I've discovered several methods for marking directly on the body. One method is to use chalk. This works especially well if you are wearing a black or dark-colored leotard. You can also use masking tape or narrow strips of any kind of flexible tape. Elastic can be used to mark the waist, but it will not work well for the rest of the body. Choose the method that works best for you.

STEP: Using the chalk or tape, mark the following areas of the front of your body with solid lines, as shown in **Diagram 2A.** (Ask your photographer to help you mark the areas of your body that you cannot reach.)

✦ *Bust point*

✦ *Underneath the bust*

✦ *Entire waistline*

✦ *Upper hip area*

✦ *Lower hip area*

✦ *Front crotch line (Mark a line on the leotard so you can see exactly how low the crotch is and where the leg begins.)*

✦ *Bottom of the knee*

STEP 2: On one side of your body, also mark the top of the leg and the bottom of the knee, as shown in **Diagram 2B.**

STEP 3: On the back of your body, mark the bottom of the fanny, as shown in **Diagram 2B.**

When you create your personal croquis, work with a friend who wants to make a croquis as well. That way neither of you will feel shy or inhibited. Choose a friend on whom you have "information." Then the two of you can sign a mutual "no blackmail" pact.

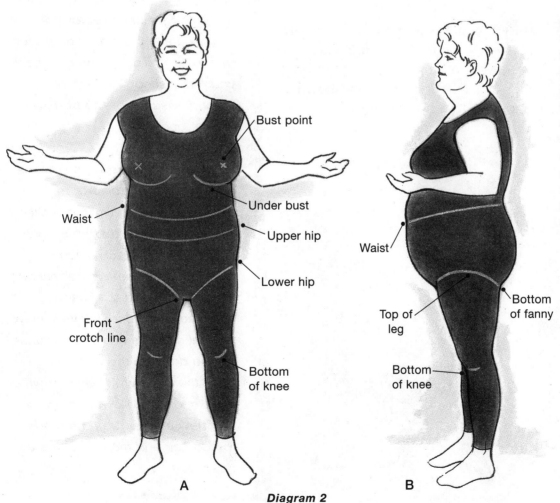

Bust point

Under bust

Waist

Upper hip

Lower hip

Front crotch line

Bottom of knee

Waist

Top of leg

Bottom of fanny

Bottom of knee

A

B

Diagram 2

Before taking the photograph, mark the joints and critical fitting areas on your body with chalk or tape. Mark the bottom of the knee on one side of your body, and mark the bottom of the fanny on the back of your body.

Snap the Picture

After you have prepared the background and marked your body, it's time to take the photographs.

ST**EP:** Seat the person taking the photos on a chair, as shown in **Diagram 3.** To get the most accurate photograph, have the photographer position the camera level with your waist.

TIP: I recommend using a Polaroid camera because you will know immediately if the photograph is in focus and whether your entire body is in the frame.

The person who is taking the photos should sit on a chair and position the camera level with your waist. That way, you will get the most accurate photographs.

ST**EP:** Stand with your back to the white or light-colored background, and spread your arms away from your body to the left and the right, as shown in **Diagram 3**. Take a photograph.

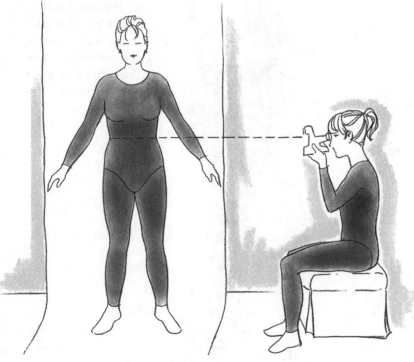

Diagram 3

SPECIAL OPTIONS

You can take the photographs of your body with transparency (slide) film instead of using a Polaroid camera. Although it will take a little more time and effort, you could then project the images onto a white or light-colored piece of paper and make a very accurate drawing of your body shape. You also could trace your facial features.

I've also seen personal croquis created using an opaque projector. This type of projector will display a standard print on paper much like a slide projector. Check your local school, library, or an audiovisual store to borrow or rent one.

If you decide to use a projector to create your croquis, adjust the distance of the projector from the surface of the white or light-colored paper so that your body fills an 8½-by-11-inch piece of paper. I use a fine-line permanent marker to outline the image because it photocopies well. Have several markers on hand because as you draw on the vertical surface, the ink flow will slow down or stop, and you will want to switch to a new marker. Use the marker to add hair and facial features as desired.

TIP: Make sure that your arms are far enough away from your body so that they don't hide any detail when you do your sketching on the finished croquis.

3 STEP: Stand with your side to the white or light-colored background with the near arm bent and the far arm and leg out of view. In this view, you can move yourself until your leg toward the back is invisible to the photographer. The best way to set up the arms in the side view is to place the arm from the shoulder down in a straight line perpendicular to the floor, and then bend at the elbow and parallel to the floor. Make sure the elbow is far enough forward so you can see your entire back, as shown in **Diagram 4.** Take a photograph.

4 STEP: Stand with the front of your body toward the white or light-colored background and your back to the camera. Spread your arms away from your body to the left and the right. Take a photograph.

5 STEP: (optional) If you have drawing talent, you may want to attempt a variety of photographs. Pose with your right hand on your hip and your left arm bent at the elbow with the palm of your hand facing upward in a traditional model stance, as shown in **Diagram 5.** Extend one leg slightly. This stance is held so that the different details of a garment are visible when you sketch them on this view; however, it is more complicated to draw on this view than on the working croquis.

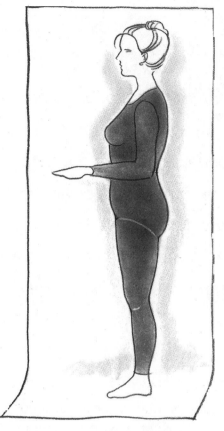

Diagram 4

To get a side view, stand with one side of your body to the white or light-colored background with the near arm bent and the far arm and leg out of view. Make sure your elbow is bent and far enough forward so you can see your entire back.

Diagram 5

You may want to take a variety of photographs. Try posing in a traditional model stance. Extend one leg slightly and place your right hand on your hip, then bend your left arm at the elbow, and turn the palm of your hand upward.

Wit & Wisdom

The purpose of making a croquis is not to get terribly involved in the process or to make it perfect but to do the best you can and move on. Have a clear eye and a kind heart when taking and viewing the photos and croquis. Remember, this is not a value judgment—it is only a tool!

Enlarge and Copy the Photo

Now that you have your photos, you will use them to get a working croquis by tracing the outline of your body onto a piece of tracing paper. The easiest way to do this and the method I have used for many years is to proceed to the local photocopy machine. Most of you can readily find a photocopy machine that has enlargement capabilities, and the results you get from it will be suitable for our purposes.

STEP: As you enlarge the photo on the photocopy machine, the definition between black, gray, and white will fade, everything will look only black and white, and many of the markings will disappear. To enhance your body areas, use white correction fluid on the finished photos to mark the location of the bust, waist, top of legs, bottom of buttocks, and so on, if the original markings don't show up well in the photo.

STEP: Using the photocopy machine that has enlargement capabilities, enlarge each photo—the front, the side, and the back—several times. To do that, make one enlargement of each photo. Place each copy in the photocopy machine, and enlarge it again. Repeat this process until each view fills an 8½-by-11-inch sheet of paper, as shown in **Diagram 6.**

Diagram 6

Using a photocopy machine that has enlargement capabilities, enlarge each of the photos several times, until each view fills an 8½-by-11-inch sheet of paper.

STEP: Place an 8½-by-11-inch sheet of tracing paper on top of the largest photocopy of the front of your body. Trace the outline of your body, and mark the location of the bust, the waist, and the top of the legs with light dotted lines, as shown in **Diagram 7.** Also trace the side and back views, and mark the location of the bust, waist, top of legs, and fanny.

You've seen the idealized version of a model body in pattern books, magazines, and newspapers. The shoulders stick out farther than the hip bones. The tummy is tucked behind the hip bones. The head sits on top of a long neck. The legs seem to go on forever. This body is 6 feet tall and probably weighs less than 100 pounds, and *nothing* jiggles. This body is not a real person. In fact, most of the photos you see—even those of the most famous and gorgeous models—have been computer enhanced. Can you name one person you actually know who is built this way? Why waste your time wishing and hoping your body will duplicate this nonexistent female specimen? Let's get on with fitting and flattering the body that *you* own.

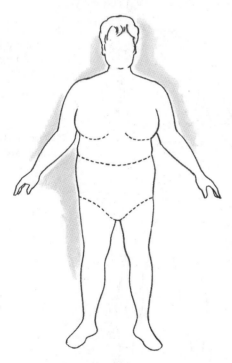

Diagram 7

Using the largest photocopy of your body, trace the outline of your body on a sheet of tracing paper, and mark the location of the bust, the waist, and the top of the legs.

TIP: I use a colored fine-line permanent marker because it leaves a light outline. Each photocopy machine will produce different results, so experiment with pens of different colors and thicknesses. If possible, you want the finished line to appear gray instead of black. Repeat this step for the side and back views of your body. These tracings are your original croquis.

STEP 4: Using the photocopy machine, make multiple copies of your croquis, especially the front view. Most of the time you will sketch your fashion illustrations on the front view of your body. If you are deeper than you are wide, you should make multiple copies of the side view and use that as often as you use the front view.

Examine Your Body

It is important that you know how one section of your body relates to another. To do this, add horizontal and vertical lines to one set of the finished croquis, as shown in **Diagram 8.** The lines help you see the length and depth of different areas of your body.

STEP 1: On one copy of your front croquis, use the permanent marker to draw a horizontal line at the top of the shoulders, as shown in **Diagram 8A.** Then draw a horizontal line at the waist and a horizontal line at the hips.

STEP 2: On one copy of your side croquis, use the permanent marker to draw a horizontal line at the bust point and a horizontal line at the waist, as shown in **Diagram 8B.** Then draw a vertical line through the lengthwise center of the body. Draw a vertical line that intersects with the back of the waist, and draw a vertical line parallel to the front of the thigh.

STEP 3: On one copy of your back croquis, use the permanent marker to draw a horizontal line at the waist, as shown in **Diagram 8C.** Draw vertical lines from the shoulder joint to the outside of the hips on

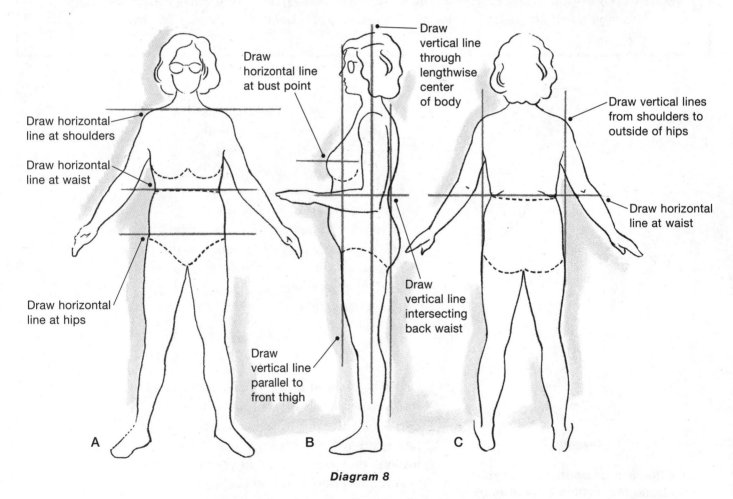

Diagram 8

It is important that you know how one area of your body relates to another. To help you see the length and depth of different parts of your body, add horizontal and vertical lines to one set of the finished croquis.

each side of the body. Your lines may be different than those shown in **Diagram 8C.** If your hips are wider than your shoulders, your lines will form more of a pyramid shape.

Use Your Croquis

Now you're ready to use your personal croquis to plan successful garments that will complement your individual figure. By drawing clothing on an actual likeness of your body, you can check the true proportion of the garments to your body shape.

After you have drawn an outfit on your croquis, go away from it for a while and then come back to look at it again later. That way you will see the garment more objectively. Better yet, draw several versions of the garment or outfit, and pin them up somewhere so you can glance at them occasionally. This method will help you see which view is best for your body shape. You may discover additional changes that may make the garment even better by sketching design elements, such as collars, tucks, darts, sleeves, cuffs, pleats, yokes, buttons, or decorative closures, on the different versions of the garment.

TIP: I have clients who make multiple sketches of their garments and use colored pencils, marking pens, or crayons to color the garments. This helps them to make color decisions easier.

Remember, you are trying to look at the overall proportion of your body so that you can get a rough idea of how different garment designs will look on you.

"Know how one section of your body relates to another."

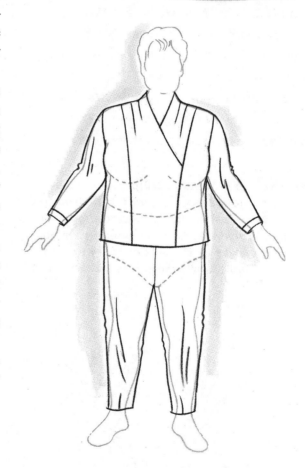

Now that you have created your personal croquis, you can make multiple photocopies and sketch garments on them to get a rough idea of how different garment designs will look on your body.

Knowing how the garment will look on your individual body shape will help you feel more confident as you work on your project.

OBSERVING YOUR CROQUIS

An important step in learning how to fit your individual body shape is to be able to observe your personal croquis carefully and to notice how it is different from the pattern companies' standard body form. This exercise is designed to help you learn to look at where your body curves or doesn't curve, where it is straight, and where it is thick or thin.

Look at the three croquis in **Diagram 1.** Pretend you are looking at the body of your very best friend, not yourself, so you won't

Observe the croquis in Diagram 1 carefully and notice how it is different from the pattern companies' standard dress form in Diagram 2. Look at where your body curves or doesn't curve, where it is straight, and where it is thick or thin.

be tempted to make this a critical exercise.

Compare **Diagram 1** to the three croquis of the standard size-12 dress form, as shown in **Diagram 2.** (Don't forget you are comparing your friend to a body that is 5 feet 7 inches.) Look at the shoulders. You must look at both the front and side views so you can see whether or not the shoulders are sloping downward. If they appear to be sloping downward, you must be able to determine what is causing the slope. Is it merely a pronounced trapezoid muscle at each side of the neck, as shown in the front and back views in **Diagram 1,** or do the shoulders actually curve downward? Or are the shoulder balls arching forward when you look at the side view, as shown in **Diagram 3?**

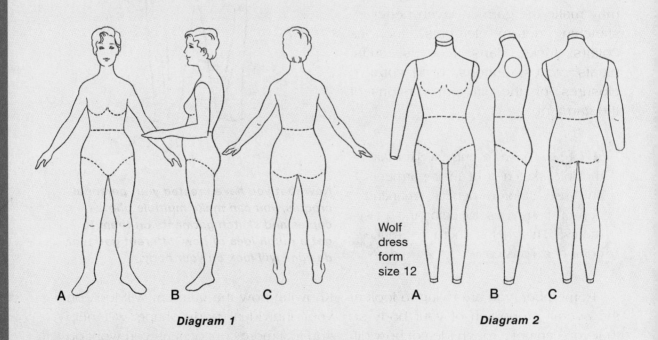

Wolf dress form size 12

Diagram 1

A   B   C

Diagram 2

A   B   C

Now look at the shoulders in relationship to the hips and in relationship to the waist. Are the hips truly large, or does a tiny waist make the hips appear larger, as shown in **Diagram 4?** Is the waist really large or are the hips slim? As shown in **Diagram 5,** slim hips often are accompanied by a straight waist, which makes the waist appear large.

If you lack hip fluff, which is the pad of flesh that sits on your hip just below your waist, your hip and thigh area will be accentuated, as shown in **Diagram 6.**

Now, compare each area of your croquis to the croquis of the standard size-12 dress form until you are sure you see the spatial differences between yourself and the expectations of the pattern companies. You may be larger or smaller than a size 12, but the general outline will remain the same.

Remember, none of us is built like another or like the perfect dress form, so when you look at your croquis, you're going to look at it carefully and in a loving way.

Diagram 3

When you examine your croquis, it is important that you look at both the front and side views. If your shoulders appear to be sloping downward on your front view, you may find, by looking at your side view, that your shoulder balls actually arch forward, as shown here.

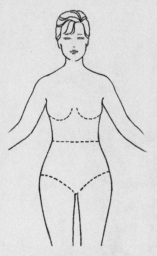

Diagram 4

Examine your croquis carefully. Look at your shoulders in relation to your hips and in relation to your waist. Are your hips really large, or does your tiny waist, illustrated here, just make your hips appear larger?

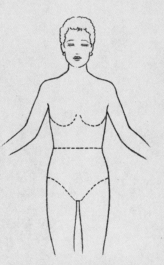

Diagram 5

Be honest with yourself when you look at your croquis. Is your waist really large or do you just have slim hips like this woman? Women who have slim hips often have a straight waist, which makes their waist appear large.

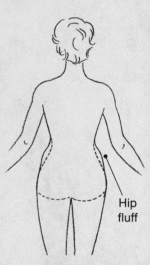

Hip fluff

Diagram 6

If you don't have hip fluff—that pad of flesh that sits on your hip just below your waist—your hip and thigh area may look larger than it really is.

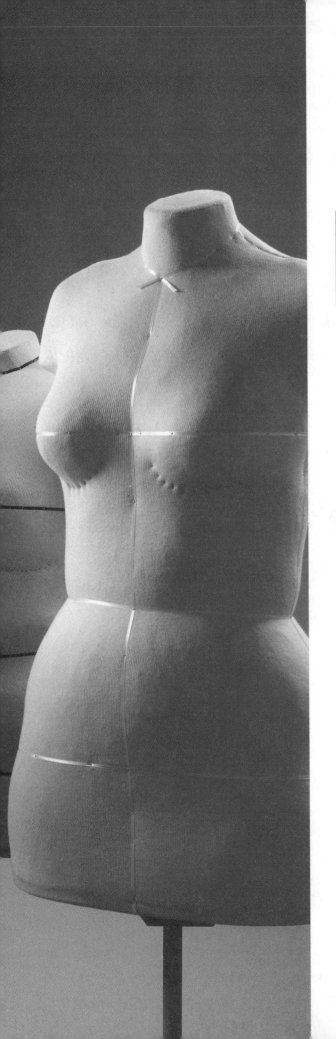

Three-Dimensional Fitting

To fit the three-dimensional human figure, you must carefully examine it to determine where it needs more or less fabric. You must know where and how your body differs from the pattern companies' fit models, and you must look at your entire body instead of focusing on one specific area.

Take a Closer Look

Before you can begin to fit garments to your body, you must be able to observe its shape from the front, the sides, and the back.

You have created your croquis, and now it is time to look at your body very closely. It's difficult to observe the real shape of your body because you can only see yourself two-dimensionally in a mirror. But your body is not two-dimensional, it is three-dimensional, and to fit garments with accuracy, you must find ways to look all the way around your body.

It's difficult to observe the real shape of your body when you look into a mirror, so use your croquis to help you think about your body three-dimensionally.

at Your Body

Two-Dimensional Patterns

Unfortunately, most commercial patterns are designed for two-dimensional bodies. Patterns designed two-dimensionally use width and length as the primary components for creating the shape of the garment. But remember that the bodies of the pattern companies' fit models are very tall, very thin, and only slightly wide. The pattern companies don't have to take into consideration the depth of a garment.

Moreover, women with that thin and tall body style are estimated to make up less than 5 percent of the population. That's why the rest of us have trouble making garments that fit—we forget that our bodies have more depth. This oversight prevents us from achieving the perfect fit.

The belief that we can use flat patterns and simply shape the edges of the paper leaves the depth component out of the pattern-making process. The oversimplification of pattern design is one reason we have so much difficulty fitting ourselves.

Thinking Three-Dimensionally

Before you can begin to fit a garment to your body properly, you must concentrate on thinking three-dimensionally. When we insert our three-dimensional bodies into two-dimensional designs, we find there are lumps and curves in areas

> "You must find ways to look all the way around your body."

for which many commercial patterns don't allow. The pattern piece cannot contour to the curves on the body, and therefore the garment doesn't fit.

When you make pattern alterations, it is very important that you understand where your body differs from the body of a fit model. Most sewers have learned that the only place to add to a pattern is on the sides. But even if we make the pattern wider or narrower, that doesn't necessarily mean the pattern will fit the shape of our bodies.

My analogy to wallpapering a beach ball in the "Wit & Wisdom" box on page 6 shows you that if you use one big piece of fabric and your body is round, it will be difficult to get the fabric to fit your body smoothly.

We must use darts, pleats, tucks, or additional seams—what I call "opportunities for fit"—to get the fabric to shape and hang attractively over our bodies. (For more information, see the chapter "Opportunities for Fit" on page 74.)

Wit & Wisdom

I hate the term "flat-pattern design."
If human beings were flat, this method
of designing garments would work every
time. I have long suggested that we go
out into the street, lie down, and have
ourselves run over by a steamroller.
That way, we'd all be truly flat, and
garments would be much easier to fit!

Norma Wolf

How does your body shape compare to Norma Wolf's, and *who* is she? Norma is the imaginary average woman whom pattern companies use as the "norm" when they create their garment designs. But, really, who is completely "normal"?

Norma's last name is Wolf, as in the Wolf dress form. The Wolf dress form is the standard body form used by commercial pattern companies and ready-to-wear designers. The Wolf dress form is a very smooth, perfectly proportioned body that is shaped so that garments hang on it attractively. Very few human beings have a body that resembles the Wolf dress form.

In "Observing Your Croquis" on page 26, I asked you to observe your croquis and compare it to the pattern

Norma Wolf is the imaginary average woman for whom pattern companies create their designs.

companies' standard body form—the Wolf dress form. If you have not already observed your croquis carefully and compared it to the Wolf dress form, you must take the time to do that now. It is very important for you to see how your body differs from the industry's—or Norma's—standard shape.

Once you compare your body shape to Norma's, you will more clearly understand where the commercial pattern companies expect the fashion fabric to cover the human body. Then you will begin to see where you actually have to add or take away fabric to cover your own body.

What, No Tummy?

While visiting a designer's studio near my home in California, I saw a line of Wolf dress forms ranging from size 6 up to size 22. The thing that fascinated me about these dress forms was that the size 22 didn't have a tummy. I still haven't figured out how someone can be a size 22 and not have some kind of a tummy—unless she is 7 feet tall. In fact, most women, whether small or large, have tummies.

Perhaps you have a protruding tummy. If you do, you are bigger in the area below your waist in the front of your body than in the back of your body. But most commercial patterns allow for an equal amount of fabric in the front and the back of the body.

To cover a protruding tummy, you must adjust your pattern to add more fabric to the length and width of the front of the garment. If you don't do this, your tummy will pull the fabric it needs from another area of your body, and the garment will not fit correctly.

Looking Good
Observe, Don't Judge

Most patterns are made for a human figure that is wider than it is deep. Look at the Wolf dress form, and remember that this is the form that is used as the standard for the industry.

The body represented by this form:

+ Is 5 feet 7 inches tall
+ Is very, very lean and narrow
+ Has a shoulder that goes from the neck straight out to the ball of the shoulder
+ Has an underarm that has very little indentation
+ Is gently curved at the bust
+ Has a B-cup bustline
+ Is smaller in the bust than in the hip area
+ Has a front chest that is smooth and flat
+ Is shallow in the rib cage
+ Has a flat tummy
+ Has an angle coming off of the waist that is a gentle slope
+ Has no bumps or lumps anywhere

It is simply unrealistic to compare your body to the Wolf dress form and make a value judgment. Our genes make decisions before we are born about where and how our bodies will curve and shape. Being short, tall, large-, or small-boned is set by nature.

As we grow bigger or older, the effects of nature become even more dramatic. During the 1990s, as the majority of the general public—specifically the "baby boomers"—aged, research on women's body shapes was published by the American Society for Testing and Materials Institute for Standards Research. This research, which was published in 1993, found that the bodies of women aged 55 and over exhibit many similar body shape characteristics and have similar fitting problems.

The Gold dress form was developed specifically for older women, as a result of research by William Rankin, owner of Dress Rite Forms. As reported in the newsletter *The Creative Machine*, the Gold form was designed to duplicate the average body of a woman aged 55. Although the Gold form may resemble your body more closely than the Wolf form, no matter what your age, neither of these forms will exactly duplicate your body shape.

Don't waste time making a value judgment on how your body differs from the Wolf dress form, but do take time to observe your body very carefully.

The Wolf form is the standard used by the ready-to-wear industry and pattern companies, while the Gold form more closely resembles the bodies of most women over the age of 55.

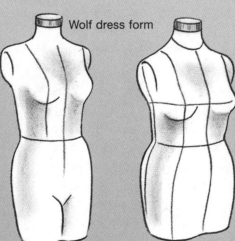

Wolf dress form

Gold dress form

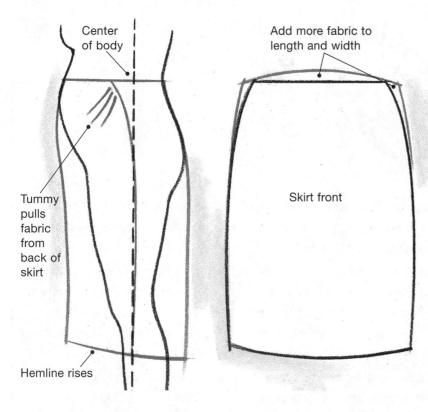

You have to add more fabric to the length and width of a skirt in the waist area if you have a protruding tummy. If you don't add fabric, your tummy will pull what it needs from another area of your body.

Garment Horizons

An easy way to determine whether your clothes fit your body is to look at what I call the "horizon" on a garment.

If you look at the bottom of someone's skirt, jacket, or blouse from a distance (remember, this is how all of us see each other), you may see that the garment hangs longer in the front and shorter in the back. That garment does not have a smooth "horizon."

Most sewers try to fix that irregularity during the hemming process. But hemming won't cure the problem because the lengthwise grain and crosswise grain of the fabric will be off. Although the hem may appear even, the skirt might push against the front of the leg and stand out in the back. There also would likely be wrinkles and pulls from the top of the skirt. You must correct the drape of the garment for the hem to hang evenly.

Grain is a key component in the way a garment hangs on your body. Most sewers know how to use the straight-of-grain lines on a pattern. But remember the grainlines only come into play when the garment is hanging off the end of the bust, off the fullest roundest part of the back, or off a fluffy high hip.

Using a skirt as an example, you can see why the topography of your body will affect the horizon of a garment. If you have a large tummy, the front of your skirt will ride higher, raising the hem in the front of the skirt.

If your waist is lower in the front of your body than in the back, which frequently happens with fuller-figured women, the hemline will be lower in the front than in the back.

If your waist is lower in the front of your body than in the back, the hemline of your garment will also be lower in the front than in the back.

If you have a very full bottom, the fabric in your garment has to get out and over your bottom, raising the hemline in the back.

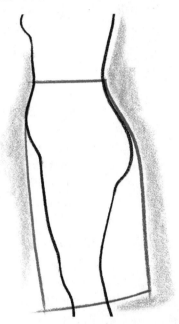

If you have a very full fanny, your garment has to get out and over your body, which will raise the hemline in the back.

Commercial patterns place great emphasis on the lengthwise grain of the fabric but little on the crosswise grain. If your body shape is pulling the fabric off the crosswise grain, the hem of your garment will never hang evenly. So, it's important that you learn how to create even horizons.

As I mentioned earlier, we have only seconds to create a good first impression, whether it's the first time we meet someone or when we walk up to an old friend. What the other person sees first is just your general body outline. When clothing hangs correctly, it falls smoothly and looks straight along the bottom edges. That is one of the first things another person will notice.

You must begin to look not only at the width but also at the length of garment pieces so that you can make them to fit your individual body. Most of these alterations will be made before you begin to construct the garment. (See "Jane" on page 210.)

Exercise in Understanding

By now I've helped you to understand that the human body is not as smoothly curved as the pattern companies' ideal.

If you are still not convinced, here is a measuring exercise that will help you understand how the bumps on our bodies affect the fit of a garment.

STEP 1: Gather the following tools: a leotard and tights, a chalk hem marker, a tape measure, a pencil or pen, and a simple skirt pattern.

STEP 2: Wearing the leotard and tights, use the chalk hem marker to make marks all the way around your legs just below your knees, as shown in **Diagram 1.**

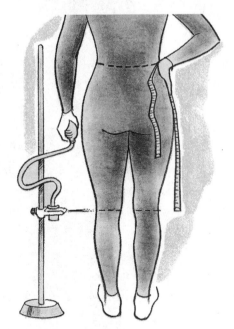

Diagram 1

After using a chalk hem marker to mark your legs on all sides just below your knees, hang a tape measure from your waist with the zero at one of the chalk marks on your leg, and record the measurement at your waist. You may find that your waist rises or falls at different parts of your body.

3: STEP: Hang the tape measure from your waist with the zero at the chalk mark on your leg, as shown in **Diagram 1**. Record the measurement at your waist on the illustration of the skirt front on the pattern guide sheet, as shown in **Diagram 2**.

Record the measurements that you take at your waist on the illustration of the skirt front on the pattern guide sheet. That way, you can refer to the guide sheet when altering your pattern.

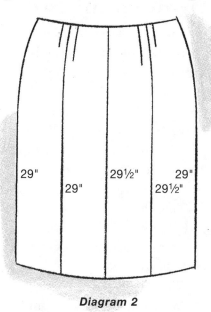

29" 29" 29½" 29" 29½"

Diagram 2

4: STEP: Continue to measure in this manner around your body in one-eighth sections, and record the measurements on the illustrations of the skirt front and back on the pattern guide sheet.

5: STEP: Measuring from the bottom, check the same areas on the skirt front and back pattern pieces, and record those measurements.

6: STEP: Compare your body measurements with the pattern piece measurements. You will discover what the pattern company expects those distances to be and what your body actually measures. If your waist happens to drop down in the front or you have a very full fanny, your measurements are going to be much less than the pattern in the front or much longer than the pattern in the back.

FROM BROWN TOWN TO GREEN TOWN

To understand how the bumps on our bodies affect the fit of a garment, I use my "From Brown Town to Green Town" analogy. If you're driving on a road between Brown Town and Green Town and the road is flat and straight, the distance between the two towns might be 10 miles. If there is a hill in between Brown Town and Green Town, you'd have to drive over it, and the distance between the two towns would now be 12 miles. But it could be that there is

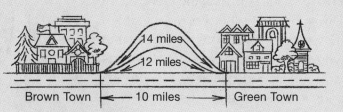

The distance between Brown Town and Green Town depends on the road you take.

a great big mountain between Brown Town and Green Town, so now you have to go up and over 14 miles of road. Got the picture?

Your Body as a Whole

Once you learn to look at your body as a whole, you must fine-tune those skills to look at every detail of your body mass and structure.

It is important for you to develop an eye for where you have more or less body mass. It is also important that you compare both the front and the back sections of your body and then look at your body as a whole rather than focusing on one specific area.

Frequently, fit is explained using isolated sections of the body—if you have wide shoulders, do this; if you have narrow hips, do that; if you have wide hips, do this—rather than using the entire body. To help you fine-tune your three-dimensional thinking, I will examine some specific fitting challenges.

Barbara knows she has a small waist and full hips, and she's learned how to alter her patterns to fit her specific body shape.

Side View

Fitting the upper area of the body can be confusing because most sewers only look at themselves straight on in a mirror. From that point of view, your shoulders may look straight and horizontal to the floor, and yet you see pleats of fabric at the shoulder. But when you look at your shoulders from the side, you might see that your shoulder ball—the actual bony skeleton—is very small.

Because the depth of the shoulder ball is not taking up the excess fabric, the fabric will hang down around the shoulder, creating pleats. The fabric would do the same thing if your shoulders sloped downward. So the fabric must be used up by what's underneath it, or it will collapse in folds.

As we get older, our normal bust, waist, and hip measurements may not change, and we can weigh exactly the same, but nothing seems to fit us anymore. That's because the structure of our spine and our overall body changes. Women get kind of rounded over, narrower, and shorter in the front, and longer, rounder, and fuller in the back. Frequently women's shoulders rotate forward a little bit. This is the natural evolution of our bodies, and even with regular exercise and proper posture, it happens.

If you follow the instructions given by the commercial pattern companies and use only bust, waist, and hip measurements, you will not observe this phenomenon and will not allow for it in the fitting of your garment. That is why you must not only take the three core measurements—bust, waist, and hip—but also observe your entire body if you want to achieve a better fit.

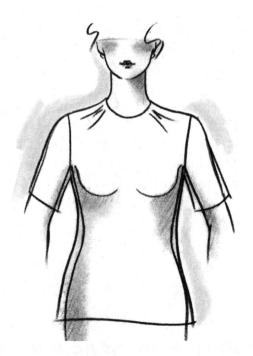

When you look into a two-dimensional mirror, your shoulders may look straight and horizontal to the floor, but you may see fabric pleats or wrinkles at the shoulder.

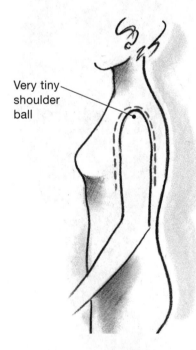

Very tiny shoulder ball

When you look at your shoulders from the side, you will see that your shoulder ball—the actual bony skeleton—is very tiny and does not take up the excess fabric in the garment.

Rear View

The shoulder blade area—what I call the chicken wings—of a woman's back is sometimes very pronounced.

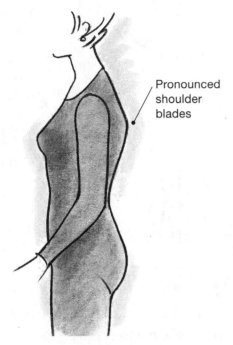

Pronounced shoulder blades

If you have very pronounced shoulder blades, fitted garments may pull and bind across your back. You will have to add fabric in that specific area to get a good fit.

If this is one of your problem areas, fitted garments may pull and bind across your back. You need to add fabric in that specific area.

Examine your back view croquis to see if your chicken wings are a prominent part of your body shape. This will help you decide if the inches in your bust measurement are taken up in the front or the back.

Your Depth

I've told you that you must learn to take into consideration the depth of your body as well as its length and width. Let's take a look at the bust. All commercial patterns are made for women with a B-cup bra size. If you are larger or smaller than a B cup, the distance around your body is going to be larger or smaller, and the distance from your shoulder over the top of the bust to the waist will be larger or smaller.

I'll use an example of a fuller bust. The bust point, or fullest part of the bust, on a B cup is about 1 to 1 ½ inches away from the chest cavity.

If you have a cup size larger than a B, you must add an additional ½ inch of depth for each additional cup size.

If you have a D cup and find you need more room in the garment, you can't just add the fabric on the sides. That added fabric is not going to actually change the contour of the garment. The garment will go around your body, but it will not hang correctly because your body is deeper in the front and pulls the fabric toward the bust. The back is not wider and does not need additional fabric.

The additional fabric must be added where you need it. A full bust needs width, but don't forget to check the length. Going out and over the bust may leave the front of the garment shorter than the back.

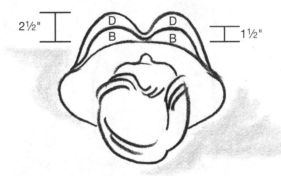

If you look at a woman's body from a bird's eye view, you will see that the fullest part of the bust on a woman with a B cup is about 1 to 1 ½ inches away from the chest cavity. Each additional cup size adds ½ inch of depth to the body.

ADDING AND REMOVING FABRIC

This true story will give you an idea of how to go through the process of adding fabric to or removing fabric from your pattern.

Gena, photographed on page 46 holding the tape measure, wears a DD bra. One day she entered my fabric store and told me she wanted to make a simple little sundress with a halter top. I measured from the center of her chest over the fullest part of her bust and to the side seam, and I noted that measurement. I measured from the top of her shoulder over the fullest part of her bust to the bottom of her bust, and I noted that number.

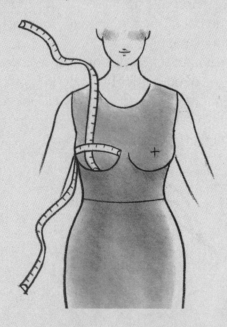

To get an accurate bust measurement for a halter top, I measured from the top of Gena's shoulder over the fullest part of her bust to the bottom of her bust and from the center of her chest over the fullest part of her bust to the side seam.

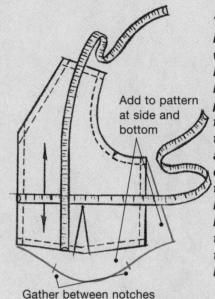

Add to pattern at side and bottom

Gather between notches

To determine if the pattern would fit Gena, I measured the bodice front pattern piece from the bottom to the shoulder and from the center front to the side seam line. I found she had to add to the pattern at the side and the bottom.

Then I measured the bodice front pattern piece in the same areas.

When comparing Gena's body measurements to the pattern itself, we discovered that the bodice wouldn't go over her bust. Plus, the line on the pattern that is supposed to hit the bottom of the bust probably was going to hit her at midbust. Since she wore a DD bra, at least another 1½ inches was needed because of the difference between a B cup (the pattern standard) and her cup size.

So we had to add to the pattern on the side and at the bottom, as shown in the illustration above. Note the curved and angled pieces—the more curved the body is, the more curved the pattern pieces should be.

But to fit the top of the skirt to the bottom of the bodice, the top had to have a dart, tuck, or pleat to remove the excess fabric. That allowed for sufficient fabric to go over the bust without the entire garment getting too big.

A small bust causes exactly the opposite problem. If your cup size is smaller than a B cup, your body will not be as deep as the pattern design. This will cause the front to droop. Most sewers see this as the center front being too big around the body, but the truth is that it is the length of the garment from the shoulder to the waist that causes the excess fabric.

For anyone with a very small upper torso, whether it comes from a small bust, tiny shoulders, being petite (under 5 feet 4 inches), being short-waisted, being hollow below the shoulder, or whatever causes most of your clothes to fold or gape in the front, you must remove that excess fabric from the

If you have a shallow chest, remove fabric from the upper chest area of the front pattern, and if you remove fabric from the garment in the upper chest area, you must also remove a corresponding amount from the sleeve. If you have thin arms, remove fabric along the length of the sleeve; if you have full arms, remove it from the sleeve cap area.

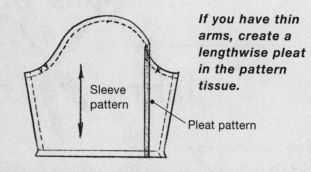

Sleeve pattern

Pleat pattern

If you have thin arms, create a lengthwise pleat in the pattern tissue.

Taper toward back

Slash pattern, and overlap pieces

Sleeve pattern

If you have full arms, slash the pattern horizontally, and overlap the pieces on the front of the sleeve, tapering toward the back of the sleeve.

front of the garment. And if you remove fabric in the upper chest, you must also remove a corresponding amount from the sleeve. If you have thin arms, you will remove fabric along the length of the sleeve by creating a lengthwise pleat in the sleeve pattern.

However, if you have a full upper arm, you will remove fabric from the sleeve cap area by slashing the pattern horizontally and overlapping the pieces on the front of the sleeve, tapering toward the back, where none is removed.

I read a set of pattern instructions that emphasized that you must make the same alterations all the way around your body. This practice does not allow for the individual contours of a body. Many of us are full in the back and small in the front so we must use common sense and alter the pattern where our body needs it.

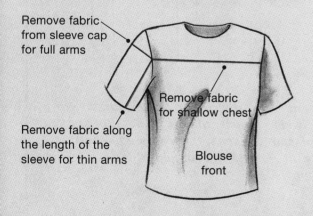

Remove fabric from sleeve cap for full arms

Remove fabric for shallow chest

Remove fabric along the length of the sleeve for thin arms

Blouse front

Looking Good

Fabric Contours

To help you visualize how fabric can be contoured to cover our three-dimensional bodies, let's look at how bottles of different shapes can be covered with fabric.

To cover the bottle illustrated below with fabric, two pieces of fabric can be sewn along the sides and across the top, leaving an opening for the neck, so that the fabric fits over the shoulders and hangs easily on the bottle. This method works on this shape of bottle, which is wider than it is deep.

The container illustrated below also has a neck, but the bottle is round and cannot be covered with fabric that is sewn in the same way. If it were, the fabric would pull up and would not hang correctly.

The top of the fabric needs to be contoured with darts, pleats, or additional pieces to create a shape that will fit the bottle.

Cheryle Custer, whose body is as deep as it is wide, is wearing a blouse in the photo on page 142 that is a wonderful example

of fabric contours. The first blouse she made was bulky and shapeless; in addition, she could not raise her arm because to make the blouse large enough to fit around her body, the end of the blouse shoulder was beyond the end of her own shoulder. We added darts at the shoulder seams about 2 inches from her neck on the front and back of the blouse. These darts helped to contour the garment to allow for the depth of her body. (For details on Cheryle's blouse, see page 174.)

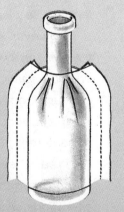

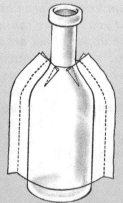

This bottle, which is wider than it is deep, can be covered easily by stitching two pieces of fabric together, leaving an opening for the neck. The fabric fits over the shoulders and hangs easily on the bottle.

This bottle is round and cannot be covered as easily as the wide bottle. When the fabric is placed on the round bottle, it pulls up at the neck and doesn't hang correctly.

If the fabric is contoured with darts, pleats, or additional pieces, it creates a shape that fits the round bottle.

Your Height

Commercial pattern companies assume all of us are 5 feet 7 inches tall. Although they provide lengthen or shorten lines on their paper patterns, those lines are definitely not always placed correctly for every body. The pattern companies assume that you get longer all the way around your body, and therefore you have no guarantee that you will get the length where you need it.

When we make alterations to a garment pattern, we are trying to insert the human form into the flat pattern paper. Remembering the "From Brown Town to Green Town" explanation (see page 36), the length of a garment is affected by part of your body's being deeper or shallower than expected. You do not want to lengthen the pattern the same distance all the way around, but only alter it where you need it.

If you get deeper in one area such as a fuller tummy or abdomen and you lengthen all the way around the garment, the sides will hang longer because there is less of your body in that area.

Another example is someone with a very full outer thigh. This person needs to slash the pattern from the side seam cutting line to the crotch seamline and spread it open.

This will lengthen the pattern only on the outside of the leg, allowing for the additional length necessary to go out and over the full outer thigh area. (For details on how to fit this troublesome area, see "Jan" on page 214.)

Mirror, Mirror

Another way to determine where you need to add fabric to your patterns is to find out exactly where your garments are generally misaligned. Start by putting on the following pieces of clothing one at a time, and look at yourself in the mirror. Wiggle around and don't pull the garments back into position. This will help you see how your clothes want to hang on their own.

Start by putting on your favorite pair of pants, and check out the side seams. Do they hang straight from the waist or do they slant forward or backward? (See "Garment Horizons" on page 34.)

The way the fabric pulls is another hint as to which way your body differs from the pattern and where you need to add extra fabric. Whichever side the garment is pulling toward obviously needs more fabric.

While you are evaluating your garments, you must remember that excess length and width can both make a garment droopy. If you've ever put on a garment, looked at a specific area, and wanted to reach out and squeeze out

Slit pattern from side seam to crotch seam and spread open

Pants front pattern

If you have a very full outer thigh, slash the pants pattern from the side seam to the crotch seamline and spread it open.

Wit & Wisdom

Many areas of commercial patterns are drawn using straight lines when they really ought to be drawn with a curve. The next time you create or alter a V-neck design, try drawing the neckline with a slight curve down to the point. You will find that your blouse or dress will lie flatter and look straighter on your body.

If your vest hangs lower in the front than the back, slip your hand inside the vest. If the vest hangs correctly, then you probably have a hollow chest.

extra fabric, then there is an area of your body that probably doesn't have as much substance as the garment or pattern manufacturer expects it to have.

Because of its small area, a vest is a very good garment to check. If you put on a vest and it hangs down lower in the front than in the back, then perhaps you have a bust smaller than a B cup, a hollow chest, or tiny shoulders. By slipping your hand inside the vest to fill the hollow part of your chest just below your shoulder, as shown in the illustration above right, you should see the front hemline rise.

If your hand fills up the space, your body straightens out visually, and the vest hangs correctly, then this is probably one of your fitting challenges. If you find that you have this problem, you are not alone—many women have this fitting challenge.

To determine how to correct this problem, look in the mirror, pinch out the excess fabric in the upper area of the vest, make a pleat, and pin it in

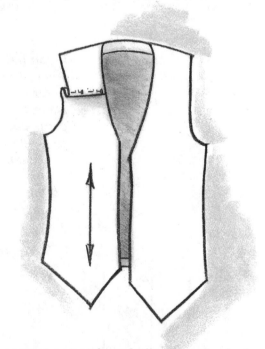

To correct a vest for a hollow chest, pinch out the excess fabric in the upper area, and pin it in place. Pin out the same amount on the vest front pattern.

Looking Good

Small Squares for Round Bodies?

A sloper is a close-fitting garment with little or no ease. Commercial sloper patterns are designed to fit the Wolf dress form perfectly. Generally shown in the back of a commercial pattern book, the sloper can be a dress or pants pattern. The pattern companies suggest that you create your personal sloper from gingham check fabric.

If you make a sloper according to your measurements and try it on, the sloper should help you see how your body differs from the measurements on the pattern companies' size charts. Remember, you may have body mass in different places than the pattern company expects.

Unfortunately, using gingham check fabric forces sewers to concentrate on making the lines straight instead of fitting the body.

Creating a sloper can be a useful experiment, especially if you have a friend to help you, but don't succumb to the urge to use plaid or checked fabric.

You may not be as round as I am, but it is still not helpful to use checked fabric on a round body since the lines will not be straight, as you can see here.

place. Depending on your body shape, you may have to pinch out from ¼ to ¾ inch.

Stand up and see if the vest hangs correctly. Basically, you're removing the fabric where you don't have the body to fill it out. You will pin out the same amount on your vest front pattern.

Alternatively, the back of the vest could be using more fabric than the front, causing the back to rise and the front to appear longer. This could be caused by a pronounced muscle between the neck and shoulder or a full upper back, or your head may sit forward on your body. The solution to this fitting problem is that you need more length in the back of the garment.

Again, I must emphasize that this is yet another reason for doing the croquis. Only by looking at your *entire* body and its shapes and contours will the puzzle of fit begin to make sense. (See the chapter "Create a Croquis" on page 14.)

Measuring Your Body

You must have accurate body measurements to create a garment that fits well. Because it's extremely difficult to measure your own body, find a friend and spend an afternoon measuring each other as Gena and Eileen are doing here. Inaccurate measurements are useless, so relax, grab a friend, and let her handle the tape.

Measure Accurately

Your body measurements are not a value judgment, they are a tool—a very important tool that you need to sew better-fitting garments.

It is important to have an accurate and comprehensive list of your body's measurements. Each of us is a unique human being, and as one of my longtime heroines, Miss Piggy, used to say, "You gotta go with what you got."

Have you ever tried to measure your own body? Did you feel like a human pretzel just trying to read your hip measurement? To get a great fit, you must have accurate measurements, so ask a friend to do the measuring for you.

Before you can begin to fit a garment to your body, you must determine where your body contours—where it goes in, out, up, or down. To do this, you have to measure each area of your body carefully and assign a number to it. This is the next step in the process of solving the puzzle of how to fit garments to your individual body shape.

The Buddy System

To get a great-fitting garment, you need accurate body measurements, but you cannot fit what you cannot see. It is extremely difficult to measure your own body because you have to twist and turn while trying to hold and arrange the tape, and that only gets you inaccurate measurements. Plus, measuring areas such as your back length is next to impossible to do by yourself. Therefore, it is imperative that someone else measures you.

Sewers can be very critical of themselves. They don't want anyone—even the best of friends or a family member—to know what their true measurements are. If you feel the same way, I recommend that you find a sewing buddy you are comfortable with and who will allow you to measure her at the same time.

Inaccurate measurements are useless, so please relax and let someone else handle the tape.

Assemble the Tools

Gather the following tools to take your body measurements accurately:

◆ *Sewing buddy*

◆ *Leotard and tights (optional)*

◆ *Chalk*

If you are squeamish about reading the numerals on the tape measure, try using the metric side. As you measure, don't pull the tape tight, and don't suck in your waist or tummy. If you do, you will get an artificially small measurement. The more accurate your measurements are, the more helpful they will be.

◆ *Elastic (optional)*

◆ *Copy of the "Measurements Worksheet" on page 52*

◆ *Pen or pencil*

◆ *Tape measure (preferably 110 inches long)*

◆ *Chair*

◆ *6-by-24-inch see-through ruler*

Be Prepared

If you want to get precise measurements, take time to get prepared. These measurements are an important part of the foundation you must lay to achieve easy, accurate fitting.

STEP 1: Put on the leotard and tights over your normal undergarments. The leotard should fit close to your body but not be so tight that it moves your flesh around.

STEP 2: Use the chalk to draw a line on the leotard along each shoulder ridge from the neck to shoulder pivot joint, as shown in **Diagram 1** on page 50.

Draw a chalk line on the leotard along each shoulder ridge from your neck to the shoulder pivot joint.

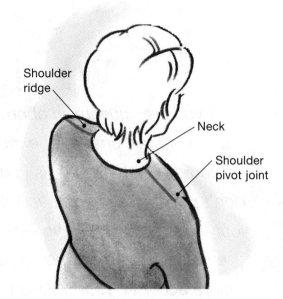

Shoulder ridge

Neck

Shoulder pivot joint

Diagram 1

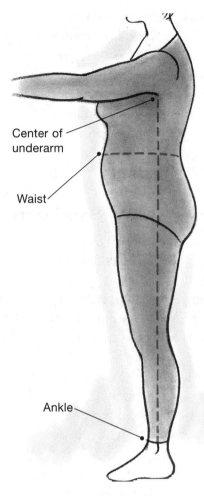

Center of underarm

Waist

Ankle

Diagram 2

STEP: Find the center of your underarm. Use the chalk to draw a line on each side of your body from the center of your underarm to your waist and down to your hip, as shown in **Diagram 2.** Extend the chalk line down the side of your leg to the outside of your ankle. Then draw a line around your waist. You may prefer to tie a narrow piece of elastic around your waist to define it more accurately, but don't tie it too tightly.

STEP: Make a few photocopies of the "Measurements Worksheet" on page 52 so that you can use it whenever you take your measurements.

Measuring

Plan on taking at least an hour to measure your friend and yourself. Have a chair handy so you can get as close to eye level as possible in each area. Make sure the tape is against the body and level, but don't pull it so tight that it causes a dent in the flesh. Take your time and write down each measurement on the worksheet as you go.

Draw a chalk line from the center of the underarm straight down the side of the body to the outside of the ankle. Draw a chalk line at the waist.

STEP: Measure your height. Most pattern companies assume you are 5 foot 6 inches or 5 foot 7 inches tall.

STEP: Measure around the base of the neck with the tape measure standing on edge, as shown in **Diagram 3,** as if you were wearing a close- but not tight-fitting necklace.

STEP: Measure the top of the shoulder from the point where it meets the neck to the shoulder pivot joint, as

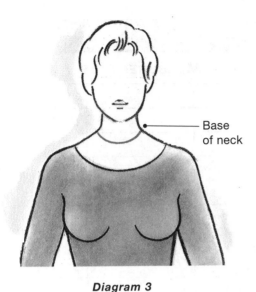

Diagram 3

Stand the tape measure on edge, and measure around the base of the neck as if you were wearing a close-fitting necklace.

shown in **Diagram 4.** To find the shoulder pivot joint, lift your arm straight up to the side, and using your fingertips, feel the pivot hinge at the end of the shoulder. Measure to that point.

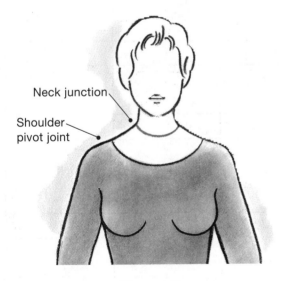

Diagram 4

Measure the top of the shoulder from the junction at the neck to the shoulder pivot joint.

"The numerals on a tape measure are simply tools."

STEP 4: Measure the bustline by putting the tape around the bust beginning at one of the chalk lines on your side, as shown in **Diagram 5.** Note the whole bust measurement and write it on the worksheet.

STEP 5: While holding the tape measure in place at the bustline, have the person doing the measuring move to the other side of your body, and note the front half of your bust measurement. Write it on the worksheet. Subtract that amount from the whole bust measurement, and write the difference—the back bust measurement—on the worksheet. Mark your cup size on the worksheet also.

Beginning at one of the chalk lines on your side, measure the circumference of the bust.

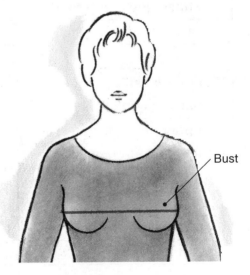

Diagram 5

MEASUREMENTS WORKSHEET			
MEASUREMENT AREA	**MEASUREMENTS**		
DATE MEASUREMENTS TAKEN			
1. Height			
2. Neck			
3. Shoulder			
4. Bust total			
Front			
Back			
Cup size			
5. Waist total			
Front			
Back			
Higher or lower in front			
6. Upper hip total			
Distance from waist			
Front			
Back			
7. Lower hip total			
Distance from waist			
Front			
Back			
8. Fullest lower hip total			
Distance from waist			
9. Bust point			
10. Front length			
11. Back length			
12. Upper arm circumference			
13. Forearm circumference			
14. Sleeve length			
To the elbow			
15. Outside leg length			
Right			
Left			

52

STEP: Measure the circumference of your entire waist starting at your side, as shown in **Diagram 6.**

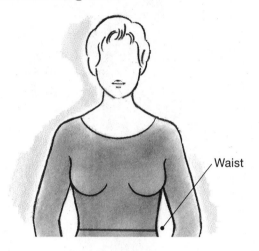

Diagram 6

Starting at your side, measure the circumference of the waist.

STEP: Holding the tape in place, have the person taking the measurements rotate around to the other side of your body, and note the front half of your waist measurement. Write it on the worksheet. Subtract that amount from the total waist measurement, and write the difference—the back of the waist measurement—on the worksheet.

TIP: To get a perfect fit at the waistline, you must compare the measurement of the front of your waist to that of the back. That way you'll be able to alter your patterns to allow for more fabric in the area that needs it. By providing sufficient fabric at the waistline, you will ensure that your side seams will hang straight. In Jane's "After" skirt on page 150, she dropped the front waist, took out fullness from the back, and added it to the front to give the skirt an even drape.

Wit & Wisdom

I like to tease sewers who guard their dress size. If you don't want anyone to know your true size, write to me, and I will send you a size 6 tag for you to sew into your next garment. But why bother, unless you plan to put the size tag on the outside. Others won't know or care what size you are wearing—they will just see how wonderful you look.

STEP: Look at your croquis side view to see if your waist appears higher or lower in the back of your body compared to the front of your body. To get an accurate measurement, have your sewing buddy sit parallel to your waistline. Have her hold a see-through ruler at the side of your body, aligning one of the inch-mark lines with the front of your waist, as shown in **Diagram 7** on page 54. Have her measure how much higher or lower your waist is at the back of your body, and note this figure on the worksheet.

STEP: Most commercial patterns and fitting texts suggest you measure the hips 7 to 8 inches below the waistline, but that doesn't give you a clear picture of the shape of your body below your waist.

It's important to measure both the upper hip and the lower hip to enable you to fit a pattern in these frequently troublesome areas. By comparing the pattern measurements with your upper and lower hip measurements, you will be able to

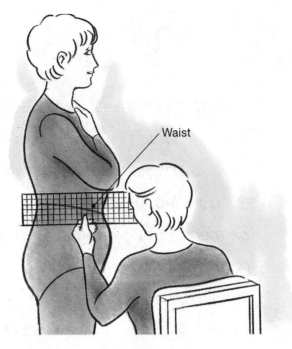

Diagram 7

To determine if your waist appears higher or lower in the back of your body compared to the front of your body, your sewing buddy should sit in a chair and align one of the inch lines on a see-through ruler with the chalk mark on the front of the waist. Measure how much higher or lower your waist is at the back of your body.

adjust the pattern as needed to ensure that you have enough fabric to allow the garment to hang attractively from the hips.

Some people, including me, have what I call hip fluff—that little ridge of flesh that poufs out just below the waist—which is usually the widest point of their upper hip measurement. Determine how far below the waist the upper hip measurement occurs. About 3 inches behind the side seam, measure the distance from the waist to where the upper hip begins, as shown in **Diagram 8.**

STEP: Measure the circumference of your upper hip, starting at your side, as shown in **Diagram 9.**

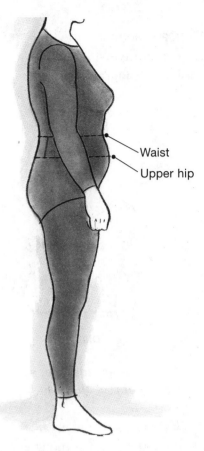

Waist
Upper hip

Diagram 8

Measure the distance from your waist to where the upper hip, or the widest part of your hips, begins.

STEP: It is helpful to have a front-to-back comparison in the upper hip area also so you can allow more fabric in that area if needed. Holding the tape in place, have the person taking the measurements rotate around to the other side of your body, and note the front half of your upper hip measurement. Write it on the worksheet. Subtract that amount from the total upper hip measurement, and write the difference—the back of the upper hip measurement—on the worksheet.

STEP: Some of us have large tummies and fluffy upper hips but no fannies, so, as I mentioned earlier, a hip

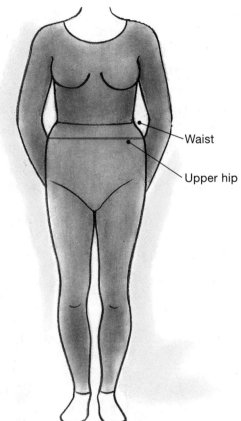

Diagram 9

Starting at the side of your body, measure the circumference of your upper hip, and write it on your worksheet.

measurement taken at the traditional 7 to 8 inches down from the waist is not at all useful. As in the upper hip, you also need to know how far down the lower hip occurs. Measure the distance from the waist to where the lower hip begins at the fullest part of your fanny, as shown in **Diagram 10**.

TIP: The person doing the measuring should be seated on the chair. That way, she will be able to feel the hip socket bump on the side of your body and see the fullest part of the buttock.

STEP: Measure your lower hip circumference, starting at your side, as also shown in **Diagram 10**.

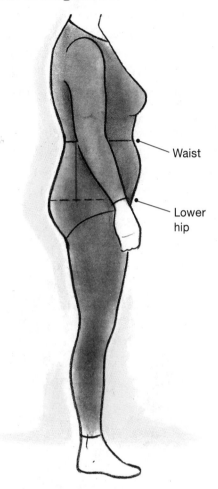

Diagram 10

Measure the distance from the waist to where the lower hip begins, and then measure the lower hip at the fullest part of the fanny.

STEP: It is also extremely helpful to have a front-to-back comparison in the lower hip area so you can allow more fabric in that area if needed. Holding the tape in place, have the person taking the measurements rotate around to the other side of your body, and note the front half of your lower hip measurement. Write it on the worksheet. Subtract that amount from the total lower hip measurement, and write the difference—the back of the lower hip measurement—on the worksheet.

STEP 15: The next measurement you may want to take is the fullest lower hip, frequently referred to as the "saddle bags." This measurement is for people who carry weight on the outside of their legs. Not everyone needs to take this measurement, but if you do, it will help you to make better-fitting pants and skirts.

Measure the circumference of the fullest lower hip, and measure its distance down from your waist at the side seam, as shown in **Diagram 11.**

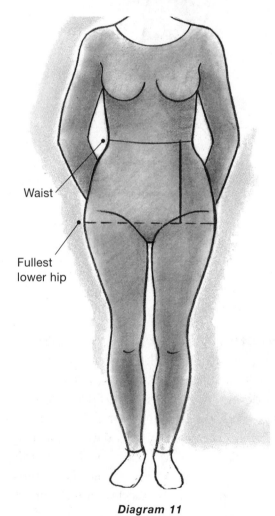

Diagram 11

Measure the distance from the waist to the fullest lower hip, and then measure the circumference of the fullest lower hip.

STEP 16: To determine the position of the bust point, measure the distance from the point where the neck meets the shoulder, straight down and to the fullest point on the bust, as shown in **Diagram 12.** Then measure the front length from the neck, over the bust, and down to the waist directly below the bust point. Record these measurements on the worksheet.

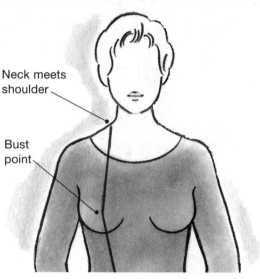

Diagram 12

Determine the location of the bust point, and then measure the length of the front of the upper body from the neck, over the bust, and to the waist.

STEP 17: Measure the back length from the point at the base of the neck, over the center back, and down to the waist, as shown in **Diagram 13.**

STEP 18: Measure the circumference of the fullest part of the upper arm, as shown in **Diagram 14,** which is sometimes referred to as the biceps. Then measure the circumference of the forearm. If you like to push up your sleeves, you will find that the forearm measurement will help you ensure that your sleeves stay up.

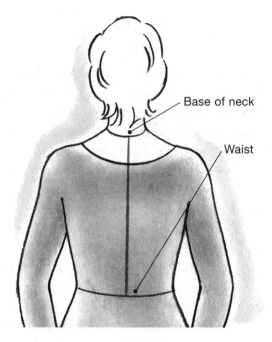

Diagram 13

Measure the length of the back from the point at the base of the neck over the center back to the waistline.

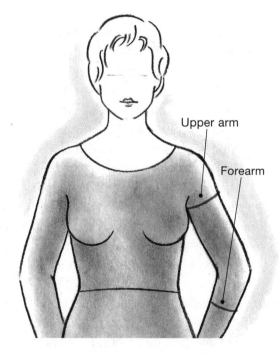

Diagram 14

Measure the circumference of the fullest part of the upper arm, and then measure the circumference of the forearm.

STEP: Measure the sleeve length from the shoulder pivot joint over the elbow and to the base of the wrist bone, as shown in **Diagram 15.** (To find the shoulder pivot joint, see Step 3 on page 50.) The elbow should be slightly bent but not bent so far as to exaggerate the length of this measurement. Then measure the length of the arm from the shoulder pivot joint to the elbow.

Measure the sleeve length from the shoulder pivot joint, over the elbow, to the base of the wrist.

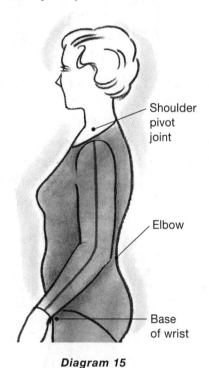

Diagram 15

TIP: Some women will discover that they fluctuate by several pounds during their monthly cycles. Some garments are comfortable at certain times during the month but are not comfortable at other times. If you feel bloated, write this on the "Measurements Worksheet" and remeasure another day. Only you know how you want to feel in your clothes. You must decide if you are willing to wear your clothes tight on days you feel bloated or loose on other days.

Wit & Wisdom

You may want to think about how your weight fluctuates during the day. If your garments feel tighter in the evening, you might want to try measuring yourself at two different times during the day.

STEP: Measure the outside leg length on top of the chalk line from the waist over the farthest point on the outside of the thigh down to the bottom of the ankle, as shown in **Diagram 16.** You may want to measure the outside of both legs, in case one leg is slightly shorter or longer than the other.

Measure the outside leg length on top of the chalk line from the waist to the bottom of the ankle.

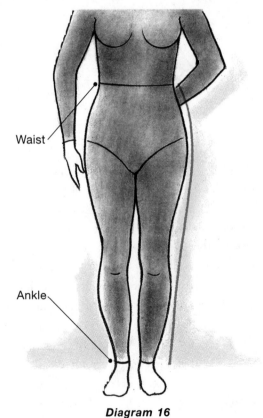

Waist

Ankle

Diagram 16

Compare Your Measurements

Fabulous as you are, you will now be able to see exactly where your body differs from commercial patterns, and you can make better decisions about where to add or subtract fabric to create a proper fit.

Remember, commercial patterns are made for a B-cup bust, and if you are fuller than that, it takes more fabric length as well as width to get over the extra fullness of your body.

Now that you have recorded your measurements, you must compare them to the idealized body form used by pattern companies. Each pattern company uses slightly different standards. Several brands of European patterns include full sets of measurements for a wide variety of sizes with each of their patterns. Some of the domestic patterns don't provide quite as many measurements.

I formulated the measurement table on the opposite page when I created my own pattern line. It is an average of all the commercial patterns currently on the market. Photocopy this table and highlight the numbers closest to your actual measurements. Don't be surprised if few of your measurements fall into the same size range.

Do not be negative!! These measurements are not a value judgment. You now have another tool that will help you create great-fitting garments. You know exactly where your body contours and by how much. You know where you need to add more fabric or where you need less fabric.

In subsequent chapters I will explain how to interpret these numbers and how to use them to create a wardrobe that fits you perfectly, but next you will learn how to choose the correct fabric for a garment and why that is critical to getting a good fit.

AVERAGE COMMERCIAL PATTERN MEASUREMENTS

Size	Height	Neck	Shoulder	Bust	Waist	Hip	Bust point	Front length	Back length	Upper arm	Sleeve length	Outside leg length
X-Small												
Size 6	5'7"	13¼" (33.6 cm)	4¾" (12 cm)	31" (78.7 cm)	23¾" (60.3 cm)	34" (86.4 cm)	9¾" (24.8 cm)	16¾" (42.5 cm)	15¾" (40 cm)	9¾" (24.8 cm)	22¾" (57.8 cm)	41¾" (106 cm)
Small												
Size 8	5'7"	13½" (34.3 cm)	4¾" (12 cm)	32¼" (81.9 cm)	24½" (62.3 cm)	34¾" (88.3 cm)	10" (25.4 cm)	17" (43.2 cm)	15¾" (40 cm)	10¼" (26 cm)	23¼" (59 cm)	41¾" (106 cm)
Size 10	5'7"	13¾" (34.9 cm)	5" (12.7 cm)	33½" (85.1 cm)	25¼" (64.1 cm)	35½" (90.2 cm)	10¼" (26 cm)	17¼" (43.8 cm)	15¾" (40 cm)	10¾" (27.3 cm)	23¼" (59 cm)	41¾" (106 cm)
Medium												
Size 12	5'7"	14¼" (36.2 cm)	5" (12.7 cm)	34½" (87.7 cm)	26¾" (67.9 cm)	37" (94 cm)	10¾" (27.3 cm)	17¾" (45.1 cm)	15¾" (40 cm)	11" (27.9 cm)	23¾" (60.3 cm)	41¾" (106 cm)
Size 14	5'7"	14½" (36.9 cm)	5" (12.7 cm)	36¼" (92 cm)	28½" (72.4 cm)	38½" (97.8 cm)	11" (27.9 cm)	18¼" (46.3 cm)	16" (40.6 cm)	11½" (29.2 cm)	23¾" (60.3 cm)	41¾" (106 cm)
Large												
Size 16	5'7"	15" (38.1 cm)	5" (12.7 cm)	37¾" (95.9 cm)	30" (76.2 cm)	40⅛" (101.9 cm)	11½" (29.2 cm)	18½" (47 cm)	16¼" (41.2 cm)	11¾" (29.8 cm)	24" (61 cm)	41¾" (106 cm)
Size 18	5'7"	15½" (39.4 cm)	5¼" (13.3 cm)	39½" (100.4 cm)	31½" (80 cm)	41¾" (106 cm)	12¼" (31.1 cm)	19½" (49.6 cm)	16¼" (41.2 cm)	12" (30.5 cm)	24" (61 cm)	41¾" (106 cm)
X-Large												
Size 20	5'7"	15¾" (40 cm)	5¼" (13.3 cm)	41" (104.1 cm)	34" (86.4 cm)	43¼" (109.8 cm)	12¼" (31.1 cm)	19½" (49.6 cm)	16½" (41.9 cm)	12¼" (31.1 cm)	24" (61 cm)	41¾" (106 cm)
Size 22	5'7"	16¼" (41.2 cm)	5½" (14 cm)	43¼" (109.8 cm)	36¼" (92 cm)	45" (114.3 cm)	12½" (31.8 cm)	19¾" (50.2 cm)	16½" (41.9 cm)	12½" (31.8 cm)	24" (61 cm)	41¾" (106 cm)
XX-Large												
Size 24	5'7"	16½" (41.9 cm)	5½" (14 cm)	45½" (115.6 cm)	38½" (97.8 cm)	47¼" (120 cm)	13" (33 cm)	20" (50.8 cm)	16½" (41.9 cm)	13" (33 cm)	24½" (62.3 cm)	41¾" (106 cm)
Size 26	5'7"	17" (43.2 cm)	5¾" (14.6 cm)	48" (121.9 cm)	41" (104.1 cm)	50" (127 cm)	13½" (34.3 cm)	20¼" (51.4 cm)	16½" (41.9 cm)	13½" (34.3 cm)	24½" (62.3 cm)	41¾" (106 cm)
XXX-Large												
Size 28	5'7"	17¼" (43.8 cm)	5¾" (14.6 cm)	50½" (128.3 cm)	43¼" (109.8 cm)	52" (132.1 cm)	13¾" (34.9 cm)	20¾" (52.7 cm)	16½" (41.9 cm)	14¼" (36.2 cm)	24½" (62.3 cm)	41¾" (106 cm)
Size 30	5'7"	17¾" (45.1 cm)	5¾" (14.6 cm)	52¾" (134 cm)	5½" (115.6 cm)	54¼" (137.8 cm)	14¼" (36.2 cm)	21¼" (53.9 cm)	16½" (41.9 cm)	14½" (36.9 cm)	25" (63.5 cm)	41¾" (106 cm)

From Fabric to Fit

To create a stylish garment with a great fit, you must develop a working knowledge of fabrics and their properties. You must investigate, check, test, and feel a wide range of fabrics and garments. Fabric choice affects how a garment fits, feels, and hangs on your body, and it affects the construction process as well. You can use most weights, drapes, textures, and types of fabric if the pattern you choose has the correct amount of ease for your body.

Selecting Your Fabric

Choosing the correct fabric for a garment is critical to getting a good fit.

Make an elegant fitted jacket with princess seams and two-piece sleeves from the stiff wool fabric (center), but use the drapey rayon (left) for a comfortable loose-fitting pantsuit.

I wish I could take each and every one of you into my fabric store. I would show you all of the different fabrics and let you feel them as I describe them to you.

But since that is not possible, I want you to take time to reach into your fabric stash and pull out lots of different fabrics. Hold them in your hands, stroke them, and feel them. Then go into your closet and feel the clothing that you currently own—especially those garments that you love to wear.

To be able to create stylish, attractive garments that fit your particular body shape, you must have a basic knowledge of fabrics and their individual properties.

Tools for Choosing Fabric

To help you make the right decision when selecting fabric, I developed two guidelines that are essential tools. Learn them and remember to use them.

Fabric Selection Tool Number 1: The thicker, the crisper, the heavier the fabric, the closer to the body the garment should be, and there should be more opportunities for fit.

An Austrian boiled wool jacket is the perfect example of a garment made from a really thick, heavy, stiff fabric.

An Austrian boiled wool jacket must have a variety of fitting devices to get the fabric to bend around a human body.

This jacket is made up of many pieces. It has princess seams, a seam up the center back, and two-piece sleeves. All of those fitting devices are used because the wool fabric is so stiff it can't bend around a human body.

Fabric Selection Tool Number 2: The thinner, the softer, the drapier the fabric, the more volume the garment must have.

For example, you love the simple gored skirt that you made from rayon, but now you want to make the same skirt out of a chiffonlike fabric. To do this, you have to add many more pieces of fabric or more

gores to the skirt in order to get it to hang correctly on your body.

Without the additional fabric, the chiffon skirt looks skimpy and pulls against your body. Unless you have a true Wolf dress form body, a close-fitting chiffon garment shows off every bump on your body.

To get a skirt made from a very drapey fabric like chiffon to hang correctly on your body, it must be made of many gores or pieces of fabric.

You can avoid the following sewing blunders by using my fabric selection tools.

You make a blouse from a crisp fabric such as crisp cotton or medium-weight linen, and it fits fairly close to your body. You just love the way the blouse looks on you. So, you decide to use that same pattern to make a blouse from rayon challis.

BECOME FABRIC SAVVY

Fabric choices are very individual. The table in "Develop Your Tactile Memory" on page 64 will help you combine fabric and patterns. You can use most weights, drapes, textures, and types of fabric if the pattern you choose has the correct amount of ease for your body.

As you work through this chapter, you must actually investigate, check, test, and feel fabrics and garments. That way you will develop a working knowledge of fabrics and their properties.

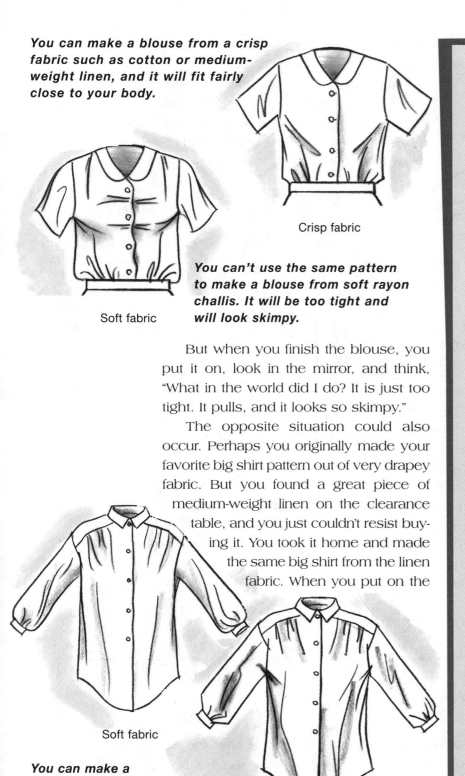

You can make a blouse from a crisp fabric such as cotton or medium-weight linen, and it will fit fairly close to your body.

Crisp fabric

Soft fabric

You can't use the same pattern to make a blouse from soft rayon challis. It will be too tight and will look skimpy.

But when you finish the blouse, you put it on, look in the mirror, and think, "What in the world did I do? It is just too tight. It pulls, and it looks so skimpy."

The opposite situation could also occur. Perhaps you originally made your favorite big shirt pattern out of very drapey fabric. But you found a great piece of medium-weight linen on the clearance table, and you just couldn't resist buying it. You took it home and made the same big shirt from the linen fabric. When you put on the

Soft fabric

You can make a wonderful big shirt out of very drapey fabric.

Crisp fabric

Make the same shirt from medium-weight linen and it will be much too bulky.

DEVELOP YOUR TACTILE MEMORY

To select fabrics confidently, you must develop your tactile memory. Tactile memory means that by feeling a piece of fabric you can relate it to a garment that you own and how that garment feels. By developing your tactile memory, you will be able to make an educated guess as to whether or not a particular fabric will work with your pattern.

To develop your tactile memory, follow the instructions in the table on the opposite page to determine whether a piece of fabric is drapey, soft, and supple, or crisp, thick, and heavy. Choose garments from your wardrobe that you love, and hang them, pluck them, squeeze them, and touch them to discover what kind of fabrics you prefer to wear. Perform these four tests on a wide variety of your stash fabrics to discover how they feel. Then use these tests to check the next fabric you want to use in a garment.

THE TEST	HOW YOU DO IT	IF IT'S DRAPEY, SOFT, SUPPLE FABRIC...	IF IT'S CRISP, THICK, HEAVY FABRIC...
Hang	Pinch the fabric as close to the center as possible and see how it drapes. Don't test the fabric near edges, selvages, interfacing, or seams as these variables increase the body and rigidity of the fabric.	It hangs like a waterfall. There are no angles or edges. The drapier the fabric, the narrower the fall.	It does not fall on its own and bends with hard angles.
Pluck	While the fabric hangs, pull up one side and see if it falls down or stays out to the side.	It falls down easily.	It tends to stay where it is pulled.
Squeeze	Grab a handful of the fabric and squeeze it in your hand.	It molds to the shape of your hand. You should not feel resistance or rubbery bounce. It does not take up much space in your hand.	It does not shape to your hand, and the mass does not diminish. There may be a spongy resistance to crushing.
Touch	Run your fingers over the surface of the fabric. (This is the least important tactile test of a fabric, and yet it is the one most sewers do first.)	The surface does not resist your touch and is very flexible. This is the variable that can fool you. Be sure to use the hang, pluck, and drape methods as your primary tests.	The surface may feel stiff, unyielding, and even rough, but it can also be brushed or washed or have a soft pile.

"Use soft fabric in an area you want to de-emphasize."

shirt, you found the new shirt felt huge and much too bulky.

Both of these discouraging scenarios are caused by choosing the wrong fabric for a garment design. A garment that is stitched from a drapey, supple fabric needs more ease, or room for movement, and a garment that is made from a crisp, heavy fabric needs more opportunities for fit—darts, seams, or tucks, for example. (Opportunities for fit are discussed in full starting on page 74.)

Choosing Fabric Wisely

The back of a commercial pattern envelope usually provides general fabric recommendations for the style of garment. It's not important that you look for the specific fabric name. Instead, you have to decide whether you want a fabric that hangs and drapes or whether you want a fabric that is crisp and stands away from your body, like one used for a stand-up collar.

A good example of how fabric can affect a garment design is in pants. If you purchase a pair of jeans, the denim fabric is thick and heavy and does not have much drape. The denim is very stiff, and when you pull the jeans from the clothes dryer, you can almost stand them up in a corner. Fabric of this type must be worn very close to the body.

But if you purchase a pair of tailored slacks, they might be made from a gabardine fabric that is much drapier than denim and a lot thinner. Thinner fabric needs to have more ease and hangs looser and drapier.

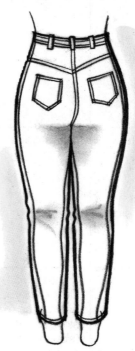

Jeans are constructed from denim fabric that is thick and heavy and does not have much drape. Since denim is a stiff fabric, it must be worn close to the body.

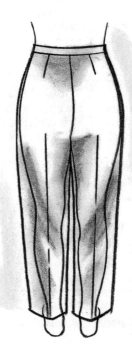

Tailored slacks might be made from a gabardine fabric, which is much drapier than denim and a lot thinner. Garments made from this fabric must have more ease and must hang looser and drapier than denim.

If you plan an evening on the town and purchase a dressy pair of pants, you might select crepe de chine, which is extremely soft and drapey. Very thin fabric like this needs lots of ease.

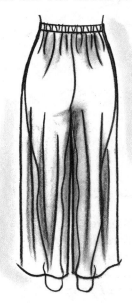

Dressy pants might be made from crepe de chine, which is extremely soft and drapey.

The fabric chosen for each of these three styles of pants determines how the pants will fit, feel, and hang on your body.

Style, Fit, and Ease

Every woman prefers a particular style of garment. You may like very loose, flowing clothing that is gorgeous and ethereal. Or you may want a more tailored and trim look for a crisp, businesslike appearance. The amount of ease needed to accomplish each of these looks is very different.

It is most flattering to use soft fabric in an area that you want to de-emphasize. Drapey fabric skims over curves and falls softly.

TIP: If you want to use soft fabric for a garment, choose a design with lots of ease. That way the volume of fabric balances the smaller area of your body.

Not only does fabric choice determine how a garment fits, feels, and hangs on your body, but it also affects the construction process. Pants made from a thinner, softer, drapier fabric have a deeper, looser crotch, while pants made from a thicker, crisper, heavier fabric have a shorter, tighter crotch seam.

You want to use crisp fabric in an area of your body where you are small so that area will look more pronounced. Crisp fabric stands away from the body and adds volume.

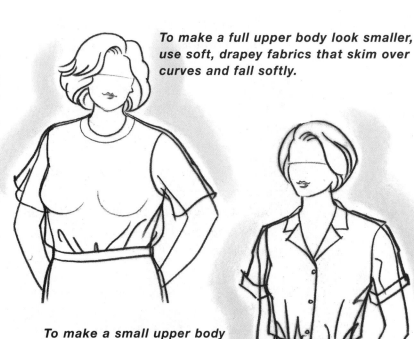

To make a full upper body look smaller, use soft, drapey fabrics that skim over curves and fall softly.

To make a small upper body look larger, use a crisp fabric that stands away from the body and adds volume.

However, most women are completely unaware of how much ease they prefer in a garment.

There are two kinds of ease—wearing ease and design ease. Wearing ease is the minimum amount of room allowed in the pattern so that you move about in the garment comfortably. Design ease is added to the garment by the designer to create the silhouette. All patterns are created with a degree of wearing ease, while some patterns have more design ease than others.

To determine how much overall ease you prefer in your garments, I recommend that you try my "pinch" test. This simple test will help you to determine how much fabric is in a garment in excess of your body measurements. Do the test every time you try on a garment that you like. The only tools that you need are your hands and a tape measure or ruler.

STEP 1: Put on a garment that is comfortable and that you enjoy wearing.

STEP 2: Pinch fabric on each side of your body at the bustline, as shown on this page.

STEP 3: Use a tape measure or ruler to measure the pinched fabric, and multiply that measurement by four because on each side of your body there is a front and back to the pinch.

TIP: You may want to ask one of your sewing buddies to help measure the pinched fabric. That way you will get a more accurate measurement.

To determine how much wearing ease you prefer in a garment, put on a garment that is comfortable and that you enjoy wearing, and pinch the fabric on each side of your body at the bustline.

STEP 4: Repeat Steps 2 and 3 at your waistline.

STEP 5: Repeat Steps 2 and 3 at the fullest area of your hips.

STEP 6: Examine the calculation for each body part, which will show you how much wearing ease you prefer in a garment.

The table on the opposite page provides general estimates of the wearing ease and design ease used by most pattern companies. It should help you select a pattern that suits your personal style.

By knowing how much ease you prefer in a garment and the properties of different fabrics, you can figure out how to make garments in the style you prefer with the amount of ease that is comfortable for you.

	GARMENT			
WEARING EASE AND DESIGN EASE ALLOWANCES IN COMMERCIAL PATTERNS				
SILHOUETTE	**Dress, blouse, vest (measure at bust)**	**Jacket (measure at bust)**	**Coat (measure at widest area)**	**Skirt, slacks (measure at hips)**
Close-fitting (fits the body snugly)	0"–3" (0–7.6 cm)	—	—	0"–2" (0–5.1 cm)
Fitted	3"–4" (7.6–10.2 cm)	3¾"–4½" (9.5–11.4 cm)	5¼"–6¾" (13.3–17.1 cm)	2"–3" (5.1–7.6 cm)
Semifitted (skims the body)	4"–5" (10.2–12.7 cm)	4⅜"–5¾" (11.2–14.6 cm)	6¾"–8" (17.1–20.3 cm)	3"–4" (7.6–10.2 cm)
Loose-fitting	5"–8" (12.7–20.3 cm)	5⅞"– 10" (14.9–25.4 cm)	8"–12" (20.3–30.5 cm)	4"–6" (10.2–15.2 cm)
Very loose-fitting	more than 8" (20.3 cm)	more than 10" (25.4 cm)	more than 12" (30.5 cm)	more than 6" (15.2 cm)

The Subtle Side of Fabric

Another key to selecting an appropriate fabric is learning to discern the subtle differences in fabrics.

Many sewers use the terms "soft" and "drapey" synonymously, but these words really don't mean the same thing. Something can be soft on the surface and not be drapey.

The surface texture of sand-washed rayons and sand-washed silks is very soft and luxurious. However, sand-washed rayon can be a very rigid fabric on the inside even though it has a nice soft feeling on the outside of the fabric. The inside of sand-washed rayon is actually so structured that it does not drape but stands away from the body slightly.

Consider the numerous kinds of velvets that are available. Although the surface of cotton velveteen is very soft and luxurious, the back of the fabric is often stiff or rigid. It has a lot of structure and does not drape. Rayon velvet or silk velvet, however, will drape over the body. The backs of these velvets are very supple and loosely woven so they curve and hang softly from the body.

There are many beautiful 100 percent cotton fabrics in fabulous prints and yummy solids on the market today. Most of these fabrics have been developed for quilting, so they have quite a lot of body in them. However, the fabrics are so beautiful that many sewers are tempted to make garments out of them when, in fact, a pattern's instructions might call for rayon or a lighter, drapier fabric.

Combining these fabrics with the wrong pattern can lead to "wadders." (If you don't know what a wadder is, see "Don't Sew Blindfolded" on page 7.)

You *must* follow the fabric guidelines on a pattern no matter how gorgeous the color, print, or texture of the fabric you really desire. The pattern companies design the garments with particular fabrics in mind. You will not be happy with the results if you do not follow their guidelines.

You cannot achieve great fit until you acknowledge the importance of fabric and take fabric differences into consideration in every one of your projects.

Looking Good

A Tale of Two Skirts

A few years ago, I saw two very similar skirts in a pattern book. Both of them had a box pleat at the center front and a few single direction pleats on either side of the center front. The backs of both skirts were gathered, and both of the patterns were size 12.

One pattern envelope indicated that the width at the bottom edge of one skirt was 109 inches, while the other pattern envelope indicated the skirt was 68 inches around the bottom.

The big difference between the two skirts was the recommended fabric. In the fullest skirt, the recommended fabrics were challis and crepe de chine, both very drapey fabrics. The narrower skirt called for wool, wool blends, and linen suiting—in other words, a much crisper, heavier fabric.

Each pattern automatically allowed for the ease in the suggested fabrics, thus the finished garments looked similar.

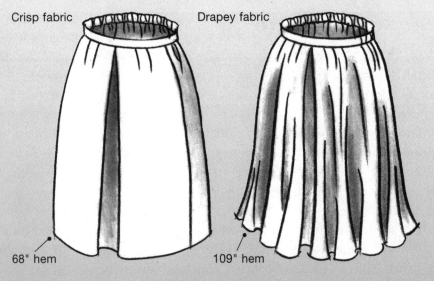

Crisp fabric   Drapey fabric

68" hem   109" hem

Two skirts can be made from two very different fabrics and yet look very similar if the patterns allow for the ease in the suggested fabrics. The pattern for the skirt on the left called for wool, wool blends, or linen suiting—in other words, crisper, heavier fabrics—while the pattern for the skirt on the right recommended challis or crepe de chine, both very drapey fabrics.

Changing the Structure of Fabric

I've given you the tools you need to select fabrics wisely. But there are other factors that come into play in the sewing process.

Three factors—interfacing, stitching, and lining—can greatly affect the performance of a fabric in your chosen design. I'll examine each one individually so that you know how you will be changing the characteristics of the fabric.

Interfacing

The characteristics of any fabric will change when it is interfaced. Just as you must develop your tactile memory for fabric, you also must develop your tactile memory for how different fabrics feel when they are used with different types of interfacing.

Before you begin to sew a garment, test several types of interfacing on each fashion fabric you're considering to see how each interfacing product affects the drape and feel of the fashion fabrics. In addition, you must make sure the type of interfacing is appropriate for the style of

A lovely rayon challis may drape gently off your hips, but add a bit of interfacing or a lining at the neckline and this fabric may become stiff and unattractive.

Wit & Wisdom

Do you know that you can use more than one kind of interfacing in a garment? I know, the pattern says 1 yard of interfacing, but you can purchase a stiff interfacing for the collar and cuffs and a softer interfacing for the front band. Different areas of the garment need different types of interfacing.

A silk crepe de chine blouse with a traditional collar requires a crisp, medium-weight interfacing.

garment, not just the type of fabric. You may use the same kind of fabric in several garments, and each might require a different type of interfacing.

For instance, you may use silk crepe de chine for blouses in several different styles. One blouse may have a mandarin collar that must have a very firm interfacing so that the collar will stand up.

To make a mandarin collar using silk crepe de chine, you must use a very firm interfacing so that the collar will stand up.

Another blouse may have a traditional collar that requires a crisp interfacing with a medium-weight structure.

A third blouse may have a V-neck with a facing that calls for just a touch of soft interfacing to prevent the neckline from drooping.

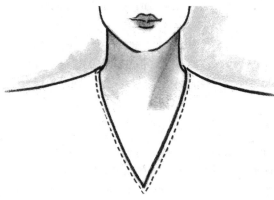

A V-neck blouse made from silk crepe de chine needs just a touch of soft interfacing to prevent the neckline from drooping.

For each of the above examples, the interaction between the fabric and interfacing are important to garment design. With thoughtful testing, you can learn to choose the correct combination for any garment.

Stitching

Every seam or row of stitching adds more structure to a garment. Each stitch is formed with a knot between the top and bottom threads. The knotted threads that hold the two layers together combine with the double or triple layers of fabric to make that area thicker and less supple.

By topstitching or edgestitching, you will cause that area of the garment to become even more crisp. Thus, when you decide to analyze the fabric on a completed garment, always analyze the fabric away from the seams.

It is not a good idea to use a standard straight stitch when sewing on very soft or stretchy fabrics because the fabric will drape and pucker around the stitching. Instead, use a narrow zigzag stitch or a double needle (the back of double-needle stitching is a zigzag stitch) to top-stitch a soft or stretchy fabric. Any of these options will allow you to use a stitch that will give with the fabric.

Lining

A garment lining serves three purposes. First, it makes it easier for you to put the garment on and take it off. Second, it covers the internal workings of the garment, and third, it stabilizes the entire garment. Even though traditional lining fabric is thin, it usually has very little give in either length or width.

When you choose a lining fabric, it must have properties that are similar to the fashion fabric. The lining will usually be softer, but it is important to keep any stretch factors in the fashion fabric and lining similar but not necessarily identical. If you are making a jacket, skirt, or pants that will be lined, and you are

"You must analyze every fabric that you buy."

using a knit fabric or modern woven fabric that has Lycra added to it for give and comfort, try using tricot or bathing-suit lining fabric. These linings will give like the garments give.

Tools Not Rules

In this chapter, I've provided a broad overview of the fabric variables that affect garment construction and fit. I know some of you were hoping for a list of what fabric to use in specific projects, but that would be an impossible task. Each of your garments, fabrics, and bodies are different, and you must learn to analyze each one of these factors.

Remember, you need the right tools to make good sewing decisions. Spend time doing your homework by analyzing each fabric you buy and all of the fabrics in your personal stash. Also, remember to analyze the fabric information on the pattern envelope. By matching the properties of the fabric to the garment design, you will be more successful in your sewing.

TIP: On fine fabrics, make your seams smoother by using fine sewing thread. Look for lingerie or fine embroidery thread.

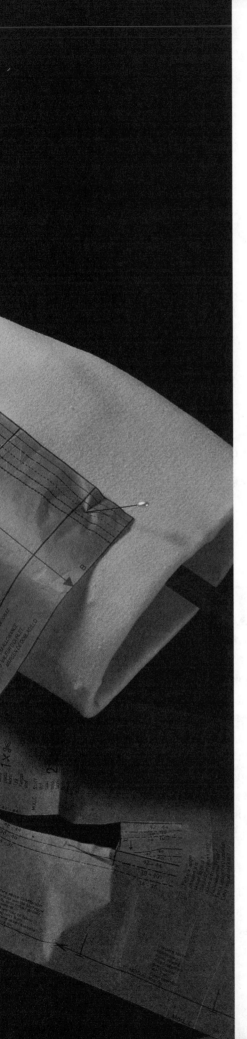

Opportunities for Fit

No matter what your size or shape, you can make gorgeous garments that fit your body. To do that, you must know where you need more fabric to cover your body and where you need less. Then you must use fitting devices—darts, pleats, tucks, gathers, yokes, and seams—to contour the pattern to fit all of your curves.

Match Fabric to Pattern

To get a great fit, you must know how to manipulate two-dimensional fabric—whether woven or knit, natural or man-made—to fit your three-dimensional body.

If your pattern does not have darts, tucks, or seams, there is just no way you are going to get a stiff woven fabric to wrap around your curved body.

Throughout most of history, fabrics were created by weaving threads and yarns together. Garments were created by combining shaped pieces of fabric, and women's clothing fit fairly close to their bodies.

During the 1960s, the world of sewing changed dramatically. Polyester fibers were knit together to create new fabrics, and those knit fabrics opened the door to a whole new way of sewing.

First, our sewing machines didn't want to handle the new fabrics, so the manufacturers invented new needles designed to stitch knit fabrics. Then new and stronger lines of thread were developed.

Most important, with the increasing availability of knit fabrics, we used simpler and simpler pattern pieces. We assembled rectangles of fabric with barely a curve in sight, and the knit fabric stretched and draped easily to fit our three-dimensional bodies.

Patterns for knit garments were simple to assemble. Many of the designs included elastic waistbands, and instead of using traditional hemming methods, we just turned the edge under and used a zigzag stitch to hold it in place.

Pattern companies capitalized on the new ease of sewing by beginning to label their patterns "easy," "easier," and "easiest." The rating applied to a pattern was based on the number of pattern pieces needed to assemble the garment. The fewer the pieces, the easier the pattern was to assemble.

Although knits no longer dominate our wardrobes, many sewers continue to work with the new natural fiber knit fabrics. There is a great variety of softer, natural fiber knits available, and the "easy, easier, easiest" patterns can still be used with these fabrics.

The Fit Era

Eventually, the knit era faded, and we returned to sewing more woven fabrics. Although the end of the knit era should have been the reintroduction of the fit era, many sewers retained some of the knit era mentality.

Have you ever seen a knit garment that was made from a pattern designed for woven fabrics? Some sections of the garment look very stiff while other areas look saggy. Patterns that are specifically designed for woven fabrics have more pieces, seams, and interfacing, all of which create the structure and increase the rigidity needed for a great-fitting garment.

> *"You must put the fabric where your body needs it."*

You can't use a woven fabric with a simplified pattern that has no opportunities for fit. The best example of this is my "wallpapering a beach ball" analogy.

Using big, flat pattern pieces on a round and curved human body is about as useful as trying to wallpaper a beach ball. If you think about covering a beach ball with a flat piece of wallpaper, it is obvious that you cannot cover the round ball smoothly. The paper will protrude in ridges and lumps. There is just no way to cover that smooth, round ball with a large, flat piece of paper—or fabric.

You simply cannot cover a round beach ball with one large, flat piece of fabric.

To fit the paper to the surface of the round beach ball, there are two options. The first is to use papier-mâché where paper is torn or cut into small pieces before it is applied to a large surface area. This is comparable to using smaller or more pattern pieces to create a garment.

To fit a flat piece of fabric to a round surface, you could cut the fabric into smaller pieces and overlap them as in papier mâché.

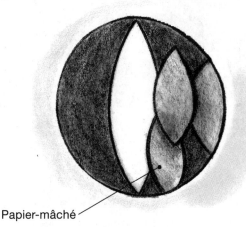

Papier-mâché

The second option is to apply the larger pieces of paper, cut into them, and overlap the edges—in other words, create darts.

By folding the flat piece of fabric and forming darts, you could cover a three-dimensional form.

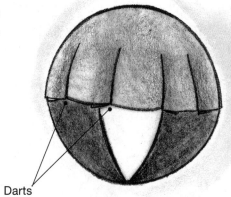

Darts

So, to fit a woven fabric to our rounded, curved, three-dimensional bodies, we have to cut it, then piece or fold it.

Choosing Opportunities for Fit

To create a garment that fits your individual body shape, you must use what I call "opportunities for fit," or fitting devices, to manipulate the pattern and the fabric.

To get a great-fitting garment, you must remove fabric from an area where you don't need it and put it in an area where you do need it. This is what keeps a garment from looking like a sack.

In any garment, you can use one or more opportunities for fit, which include darts, pleats or tucks, gathers, easing, yokes, additional pattern pieces, and princess seams. Each of these fitting devices removes excess fabric from one section of the garment and adds it to another area to contour the flat pattern pieces to fit your three-dimensional body.

THE DYNAMIC DART

The most commonly used and underrated opportunity for fit is the dart. The dart is actually a tapered seam that removes excess fabric from a specific area to allow the garment to lie smoothly over the body. A dart can be designed to remove either a small sliver of fabric or a large chunk of fabric.

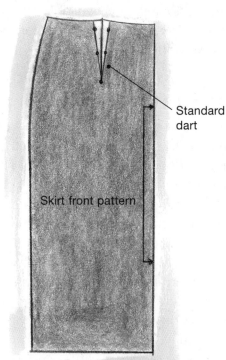

Standard dart

Skirt front pattern

The standard dart is used to remove excess fabric, allowing a garment to lie smoothly on the body.

A standard dart is straight, but to get a good fit, it often should be curved in or out. For example, if you have hip fluff, you want to use a curved dart to accommodate the curve of your body just below your waist.

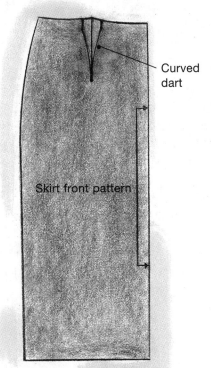

Skirt front pattern

Curved dart

A curved dart functions the same way a straight dart does, but it allows you to get a closer fit.

On those of us who have hip fluff, our curves happen sooner than on the Wolf dress form so we must use curved darts on a fitted skirt or the peplum of a jacket. (For instructions on how to plot a curved dart, see "Getting over the Tummy and Hips" on page 88.)

PLEATS, TUCKS, OR GATHERS

Pleats, tucks, and gathers are other opportunities for fit that remove fabric from one area while allowing the garment to expand in another area.

Pleats or tucks are folded sections of fabric that are anchored in place and are

Wit & Wisdom

Many women prefer a garment with an elastic waistband because the elastic waistband is comfortable and the garment looks good on their body. It looks good because the elastic creates a series of tiny little darts that hold the fabric in at the waist but allow it to spread out smoothly over the tummy and the hips.

used to accommodate a larger body mass or to allow for increased body movement. For example, increasing the size of a tuck at the shoulder allows a blouse to expand to accommodate a large bustline.

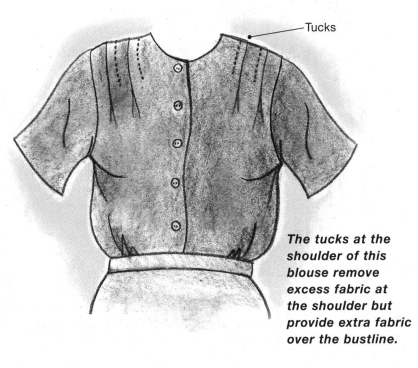

Tucks

The tucks at the shoulder of this blouse remove excess fabric at the shoulder but provide extra fabric over the bustline.

Wit & Wisdom

Hip fluff isn't the only reason the body curves closer to the waist on some women. Another reason is that some women aren't very tall. A woman who is 5 feet 1 inch has hips that curve sooner than those on the industry standard, the Wolf dress form. When buying ready-to-wear, a woman this size should buy petite clothing.

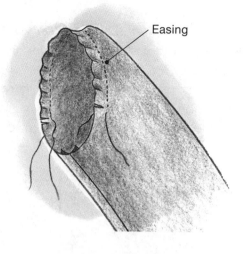

Easing is used to remove fullness from the top of a sleeve cap before it is set into a garment.

Gathering is created when a large amount of fabric is drawn up to fit into a smaller space, creating small, even pleats or folds.

Gathering works best as a fitting device on soft, supple fabrics, and it can be used to replace tucks.

Easing also removes fullness from fabric, but to a lesser degree than gathering. In easing, the fabric is drawn up without causing a tuck or a pleat. Since easing gently pulls in the fabric, you can use it to curve or contour areas such as the top of a sleeve cap.

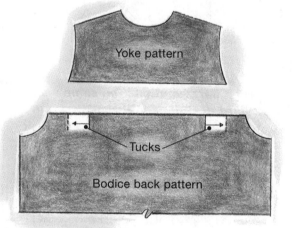

Gathers are created in this chiffon skirt when a large amount of fabric is drawn up to fit into the smaller waistband.

YOKES FOR FIT

Sewers usually do not think of a yoke as a fitting device. The standard yoke pattern has straight edges where the yoke and bodice pattern pieces are joined.

The pattern pieces for a standard yoke have straight edges.

But if you curve the bottom of the yoke pattern piece and/or the top of the bodice piece, you can add extra fabric to make the garment longer or remove fabric to make the bodice shorter. Basically, you are creating darts on the armscye, or armhole, seams. You can use this pattern change to increase the back length of a garment.

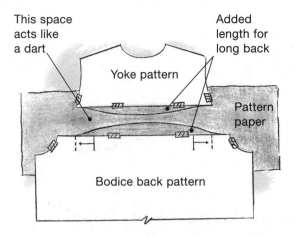

This space acts like a dart

Yoke pattern

Added length for long back

Pattern paper

Bodice back pattern

A yoke can be used as a fitting device when the edges of the yoke and the bodice pattern pieces are curved outward to provide more fabric across the back of a garment.

If you are very full-busted, you can also add to the top of the front bodice to allow for the increased length needed by the garment going out and over the bust.

SEAMS EASY

The ideal fitting device is more pattern pieces. The more pattern pieces you use to create a garment, the more opportunities for fit you have. Some sewers avoid designs that involve numerous pattern pieces. However, every pattern piece can be curved, angled, trimmed, or bumped out to conform to the shape of your body, as shown in the illustration of a pattern for a vest with princess seams above right.

Princess seams are another method of adding and subtracting fabric. Princess seams start in either the shoulder or armhole and offer many fit opportunities for many different body styles.

If you are very full-busted but small-waisted, you can use princess seams to remove the excess fabric from the waist area and still have enough fabric to cover the bust.

If your arms are very small and your bust is large, you can increase the side front piece of the bodice toward the depth of the bust point, and lengthen the front piece to match without changing the armscye so that the sleeve will still fit your body, as shown below.

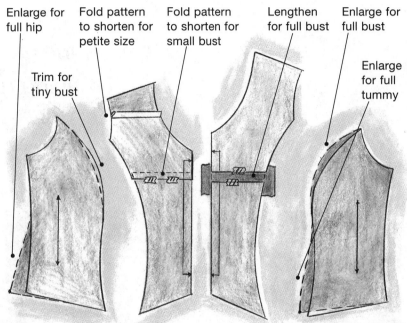

Enlarge for full hip

Trim for tiny bust

Fold pattern to shorten for petite size

Fold pattern to shorten for small bust

Lengthen for full bust

Enlarge for full bust

Enlarge for full tummy

Find Your Extra Inches

Any of these fit opportunities can be used to shape fabric to fit your individual body shape. But you must first define the source of the extra inches. You must become your own detective in the process of completely understanding your body.

If you are full through the middle of your body, you may have extra inches in your abdomen and tummy, in your back or "love handle" area, or on your sides. The extra inches may be evenly distributed or more pronounced in one area than another. Get out your croquis and your measurements worksheet, and use them to decide where you need to add fabric and where you need to remove it.

Almost every piece of your pattern can be manipulated to create a better-fitting garment.

Enlarging or Reducing

One of the most important principles of fit is determining whether a pattern is suitable for your individual body shape.

W hen choosing a pattern, you must not only decide what style you like to see on your body, but you must also take into account how you are built.

It is now time for you to examine your own body carefully to determine what opportunities for fit you can use. Sit down, look at your measurements, and look at your croquis. Where are your bumps? Where do you need more or less fabric on your body?

Do you consistently have problems with the bust being too tight? Are your garments always too tight at the waist? Does everything hang too long in the front?

Before you can choose a pattern that will be attractive on your body, you must know how you are built. Look at your croquis carefully and make notes about your body shape.

TIP: Note and write down every area on your body that consistently causes you problems in fit, whether it is in ready-to-wear clothing or in garments you create. This information will help you discover where you need to add or subtract fabric on most patterns.

Your Pattern

As I explained in "Looking Good: See the Contours" on page 5, a well-fit pattern is really a Goode's projection map of your body. To get a garment that fits you accurately, you will use a similar method of contouring the excess area out of the pattern. That way you will create a garment that hangs smoothly.

After measuring and analyzing your body, you can begin to understand what the different contours mean. Here are a series of examples comparing different areas of the body to a Wolf dress form and a few hints on how and where to make changes in your patterns.

Covering the Bust

If you have a larger bust than the industry standard Wolf dress form (a B cup), you need extra fabric to cover that area. There is just no way you can make a big, flat pattern piece fit around your three-dimensional bustline. If you pin fit the pattern to your body, you'll find that the pattern piece hangs long on the sides of your body, but it pulls up in the front.

To cover your bust, you must get more fabric on the front of your body and less fabric on the sides. If you add a dart to the pattern piece to remove the excess fabric from the side, the fabric will flow smoothly over the bust.

If you have a cup size smaller than a B, the opposite problem occurs. You will find

Large bust

Wolf dress form bust

Blouse front pattern

If you pin a flat pattern piece to your three-dimensional body, it will hang long on the sides but will pull up in the front of your body.

1½" dart added at side seams tapering to bust

By adding darts at the side seams, the sides of the blouse are pulled up, allowing the front to hang straight across the bottom.

that the front of the blouse hangs too long, and you must remove the excess fabric. To make the front shorter, you can reduce the length of a traditional dart or use a pattern with princess seams.

For example, to alter a vest pattern with princess seams for a small bust, reduce the size of the side front pattern piece at the bust point, as shown on page 84. Remember, commercial patterns are designed for a B-cup bust. Measure the length of the old and the new seams on the side front piece, and subtract the difference. That difference is the amount by

Looking Good

Measure Your Patterns

Before working with any pattern, measure the pattern tissue of your recommended size between the seamlines to get the dimensions of the finished garment. (Some pattern companies make it easy for you by printing the finished width of the bust, waist, and hips on the pattern pieces.)

Keeping the characteristics of your fabric in mind, compare the ease of the pattern with the type of ease you prefer. Adjust the ease to get the look you desire.

After you adjust the pattern, pin fit the pattern to your body, and, if needed, make further adjustments. You may even want to create a muslin test garment to ensure a perfect fit. (For more information, see "Always Test Fit Your Patterns" on page 133.)

If your pattern is not large enough or is too large, make the changes now to avoid creating a garment that doesn't fit and that you won't wear.

---

which you must reduce the length of the center front piece. Cut the center front piece horizontally, and overlap and tape the two pieces to shorten the front.

You can alter a princess seam to reduce the depth of the side front pattern to accommodate your smaller bust, but you must then shorten the seamline on the center front pattern. Measure the old and new seams on the side front pattern and subtract to find the difference. Then shorten the center front pattern by cutting the pattern and overlapping the pieces.

Reduce size at bust point

B cup
A cup

Center front pattern

Cut pattern, and overlap difference to shorten vest front

Side front pattern

You can also use princess seams to fit a large bust. The side and front pieces create enough depth to cover your bust

and taper to fit the waist. But don't forget, when a bust is deeper, it's also longer so you also must add to the appropriate area so that it goes out and over the bust. (See "Cindy" on page 181.)

Fitting the Fanny

If you have a tiny fanny, you need less fabric in that area of your garments. To reduce the amount of fabric, cut off a small amount from the top of the back skirt or pants pattern on an angle horizontally, and reduce the length of that piece. Tape the two pattern pieces together.

For pants, you also need to decrease the depth of the seat shelf. The seat shelf is the area between the fullest part of the fanny and the center of the crotch. The center of the crotch is the point between the legs from which a plumb line would fall. When the inseam is at the center of the crotch, pants hang smoothly.

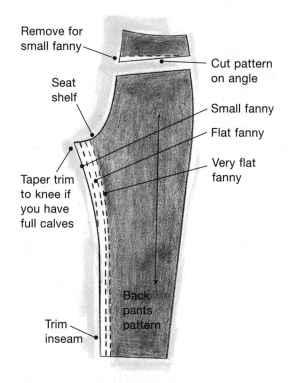

Remove for small fanny

Cut pattern on angle

Seat shelf

Small fanny

Flat fanny

Very flat fanny

Taper trim to knee if you have full calves

Back pants pattern

Trim inseam

To fit a small fanny, slash your pattern and remove the excess fabric from the back pattern piece. The flatter your fanny is, the deeper you will trim the pattern.

To decrease the depth of the seat shelf, trim off some of the inseam, as shown above. The flatter your fanny is, the more you will have to trim from the inseam. (For details, see "Karlene" on page 218.)

TIP: Most women will trim the inseam from the crotch to the bottom of the pants leg pattern. However, if you have very full thighs or calves, you can gradually taper the trim to the existing cutting line at the knee.

Another option for fitting a small fanny is to add a yoke to your skirt or pants to remove the extra fabric. That way, the yoke is not only a design detail, but also a fitting mechanism. You can also use a yoke to fit a very full fanny by adding enough fabric to go out and over your bottom. Slash and tape the back pants pat-

tern to a piece of pattern paper, as shown below. Because your fanny is wider and deeper, enlarge the pattern at the side seam, tapering to the knee area, and enlarge the bottom of the yoke at the center back, tapering to the side seam. Add a tuck to the top of the pants back pattern.

TIP: You can tape the pattern onto tissue paper or newsprint, but I prefer to trace my patterns on Mönster Paper, which is very strong and flexible and can be sewn to test the fit of the garment. (See "Resources" on page 241.)

You will also need more fabric to reach the center crotch, so enlarge the pattern at the crotch and inseam, tapering to the knee area. If you fail to enlarge this area, you will get big horizontal wrinkles across the fanny.

Before cutting the fabric, add seam allowances to the bottom of the yoke

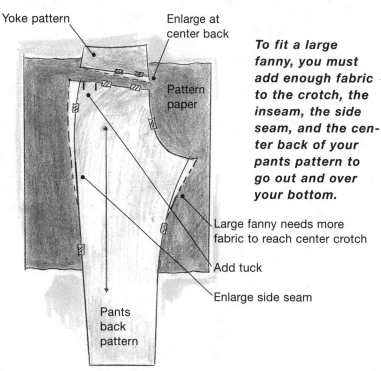

Yoke pattern

Enlarge at center back

Pattern paper

To fit a large fanny, you must add enough fabric to the crotch, the inseam, the side seam, and the center back of your pants pattern to go out and over your bottom.

Large fanny needs more fabric to reach center crotch

Add tuck

Enlarge side seam

Pants back pattern

and the top of the pants pattern. (For details on how to alter a pattern to accommodate a large fanny, see "Cynthia" on page 221.)

If something fits your fanny but is always too big in the waist, then you must make the garment to fit the fanny and increase the darts or tucks at the waist. The bigger the difference between two sections of your body, the more opportunities for fit are needed to make a smooth transition.

Your Body's Clothes Hanger

The upper torso is what I call the body's clothes hanger. Our dresses, jackets, and blouses all hang from our shoulders and out and over our three-dimensional bodies. But as I've said before, we don't all have the same dimensions.

As women get older and our backs curve a little, our backs, in essence, get longer. This long back curve can be caused by a variety of body shapes.

Your head may be thrust forward on your body, which means all of the excess length in your back is at the very top of your shoulders, or you may have ultra narrow shoulders that rotate forward.

To lengthen your garments, you can add a section to the top of the back of the garment in a fitting mechanism that I call "The Emily." I named this process after a client named Emily who constantly had struggles fitting her upper back. This fitting device, which is done strictly at the top of the garment, allows the fabric to go out and over the back curve so that the garment hangs correctly on the body. (For instructions on how to make this alteration, see "The Emily" on page 156.)

DOWAGER'S HUMP

You have a longer back if you have what is commonly called a dowager's hump or full back. In fitting sessions with students, I've frequently found that this body shape is accompanied by a shoulder that sits forward and a full upper arm.

You, too, can use "The Emily" to improve the fit of your garments. But since you have more fullness in your back and the fullness extends farther

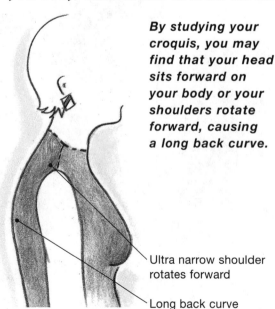

By studying your croquis, you may find that your head sits forward on your body or your shoulders rotate forward, causing a long back curve.

Ultra narrow shoulder rotates forward

Long back curve

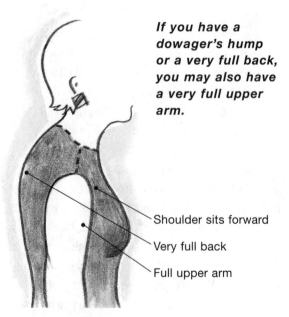

If you have a dowager's hump or a very full back, you may also have a very full upper arm.

Shoulder sits forward

Very full back

Full upper arm

down your back, you must add length and width to the garment. You can lengthen the center back seam to mimic the roundness of your back, and the garment will hang well. (See "Judy" on page 198.) You can also use a yoke, lengthening the bottom of the yoke or the top of the bodice—or both. (See "Yokes for Fit" on page 80.)

Another cause of a long back may be that the end of your shoulder angles forward, as shown on the opposite page. If this is your problem, you must lengthen the top edge of the shoulder at the back. The excess fabric resulting from lengthening the back should be removed on the shoulder seam at the outside edge.

FULL SHOULDER BLADES

Full shoulder blades are similar to the dowager's hump, but they occur lower on the body. Again, you can lengthen the center back seam (see "Judy" on page 198) or you can alter the yoke pattern as mentioned above. However, when you increase the width at a yoke, you will shape in the fullness with a pleat or a seam. (For details, see "Shirley" on page 169.)

"Add length and width to a garment to cover a full back."

LOVE HANDLES OR FLOOBIES

You may have a long back because you are blessed with "love handles"—which I call "floobies." Floobies are those fluffy parts of your body that pooch out just below your bra. The secret to fitting the back of your garments if you have floobies is to be sure to have enough fabric to cover the area. If the garment is made to be semifitted, your best choice is to use princess seams. With most other garments, you can use a yoke, but it must have plenty of fullness— gathers, tucks, or pleats—to provide enough fabric to prevent pulling across the back.

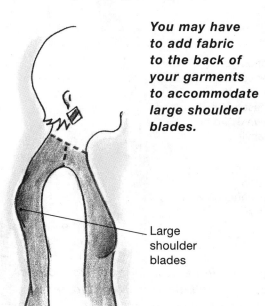

You may have to add fabric to the back of your garments to accommodate large shoulder blades.

Large shoulder blades

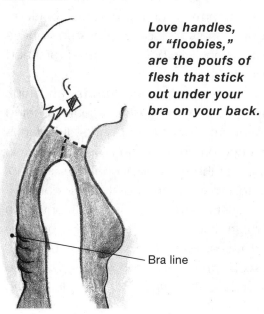

Love handles, or "floobies," are the poufs of flesh that stick out under your bra on your back.

Bra line

EXTENDED SHOULDER REACH

If you consistently complain that your garments are tight in the shoulder and arm area, it may be that you are able to rotate your shoulder farther forward than most people. It's not that your back is any bigger; it's just that you can flex farther forward. That extra reach pulls at the fabric, causing binding.

To test if you fall into this category, bring your arm across your body and see just how far you can move your shoulder ball toward your chin without turning your head to meet it. If you can get your shoulder ball relatively close to your chin, this may be your problem.

This fitting dilemma can be resolved especially well with a yoke. The fabric below the yoke can be widened without affecting the overall size of the garment—plus now you have another opportunity for a design element.

Getting over the Tummy and Hips

Like the full bust and the full fanny, you need enough fabric to go out and over your tummy and hips. Refer back to your croquis to look at the smoothness of the transition between your waist and your hips.

A commonly used tummy and hips fitting device is the dart. Usually located on the front of a skirt or pants, the dart is stitched on an angle so it pulls in excess fabric at the waistline yet allows the fabric to expand at the point of the dart.

A standard dart is traditionally a straight line from the narrowest point to the fullest part of the hip. If your body travels smoothly from your waist to your hip, this type of an angle would work well.

Unfortunately, most women have fullness at the tummy and/or hip. A garment using standard darts made from a pattern in a traditional way is just not going to fit a body with hip fluff because the widest part of the body occurs sooner than the dart releases the fabric.

Measure your pattern within the seamlines 2 to 4 inches (5.1 to 10.2 cm) below the waist, depending on where your hip fluff is located. I used 3 inches (7.6 cm) below the waist for my example. You may discover that your pattern is actually smaller than the amount of fabric needed to cover that part of your body.

A size-12 skirt pattern with standard darts expects you to have a 26-inch (66 cm) waist and 36-inch (91.4 cm) hips. Halfway between the waist and the hips, or 3½ inches (8.9 cm) down from the waist, the pattern expects the body to have 29 inches (73.7 cm) of flesh. But

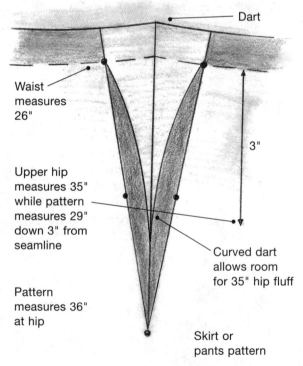

Dart

Waist measures 26"

3"

Upper hip measures 35" while pattern measures 29" down 3" from seamline

Curved dart allows room for 35" hip fluff

Pattern measures 36" at hip

Skirt or pants pattern

By changing a standard dart to a curved dart, you will allow more fabric in the area just below your waistline.

women with hip fluff may already have 35 inches (88.9 cm) of body at that point.

If you stitch a straight dart, the skirt will ride up until there is enough fabric to go over the hip fluff area. By stitching a curved dart, you will put enough fabric to go around that area 3½ inches (8.9 cm) below the waist, allowing the garment to hang over the fullness of the body. In this case, the dart should be curved, as shown on the opposite page.

To get a better fit over a full tummy or hips, you can also use a series of smaller darts, or elasticize the back waistband on a skirt or pants. You may want to elasticize the entire waistband, if needed.

Adding a Waistline Yoke

Just like the full bust and the full fanny, if you have a very full tummy, you must add enough fabric to go out and over your tummy. To get more fabric in that area, you can add a yoke to your pants or skirt pattern by following these five steps.

STEP 1: Cut a small amount from the top of the front skirt or pants pattern on an angle horizontally. Label the small pattern piece "yoke." Tape both pattern pieces to a sheet of pattern paper.

STEP 2: Draw the additional length needed to accommodate a full tummy on the top of the pants leg pattern piece, as shown above right, starting at the center-front cutting line and tapering to nothing at the side-seam cutting line.

STEP 3: Because your tummy is not only deeper but also wider, you must

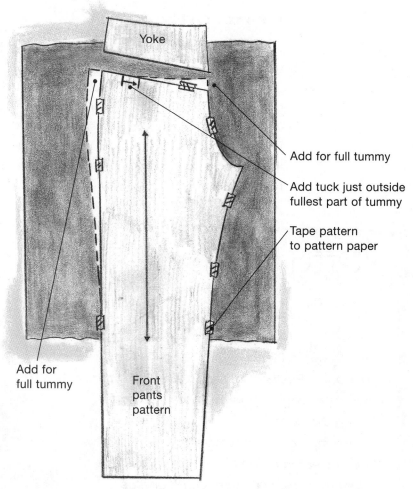

When you add to your front pants pattern for a full tummy, you must remember to add not only to the length but also to the width.

add to the side seam of the front skirt or pants pattern piece as well, starting at the top edge of the skirt or pants pattern and tapering to the knee area, as shown in the illustration above.

STEP 4: To add shape to the front of the garment, add a tuck near the side seam of the pants front just outside the fullest part of your tummy.

STEP 5: Add a seam allowance to the bottom of the yoke and the top of the front pants pattern.

Controlling the Contours

Even with plenty of planning, you may complete a garment, put it on, and it won't look quite right. This may be caused by the silhouette of your garment looking boxy and awkward. Do you wear the garment anyway and just avoid mirrors? Do you let these garments end up as wadders on the floor of your sewing room or in the Goodwill bag? You don't have to do that anymore. There are several ways to create your own opportunities for fit after the fact. I call this method "controlling the contours."

Here are a few common ways you can streamline the exterior of your garments to control the contours.

PERFECT PLEATS

Pleats are another opportunity for fitting a garment, and they can be very flattering if they hang well on your body. Pleats also help to streamline the exterior of your garments—what I call "controlling the contours."

Pleats are meant to hang straight like a pair of pleated drapes. But what if you have a tummy or hips? Picture a child or a pet hiding behind those drapes. The fabric would appear lumpy and distorted.

To allow for your three-dimensional body behind pleats, one of the folds of the pleat must be raised slightly. The angle and height of the rise depend on the garment design and your body shape.

To ensure that your pleats hang straight, follow these steps:

STEP 1: *Put on the partially assembled skirt or pants.*

STEP 2: *Grasp and pull up the outer pleat, as shown. If that causes the fold to fall smoothly over the body, pin the pleat in*

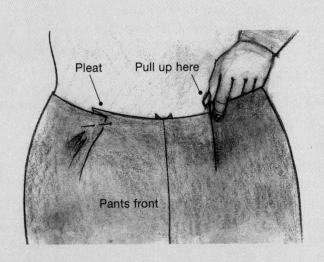

The raw edges of pleated fabric do not have to be even. You can adjust the pleats as needed so that they hang straight on your body.

place. If the fold does not fall smoothly, proceed to Step 3.

STEP 3: *Grasp and pull up the inner pleat. If that causes the fold to fall smoothly over the body, pin the pleat in place. If not, readjust the pleat until it does hang straight.*

There, you've done it—a perfectly straight pleat.

If the bottoms of your sleeves are too floppy:

STEP 1: Take a small tuck or make a small pleat at the outside of the sleeve at the hemline, as shown.

STEP 2: Make the change look more finished by stitching one or more buttons on the tuck or pleat to hold it in place, as shown. You can also stitch a shape such as a box or triangle on the tuck or use one of the decorative stitches on your sewing machine to hold the tuck in place. The tuck will add shape to your arm and control the extra fabric at the bottom of the sleeve.

If the torso of your blouse is too bulky:

STEP 1: Make an open-ended dart in the torso area of the blouse approximately at the waist, as shown. You may need to adjust the placement to make it look attractive on your body.

STEP 2: Leave the ends of the dart plain or add decorative stitches or a button. (See the photo of Cheryle on page 142.)

If the shoulders of your blouse are too full:

STEP 1: Fold a series of tiny tucks or one large tuck almost near the neckline edge to create a flange on each shoulder until the fullness disappears, as shown.

STEP 2: Stitch the tucks in place.

If the bottoms of your tailored pants legs are floppy:

STEP 1: Add a dart in the center front and the center back of each leg, as shown. The depth of the dart will depend on the garment's design, but it is best to make the dart the same depth in the front and back. Start by pinning the darts ½ inch (1.3 cm) deep and checking the look.

STEP 2: Determine the length of the darts. The length of the darts depends on the length of your legs and the hang and appearance of the pants when you take out the excess fabric. Start by pinning a 4-inch (10.2 cm) dart, gradually creating your own dart by experimenting with shorter or longer lengths.

STEP 3: Stitch each dart.

Tucks

Tuck

Open-ended dart

If you have completed the garment and still are unhappy with the fit, you can take a small tuck or pleat at the outside of the sleeve at the hemline, make an open-ended dart in the torso area of the blouse at the waist, stitch a series of tiny tucks near the neckline edge, and add a dart in the center front and the center back of each leg. Voilà!

Dart

The Fit Puzzle

No matter what your age or size, good fit means your clothing hangs well, is comfortable, and, more important, looks and feels great on you. These women love themselves and the garments they have created because they've solved their own fit puzzle. Now you can, too.

The Puzzle Pieces

Broad shoulders

Large bust

Petite

Narrow hips

Now that you have collected many bits and pieces of information about your body, it's going to take a bit of detective work to solve your specific fit puzzle.

How would you describe yourself? Are you short, are you tall, are you round, are you thin? To solve your personal fit puzzle, you must know your individual body shape.

Every human has a completely individual body shape and needs a unique set of pattern alterations. Making those alterations is more than just adding or subtracting inches from the sides of the pattern pieces, as you will learn in "Making It Fit," starting on page 130. You must add fabric where your body needs it, and you must subtract fabric where your body doesn't need it.

You must understand how your body is different from the Wolf dress form—the standard used by clothing manufacturers and pattern designers. You may determine that the differences are subtle. Therefore, the changes you make to a pattern also will be subtle. If your differences are more drastic, your pattern alterations will be more extensive.

94

Three Great-Fitting Garments

Let's begin to solve the fit puzzle by looking at three great garments. The women in the photograph on page 92 are wearing garments that they have created and that fit them well, but the garments didn't start that way.

Maureen, on the left, created her lovely rayon blouse in a hurry. To her dismay, during a pin fitting of the garment, she discovered the blouse didn't fit. The upper chest area was too long, and the blouse didn't hang properly.

Since Maureen had cut out the garment before she discovered the problem, she didn't have enough fabric left to recut the blouse front. So I helped her create an artificial opportunity for fit. I suggested she create a flange with buttons to take up the excess fabric in the upper chest area. Not only did the flange correct the fit of Maureen's blouse, but it also ended up being an attractive design detail.

Diane, in the middle, is wearing a blouse that is another example of a garment that fit better when the upper chest area was shortened. By using her croquis and examining her measurements, Diane discovered that her body differs from the industry standard in the upper chest area. If she didn't make this change, the bust area would be too low, and the front of the armscye and sleeve would bind when she reached forward.

Now, she makes this alteration on all of her bodice patterns. In addition, Diane discovered she has fairly deep, square shoulders, so she always heightens her sleeve cap.

Ruth, on the right, made this nicely contoured, 100 percent linen jacket. Unfortunately, the pattern came with a

> "Analyze your body gently to learn what flatters you."

one-piece sleeve that would have been too snug for Ruth's arms. So she took her favorite two-piece sleeve and used it instead. Now Ruth has ample room for movement. She wears this jacket regularly at work, and it's a very comfortable and stylish garment.

None of these women are tall, young, or extremely thin, yet they look great. Each of them has become adept at flattering her own body through contour and balance. They don't just make garments bigger to cover themselves up. They fine-tune the fit to camouflage the least favorite areas of their bodies, to show off their assets, and to make their clothes more comfortable. The best-fitting garments are ones that simply look correct on the body and hang evenly, and these women have achieved this objective.

Fit or Camouflage

When you consider where to add or subtract fabric, you must think about whether you want clothes to mimic the contours of your body exactly or whether you want to create an illusion, which I call camouflage. However, I'm not talking about wearing very loose, oversize clothing.

If you think one specific area of your body is flawed and you choose a garment

(continued on page 99)

HOW TO SEE WHILE LOOKING

It's very difficult to be objective about how we look. Each of us has ideas about our appearance that have been influenced by other people's opinions. For instance, if we have parents, family, or friends who always tell us that we look one way or another, we eventually begin to see things that way.

I had a client who was absolutely convinced that she had a very large fanny. For years, my client's mother told her she had a large fanny, and her sisters told her she had a "great, big bottom."

The first thing I did was get her into a leotard and take photographs of her so that I could create her croquis. My client looked at the photographs carefully, concentrating on the shape and proportion of her body. She then looked at me and said, "I can't believe it! I don't have a big bottom. All of my life my mother and my sisters told me that I had the biggest bottom they had ever seen." I said, "Of course you don't."

Because of the information my client had gotten from her family, she spent years looking through books and reading magazine articles about how to make her "large" fanny look smaller. When sewing garments and buying ready-to-wear, she chose styles that were supposed to minimize her "big bottom." She sought out and used fit instructions to make garments for her imaginary body shape, but no matter what she did,

nothing quite fit and nothing looked quite right. But by simply wearing a leotard and having her photo taken, my client came to know and appreciate her body for what it was, not what someone else told her.

A few years ago, I helped produce a videotape on my fit process, and several women who appear in this book were asked to share their body shape by being videotaped in leotards. The video team was concerned about the process. The team feared that the women would be embarrassed and that they would not go through with the videotaping session. The team discussed various ways to hide the women's identities—by covering their heads with bags, putting black bars across their faces, and so forth.

As the discussion droned on, one of the women, Jan Hyland, walked over to one of the members of the video team, put her arm around her shoulders and said, "It's OK. You don't have to be afraid to show us in our leotards. All of us like our bodies just as they are."

As you will see later in the book, I asked my students to make their garments twice—first, making only the changes the pattern instructions recommended, and, second, making the fitting changes they had learned from me. Then I asked all of them to appear in the book wearing a leotard so that you could see that underneath the clothing, they were all real women just like you.

When the photo sessions for this book were scheduled, many of the same questions arose. Would these women in a wide variety of shapes, sizes, and ages step in front of the camera wearing leotards and be at ease enough to allow their photos to be taken? As you can see, the answer was yes. You will see them in their garments on pages 137–152, but remember that they first looked at themselves and measured themselves, and only then did they choose and alter a pattern, creating a garment that truly fit their body shape.

Diane knows she has a deep and full back and a shallow chest.

Jane's waist is lower in the front than in the back.

Jan has very full, low outer hips.

Barbara's hips are almost three sizes larger than her bust and waist.

Although Shirley is full-figured, she has small shoulders.

Dolores has a small waist, a hollow back, and a full fanny.

Lynda has hip fluff and is shorter than the average pattern height.

Looking Good
Creating the Illusion

Despite what today's magazines may want you to believe, fashion models are not perfect. Even the highest-paid fashion models are fitted individually for the garments they wear on the runway.

Nature is random, and each of us is created differently. Nature is even more random in that most of us are many different sizes on the same body.

Plus, as we get older our bodies and horizons change. Our shoulder and bust horizons, which were once nice and straight, now dip forward, while our hip and waist horizons tip upward. Many women have the same measurements they have had for years and yet their clothes don't fit anymore. Each of us should be remeasured every few years or if our weight changes. As we pass the age of 50, it should be done more frequently, perhaps once a year.

As women age, their spines compress, and their backs get rounder and longer. The tummy gets more pronounced, and the fanny gets lower and flatter. In general, our side view changes more than our front or back views, and length measurements become more and more important.

I am very long-waisted, so when I make a vest, a jacket, or a blouse that's not going to be tucked in, I don't make the garment to follow my body exactly.

If I altered a pattern to fit my long waist exactly, you would see how short my legs actually are. Instead of having these garments fit me right at the waistline, I make them curve where I would prefer my waist to be if I were more classically proportioned.

Level horizon

Slanted horizon

Round back

More pronounced tummy

Lower and flatter fanny

Young woman

Older woman

A key piece of the fit puzzle is our body horizons. As we age, our bodies change, and our horizons, which once were level, are now slanted.

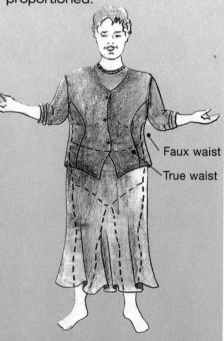

Faux waist

True waist

If you are long-waisted like me, fool the eye by curving your garments in where you'd prefer your waist to be.

style simply because it will cover up that area, you are probably making a mistake.

You won't fool anyone by wearing garments that are too big and oversized for your body. In my fitting classes, I always say, "You can tell a two-man tent from a four-man tent, even from the outside."

At the other end of the spectrum are clothes that fit too tightly. With today's stretch-knit clothing, we are sometimes tempted to wear garments that are a little too tight for us. Just because you can get into something doesn't mean that it fits. It is much more flattering to create a pleasing outline. To do that, you must look at your body overall, and that is why you created the croquis earlier.

This is not just a fit issue for women who wear size 14 and larger. It is important to women of all sizes. One time, a woman who wore size 8 joined my class "Thin Is Not the Only Way." The other members of the class were amazed and confused about why she was there, so I asked her. She said she had "chubbied up" from a size 2 and had no clue where to begin to fit this much larger, different-shaped body.

Although you may think a size 8 is a "small" size, to this woman, it was not. The number of the size is not important. The most important thing you can do to get a great fit and create an attractive garment is to analyze your body gently and to learn what flatters you—whatever your size.

Ease

Ease is another key piece of the fit puzzle. Ease is the fabric in excess of your body that creates fit and style. The amount of ease you desire in a garment depends on the fabric, your body shape, and, of course, your personal preference.

A good example of the relationship of height to ease is well-made petite clothing. Because these garments are proportioned for the smaller overall body size of the wearer, they have less ease overall than clothing specifically made for an average or tall woman.

The type of fabric you choose to use with a particular garment design on your particular body shape is also an important factor in creating camouflage. Remember, drapey fabric will skim over curves and fall softly, so it is most flattering to have soft fabric in an area that you want to de-emphasize.

Crisp fabric stands away from the body and adds volume, so you will want to use crisp fabrics in areas where you are small.

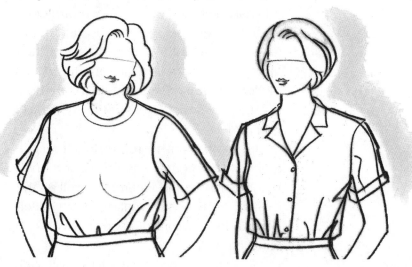

Use a soft drapey fabric to make a large bustline look smaller on your upper body.

Use a crisp fabric that will add volume to your blouse to make a small bustline look larger.

"Shoulder pads help to balance a full bustline."

TIP: The amount of ease you allow in any garment is dependent on your body type. A full figure will always need more ease than a thin figure. I happen to be a short, round human being, so when I sit down I tend to spread more than some people do. I need a lot of ease in my garments, so I can be just as comfortable sitting down as standing up.

Personal preference also plays a role in ease. Some people are simply uncomfortable when their clothing fits tightly against their bodies. To be more 'comfortable, these people should use softer fabric and allow for more ease in their garments. Others like the structured feel of clothing that presses against their bodies, thus they need less ease. Which do you prefer?

It is important to remember that the ease in a garment has to be proportioned to the height of the wearer as well as the design. Your height makes a big difference in the amount of ease that you can carry off well.

A woman who is 6 feet tall will look great in a very loose-fitting and flowing garment that has 10 inches of ease. The drape of the garment will look wonderful on her body. A woman who is the pattern norm of 5 feet 7 inches tall will look good in a garment that is very loose-fitting or one that has slightly less ease.

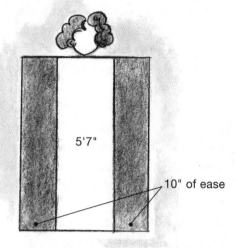

5'7"

10" of ease

A woman who is 5 feet 7 inches will look great in a garment that has 10 inches of ease since she will still look taller than she is wide.

But a woman who is only 5 feet 1 inch tall cannot wear a garment that has 10 inches of ease. There would be too much fabric on her body, and the garment would feel and look overwhelming. She would have to pare down the ease in the design by choosing a smaller size pattern or by taking out vertical sections to reduce the overall circumference of the garment.

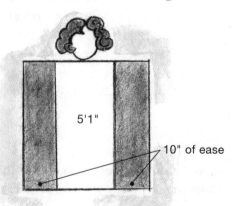

5'1"

10" of ease

A woman who is only 5 feet 1 inches will look overwhelmed in a garment that has 10 inches of ease since she will look as wide as she is tall.

Looking Good

Flatter Yourself

Shoulder pad

Fullest part of hip

Long vests, jackets, and sweaters may cover your full hips and thighs, but the shape of the garment also exaggerates the size of your hips.

You can create an attractive body outline by combining a close-fitting princess-seam jacket with shoulder pads.

To cover or to camouflage, that is the question.

Do you have small shoulders and a small waist, combined with full hips and thighs? The fashion tipsters recommend that you cover up these areas. They want you to wear long vests, sweaters, or jackets to disguise the shape of your body. But as this type of garment hangs from your shoulders over your wider hips, the shape of the garment tends to exaggerate the fullness of the hips and the thighs.

For a more flattering look, wear a close-fitting curvy top that ends just at the fullest part of the hip and always add shoulder pads to create a pleasing body outline. (For additional information on using shoulder pads as a fitting device, see "Looking Good: Wear Shoulder Pads" on page 108.)

Make notes about the amount of ease that looks good on your body shape and the amount you desire in different types of garments. Write all of the information in a small design notebook or on an index card and keep it in your handbag. You will find this information invaluable when you are selecting garment patterns, and it will help you to create a garment that fits.

Working with Patterns

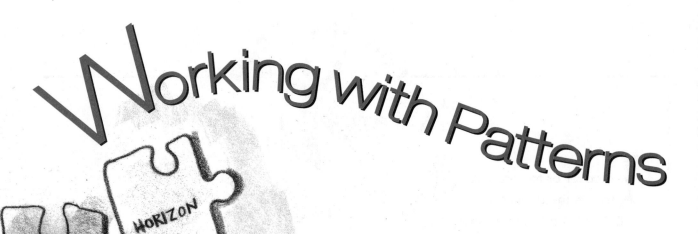

To get the fit you want, you must choose a pattern as carefully as you took your measurements. The pattern is the final piece of the fit puzzle and probably the most important.

The more information you collect about your body, the easier it will be for you to solve your individual fit puzzle.

When you choose a pattern, you must take into consideration not only what style you like but also the shape of your body. As I told you in "Opportunities for Fit," starting on page 74, one of the key principles of fit is whether the pattern suits your body shape.

Look at your croquis and the notes you made about your body. Where are you larger or smaller than your usual size? Do all of your garments fit tightly in the same area? What amount of ease do you prefer in your garments? Analyze your body. Where are you deep? Where are you shallow?

Use all of this information to help you determine where you have to add or subtract fabric to get a great fit—or a great camouflage. To ensure either a good fit or good camouflage, you must choose a pattern that has opportunities for fit—seamlines, darts, and so on.

Patterns and Sizing

One of the most frequently asked questions I hear is, "What size pattern should I purchase?" This is a valid question.

Think about shopping for ready-to-wear. You go into a department store, try on a size-14 skirt, and it fits you perfectly. Then you go to the designer boutique and discover you can fit into a size 12 in a slightly more expensive skirt and even a size 10 in a really expensive skirt. This is called vanity sizing, and over the years, it has become the standard in the ready-to-wear industry. Manufacturers have added so many inches to the standard sizes that a size 12 today would be the equivalent of a size 16 back in the 1960s.

A good example of how vanity sizing can be confusing is ordering a garment in a bridal wear shop. If you are going to be a bride or a bridesmaid, you may have a rude awakening. After the gown has been chosen, an employee of the store will measure you and probably say, "You're going to need a size 16." You'll probably gulp and start to hyperventilate because you always wear size 12.

But the companies that manufacture the gowns still use the same measurements that were established years ago. These numbers are based on measurements that were gathered as a way to ensure consistency among special-order manufacturers. And that is why commercial pattern manufacturers still use these old measurements—because they are consistent. But this method of sizing can be confusing and makes the pattern selection process especially difficult.

"Select a pattern that has several opportunities for fit."

Thank Goodness for Multisize Patterns!

After you took your measurements and compared them to my measurements table on page 59, you were probably amazed to discover that different areas of your body fell into a number of sizes. Because individual bodies fall into so many size ranges, I love multisize patterns! Multisize patterns, which include three or more sizes, allow me to make fitting decisions for each area of the body as I work.

When you work with a multisize pattern, always compare your personal measurements to the measurement table on the pattern.

TIP: When working with multisize patterns, it's important to know your bra cup size. The bust measurement on commercial patterns is the full bust measurement for a B cup. If your bust is a C, D, DD cup, or larger, the front of your body is about ½ inch larger for each cup size larger than a B.

If you make a garment to fit the full bust measurement of a person who wears a D-cup bra, then the remainder of the garment, especially the shoulders, the neck, and possibly the arms, would be too big. You are better off starting with a smaller size and adding fabric to the bust area as needed. (See "Cindy" on page 181 for details on adding to a princess seam and "Shirley" on page 169 for making a garment with a yoke.)

If your bust is larger than a B cup, you will have to add about ½ inch to the front of a pattern for each additional cup size.

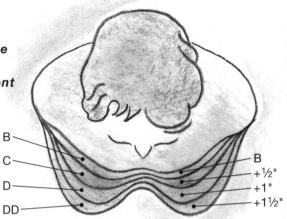

B
C
D
DD

B
+½"
+1"
+1½"

When you look at your croquis, you also may discover that the extra inches in your full bust measurement are not only due to your D cup. Look at your back bust measurement. You may find that you have a broad back, which adds inches to the back bust measurement. Again, you would use a smaller pattern size and add the fabric where you need it—some to the bust and some to the back.

TIP: You must remember that if you add to the pattern for an increase in bust size, the pattern piece also must be lengthened. If you are less than a B cup, the pattern piece must be shortened. (If you are using a princess seam, see "Cindy" on page 181. If you are adding a dart, see "The Dynamic Dart" on page 78.)

Whenever you work with multisize patterns, it is very important to know the size of your shoulders. If you have very small shoulders, everything you put on is

CAMOUFLAGING HIP FLUFF

If you have been blessed with hip fluff, you may be tempted to select an A-line skirt pattern in an effort to reduce the excess fabric from that area of your body. Unfortunately, when you use an A-line design, it is almost impossible to have enough fabric at the hip fluff level after you fit the waist.

If the widest part of your hips occurs close to your waistline—what I call hip fluff— an A-line skirt pattern will probably be too small at the upper hip.

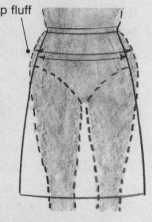

Hip fluff

To add enough fabric to the skirt, you will need your pattern, a tape measure, scissors, and pattern paper.

TIP: You can tape the pattern onto tissue paper or newsprint, but I prefer to trace the pattern onto Mönster Paper, which is very strong and flexible and can be sewn to test the fit of the garment. (See "Resources" on page 241.)

STEP 1: Measure the width of the skirt front pattern at the upper hip level, excluding the seam allowances, as shown in **Diagram 1.**

STEP 2: *Repeat Step 1 for the back skirt pattern.*

STEP 3: *Examine your measurement worksheet, and calculate what the width of the finished skirt should be, including enough fabric for comfort and drape. Use the amount of ease you preferred in a skirt that you made previously to get the results you desire.*

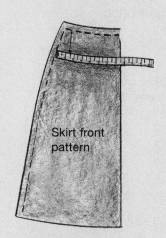

Measure the width of the pattern at your upper hip level, excluding the seam allowance.

Skirt front pattern

Diagram 1

STEP 4: *To widen the skirt front and back pattern pieces, lay the center front and back of each piece parallel and as far away from the fold as needed, as shown in* **Diagram 2.** *To add 3 inches, place the pattern pieces 1½ inches from the fold.*

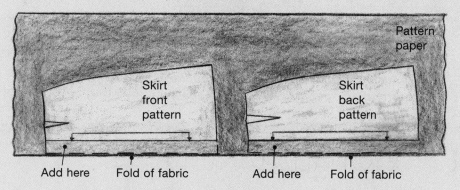

Pattern paper

Skirt front pattern

Skirt back pattern

Add here   Fold of fabric   Add here   Fold of fabric

Diagram 2

STEP 5: *Cut all of the pattern pieces from the fashion fabric, and stitch together the skirt front and back.*

Add to the skirt pattern at the fold, or if the pattern is a full front piece, cut it apart at center front and spread it on pattern paper.

STEP 6: *Gather the waistline edge of the skirt slightly to fit onto the bodice or waistband and finish assembling the skirt. The gathers will balance the proportion of your waist to your hips and will make your hip fluff look smaller, as shown in* **Diagram 3.** *This technique will also make a very small waist look larger.*

The finished skirt has a flattering fit, thanks to gathers at the waist, which camouflage large upper hips (hip fluff) by balancing the proportion of waist to hips.

Attach skirt to bodice or waistband

Diagram 3

too big in that area. You will want to use a small-size pattern for the top of your body in the shoulder and armscye areas. If needed, add to the side seams to accommodate a larger bust.

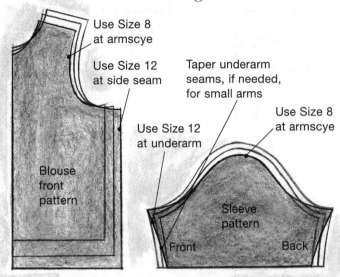

Use Size 8 at armscye

Use Size 12 at side seam

Taper underarm seams, if needed, for small arms

Use Size 8 at armscye

Use Size 12 at underarm

Blouse front pattern

Sleeve pattern

Front   Back

If you have small shoulders, you will want to redraw the cutting lines on your pattern, using a smaller size in the shoulder areas and a larger size on the side seams.

Look at your croquis. If your waist is especially small, it could be that you are narrow through the center of your body because you have a narrow rib cage. But what if you find that your waist really goes in suddenly and you are full above and below your waist? Perhaps you wouldn't want to draw attention to the fact that your waist is tiny if it makes the rest of your body look bigger.

If you have a B- or C-cup bust and small shoulders, try using one size smaller for your neck and shoulders than your bust measurement recommends.

You must also know whether you have a narrow or broad back when you work with multisize patterns. If your back looks broad on your croquis or your back bust measurement falls into a larger size range but you are a B cup or smaller, you may want to buy a pattern that is one or two sizes smaller and enlarge the back only.

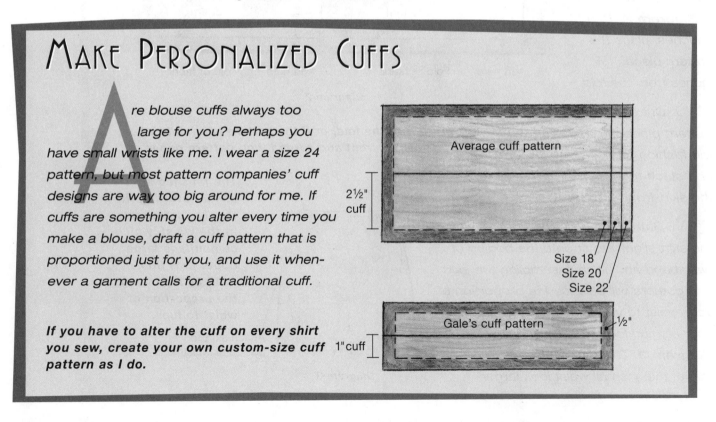

MAKE PERSONALIZED CUFFS

Are blouse cuffs always too large for you? Perhaps you have small wrists like me. I wear a size 24 pattern, but most pattern companies' cuff designs are way too big around for me. If cuffs are something you alter every time you make a blouse, draft a cuff pattern that is proportioned just for you, and use it whenever a garment calls for a traditional cuff.

If you have to alter the cuff on every shirt you sew, create your own custom-size cuff pattern as I do.

2½" cuff

Average cuff pattern

Size 18
Size 20
Size 22

1" cuff   Gale's cuff pattern   ½"

Don't Fear the Pattern Tissue

When you use my fitting method, you must change your attitude toward the pattern tissue. The tissue is not sacred! You can draw on it, cut it, tape it, or copy it. Use it, and make it work for you.

And don't think that when you change the pattern tissue, you will get a technically perfect pattern. Each of us is unique and every pattern is unique. This is not an exercise in how to make a perfect pattern, but how to make a garment that fits.

In the old days, the primary method of fitting was draping. Today, many of the best dressmakers and top designers still create couture garments using this method. This procedure involves placing the fabric on the body and pinning it in place to create a garment. Each of the pieces fits the individual human body

for whom the garment is made—and results in a garment that hangs well and flatters the wearer. Draping takes a great deal of skill, and that is not what I am proposing you do.

But you do need to accept and use the trial-and-error method. If there is one area of your body that you struggle with, you may need to add or subtract fabric in different places before you are successful.

TIP: Read "Making It Fit," starting on page 130, carefully, and make notes about your own body as you read it. You may find many of your own fitting challenges are very similar to the women featured in that chapter.

Invest in pattern paper and some inexpensive fabric, and make some test garments. Once you change your patterns, you will make garments that fit!

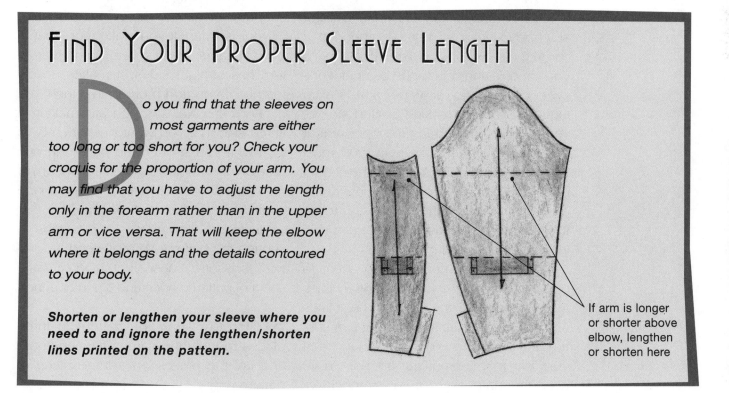

FIND YOUR PROPER SLEEVE LENGTH

Do you find that the sleeves on most garments are either too long or too short for you? Check your croquis for the proportion of your arm. You may find that you have to adjust the length only in the forearm rather than in the upper arm or vice versa. That will keep the elbow where it belongs and the details contoured to your body.

Shorten or lengthen your sleeve where you need to and ignore the lengthen/shorten lines printed on the pattern.

If arm is longer or shorter above elbow, lengthen or shorten here

Looking Good

Wear Shoulder Pads

If you have small shoulders, instead of making your garments fit that particular area, you may discover that it is more flattering if you put shoulder pads in your garments. Don't immediately say you hate shoulder pads. Shoulder pads are not just a fashion trend.

They are also an important fit mechanism.

Clothing hangs best when the shoulders are the widest part of the body. If your shoulders are narrower than your bust or your hips, if your shoulders are sloping, or if your upper arms are fuller than your shoulders, shoulder pads will give your body proportion.

The object is not to look like a fullback, but to add shape. A small, well-fitted shoulder pad is the augmentation you may need to allow your clothing to hang well on your body.

The 1-Inch Rule

When you make lengthwise changes to a pattern, you will want to maintain the correct proportion of the garment, making sure the fullness is where you need it.

A good example is a sleeve. Check your croquis and your measurement worksheet carefully. If your upper arm is extra long and you are making a fitted sleeve, you must add length to the upper arm. If you do not need extra length, you must shorten the lower arm to create the correct hem length. This will put the elbow at the proper place so it can bend easily. To do this correctly, you must make the changes in maximum 1-inch increments.

You'll find that you may not want to use the horizontal lengthen/shorten lines that are printed on the pattern. These lines assume that you are strictly adding or subtracting inches for your height and that you are not contouring the pattern to accommodate your three-dimensional shape. Usually these lines are not located exactly where you need to add length.

If your pattern piece has any side shape, you will lose the overall silhouette of your garment if you make more than a 1-inch change in one area. But if the pattern has straight sides, it makes no difference if you add more than 1 inch.

For example, say you are making a flared skirt that you want to shorten by 3 inches. If you shorten the pattern in one area or just cut the length off the bottom of the pattern, you will lose the flared shape of the skirt, as shown in **Diagram 1.**

Instead, follow these simple steps to shorten the pattern. You will need the pattern, scissors, transparent tape, a large sheet of pattern paper, and a pen or pencil.

STEP: Cut apart the pattern in three places roughly the same distance apart, and lay the pieces on a large piece of pattern paper.

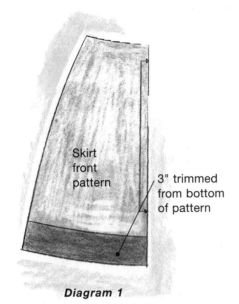

Diagram 1

This skirt pattern will lose its flare if you simply cut 3 inches off the bottom.

STEP: Align the pieces along the center front, and overlap them in 1-inch increments so the basic flared silhouette of the skirt is maintained. When you are finished making your 1-inch adjustments, tape the pieces together, and tape the pattern to the pattern paper, as shown in **Diagram 2.**

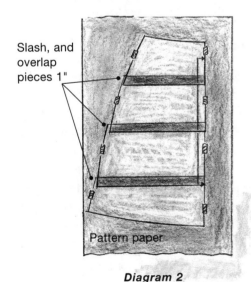

Diagram 2

To shorten a flared skirt pattern and retain its shape, cut the pattern apart in three places, then overlap the pieces by 1 inch.

STEP: Trace the taped pattern and transfer all pattern markings to the new pattern.

TIP: The edges of your pattern will be choppy and uneven, so redraw the cutting lines on the pattern paper by marking a point halfway between the cutting line on the top piece and the cutting line on the bottom piece. Gradually blend the two lines together starting and ending about 2 to 3 inches from the point, as shown in **Diagram 3.**

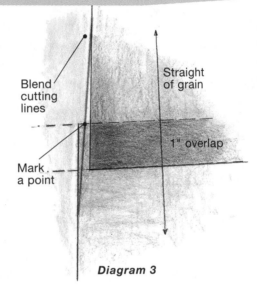

Diagram 3

Redraw the cutting lines by marking a point halfway between the original cutting lines and the new line and blending the old and new lines.

STEP: Cut out the pattern.

Don't Hem Yourself In

As I have emphasized throughout this book, there are no absolutes when it comes to getting a great fit, and I have no hard and fast rules on hem lengths.

Because I have a long torso and very short legs, some skirt lengths can make me look awkward.

By sketching on my croquis, I've found that longer skirts create the best overall proportion for my body.

Although my legs are shapely, the overall outline of my body looks out of proportion with this knee-length skirt.

I have a full midriff, so if I want to wear a dress, I prefer a one-piece, wedge-shape dress that hangs nicely from my ample shoulders and bust, as shown above right. It is a good choice for my body because it doesn't show off my lumps. With this dress style, I can wear a short skirt that sits just at the top of my knees, making my legs look longer. Each of my garments has a different length, but each is correct because of the overall proportion the garment creates on my body.

Sketch various hem lengths on your croquis to determine what hem lengths

I camouflage my full midriff by wearing a wedge-shape dress that hangs from my shoulders and bust. With this style, the short skirt length works for me.

look best with each style of garment you wear. Also take into consideration the other pieces you will wear with any garment. The length of a jacket, vest, or blouse will create different proportions on your body. Get out your croquis and test, test, test.

Seeing the Whole Puzzle

I wish I could have each of you in a class to help you work through my fitting process. I know you were hoping for the one rule that would work perfectly for you. The truth is, there are as many answers to the fit puzzle as there are sewers. Once you quit trying to find or follow the rules and develop your personal tools, you can make clothes that fit and flatter your body.

Get a sewing buddy or a group of buddies and help each other. Look through this book and see all the women who have done the process and are happy with themselves and their garments.

To determine what length of skirt looks best on my body shape, I sketched various lengths on my croquis and found that longer skirts look much better.

Looking Good

Size Your Pants

When it comes to choosing sizes for pants, a lot depends on the size of your bottom, tummy, and legs. I have very small legs, and yet I have a very full tummy.

Unfortunately, when it comes to camouflaging a tummy, some women are very unrealistic about how pants are supposed to fit. Pants that are snug enough so that they will sit against the front of their legs exaggerate a full tummy. You are better off having a little more fabric around the leg, which is much more flattering.

When I make pants or skirts, I have to add enough fabric to the front and back of the pattern so the garment hangs correctly. That is why I had you measure the front of your body and the back of your body separately, so that you, too, can make the same adjustment if needed.

Most of the pants that I wear are made from very soft fabric that has a lot of drape so that the pants hang and skim my body. Remember, use soft fabrics in an area that you want to de-emphasize. But to get this flattering look, I cannot use a pattern either as small as my legs are or as full as my tummy is, so I begin in the middle. My legs are about a size 16, and yet my tummy is a size 24, so I start

Add more for extra tummy

Pants front pattern

Add to center front for extra tummy

Add to front side seam overall

Pants back pattern

Add to back side seam overall

To get pants to hang correctly on my body in spite of a very full tummy and very small legs, I have to add to the pattern at the front side seam, the center front, and the back side seam.

with a size 20 pattern. This size will give me a little more fullness through the legs.

When I make traditional pants, they hang fairly full, and I always add darts to the bottom of the legs. (See "Controlling the Contours" on page 90.) Even if I am making stretch pants or leggings, I still make them full enough so they set away from my legs and don't exaggerate my tummy.

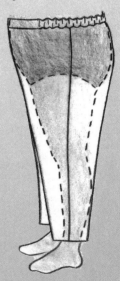

By using a size 20 pattern for my pants, I can enlarge it to fit my full tummy without the pant legs looking too full on my very small legs.

Know Thyself

Each of these women has taken the time to discover her own personal style. Now each one can sew garments that not only fit her individual body but also make her look fabulous. If you take the time to discover your own personal style, you will be able to do the same.

Determine Your

Your personal style is a combination of your look, your body, your age, your lifestyle, and how you want others to see you. When all these factors come together, your clothing will reflect who you are.

To help you to determine your own personal style, survey all of the garments and accessories in your wardrobe.

The three women—Diane, Cara, and Rosemary—on pages 112–113 look wonderful wearing the garments they made for themselves. Each garment's style is very different and complements each woman's body, personal style preferences, and lifestyle.

Personal Preferences

Diane, on the left, is an artist, pattern maker, and sewing instructor. She created her gorgeous vest from her own pattern, called The Torii Collection #100, out of textured rayon. (See "Resources" on page 241 for pattern sources.) The blouse underneath is of translucent rayon. This soft, full style works well on her tall figure. Diane loves unique and comfortable styles, and most of her wardrobe would fall in the art-to-wear category. One of Diane's specialties is stenciling, so she added her own designs on the front of the blouse to give character to the garment.

On the right is Rosemary, who made her fabulous pantsuit out of 100 percent linen. This simple outfit has great style. Rosemary also made traditional pants and a skirt, which she wears with the jacket and blouse for business. For our picture she added tailored shorts for a touch of pizzazz. This great combination of garments fits her busy schedule as a speech therapist and college instructor.

Rosemary is an avid sewer and makes a large portion of her wardrobe. Her hobbies include many handicrafts as well as clothing construction. Her wardrobe combines traditional styles with unusual touches and combinations of fabric that create a look that expresses her individuality while fitting her lifestyle.

Cara is the young woman in the center. She works for a payroll company

"Style is what makes you look your personal best."

and must dress in classic business attire. When she sews, she is not interested in the unique. Instead, she wants her garments to look like quality ready-to-wear, but with improved fit. So, Cara concentrates on contemporary fabrics with simple lines. This simple knit dress is appropriate for her age and style preference.

Diane and Rosemary are tall, and their clothing styles have a fair amount of ease. Cara, who looks the same height as the others in the picture, is actually only 5 feet 4 inches tall. (She stood on several pattern books for the photograph.) The pared-down lines of her dress are appropriate for her more petite stature.

Each of these women has spent time making decisions about how she wants her clothes to feel, look, and move, and what impression she wants to make. The result is a garment that each woman truly loves.

Define Your Look

I am the co-owner of a fabric store called The Sewing Place, located in northern California, and I am blessed with wonderful employees who are happy to help all of the customers. Recently I heard one employee ask a customer about a pattern she was purchasing.

The customer had chosen a pattern for a garment that was very loose-fitting and was designed for soft, drapey fabric. But the fabric she selected was of medium to heavy weight that had very little drape.

The customer explained that she loved the picture on the pattern envelope and was attracted by the advertising that promoted the pattern as "very easy." She loved the fabric she had chosen and did not understand how the combination was going to look.

Questioned about her style of dressing, the customer said she likes fairly structured, close-fitting clothes. With a gentle nudge from my employee, the customer eventually chose a different pattern for a garment with less ease and more pieces.

A week later, the customer returned to the store wearing the completed garment and sporting new confidence in her sewing skills and pride for making a garment that she loved. Once that customer defined the fabric and style she preferred and combined them with the right pattern, the proper alterations, and compatible fabric, it was just a matter of assembling the pieces.

My employee helped the customer make a conscious decision about what her personal preferences were and that, in turn, helped her to purchase the correct pattern.

The fabric you choose for a garment must work with the pattern. If you use medium to heavyweight fabrics with a pattern that was designed for drapey, soft fabrics, your garment will look puffy and bulky.

If you define your look, you will lessen the chances of what I call "fantasy sewing" that often leads to your making clothes that you hate to wear.

You *Do* Look Great

Many of us have favorite garments we love because everyone compliments us when we wear them. In this book, I am concentrating on getting you to make clothing that looks good on your body and makes you feel good—clothes you will wear on a daily basis.

Looking Good

Accentuate 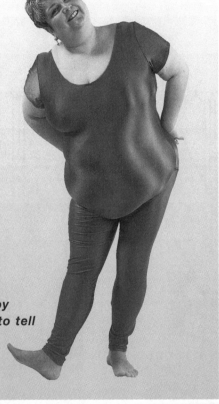 the Positive

Wait! I heard you! "I can't look gorgeous. My _____ (*fill in the blank with your particular body part*) is _____ (*too small, too large—choose one*)."

That's what you said—or thought—isn't it? I hear this every day from women of all shapes and sizes! If you would come into my fabric store, you would have to learn to accept a compliment. Otherwise, I would just have to poke you.

I sincerely believe that if you have a positive attitude about yourself, it will help you in all things throughout your life, and I want you to start to develop the positive-thinking habit now.

Here is a good way to begin. The next time someone compliments you—or your sewing—say, "Thank you," and smile. I do this myself, and you should do it, too!

As you may know by now, I enjoy breaking all the rules. As I like to tell all of my friends and sewing students, no one this short and this round should be this cute!

It is time for you to define your personal style and decide what clothes make you feel wonderful and look gorgeous.

Your body is neither good nor bad. It is simply as it is. In each person there is beauty, integrity, honesty, rhythm, depth, intelligence, and balance. All of these things make up an individual, and each individual is very special.

What is best for you—a beautiful, gorgeous, talented woman—is a very personal decision. If the current trend is severely tailored fashions in shades of taupe and black, and you have the soul of a gypsy, the fashionable look will not make you feel attractive. If a garment satisfies your soul, then it will give you an outward glow that can only enhance the total you.

As you work through this chapter on personal style and fabric preferences, do not struggle to choose the right answer because there is no right or wrong answer.

Let your heart answer the questions, and don't overanalyze. Develop a new, clear vision of yourself.

Discovering Your

You must know yourself and your personal style before you can sew for yourself.

FITTING ROOM

Refine your vision of your personal style with a day of cashless clothes "shopping."

At least once a year I want you to go to your favorite department store or shopping mall for a window shopping day. My step-by-step method will help you to develop a vision of your personal style and to learn more about yourself and your taste in clothing.

Assemble the Materials

You will need the following materials to get started with my program:

✦ *Pantyhose or knee-high stockings*

✦ *Several pairs of shoes in various styles*

✦ *Hand mirror, comb, and brush*

✦ *Notebook and pen or pencil*

✦ *Small package of straight pins*

✦ *Tape measure*

The Discovery Program

STEP: Do not take money, a checkbook, credit cards, or any other way to actually make a purchase. This frees you to look at everything and anything.

Personal Style

STEP 2: Look your best. Wear your best undergarments. Fix your hair. Wear or take pantyhose or knee-high stockings, if you prefer. Take several pairs of shoes in various styles. Wear comfortable clothing that is easy to get out of and back into, such as pull-on pants and a button-up blouse.

TIP: Bring the hand mirror so that you can check the back of your body as you try on garments. That way you won't have to twist your body to see your back clearly.

STEP 3: Pack the notebook and pen or pencil in your handbag or tote so that you can write down information and draw sketches or different styles that appeal to you. If you use a small spiral-bound artist's sketchbook as your notebook, you can easily sketch garment styles on the unlined pages. Tell the salesclerk you are planning your yearly wardrobe and will be looking at many garments, and that you will be doing any purchasing at a later date.

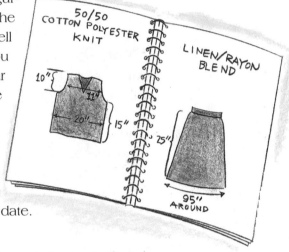

STEP 4: Try on several garments that do not seem to be the "current you" at all. Choose something you feel you would never actually wear but a secret part of you occasionally fantasizes about. You may discover that the style is actually flattering on you even though you didn't think it would work! This is an excellent way to experiment with new garment styles.

You may want to use a small spiral-bound artist's sketchbook to sketch interesting garments and make notations to use with your own designs.

You may need a tote bag to carry all of the essentials for effective window shopping—pantyhose, a notebook, a hand mirror, a comb and brush, flat and small-heeled shoes, a small box of straight pins, and a tape measure.

"Pay attention to what looks best rather than the size tag."

STEP: Try on garments that resemble patterns you are thinking of making. This will help you discover if this is a style that works for you before you spend the time and money to make it. If a garment is too large, you can use the straight pins you brought with you to adjust the areas that don't fit correctly. Pinch out excess fabric, noting how much fabric needs to be removed for the garment to look good on you, and pin it in place, as shown in **Diagram 1.** You can also use the pins to adjust hemlines.

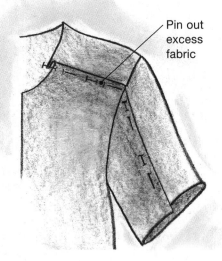

Pin out excess fabric

Diagram 1

Use small straight pins to pin out excess fabric on a blouse that is too large for you. Make sure to note how much fabric you had to remove.

STEP: Since you will not be purchasing any of the clothes you choose, feel free to try on the very best fashions. Most of us are uncomfortable trying on clothes we know we can't afford. However, you need to discover what expensive clothing is all about. Analyze the way each garment looks on you. Does the cost affect the look? Is the fabric finer, smoother, drapier, or softer? What makes it different from a lower-priced garment? Maybe it is just the details.

TIP: Don't even look at the price tags on the garments you select. That way you won't be tempted to like or dislike a style based on its price.

STEP: Try on many sizes of the same garment—the size you normally wear, one size larger, and one size smaller. Pay more attention to what looks best rather than the size tag on the garment. Be sure to write down the types of fabric you prefer.

TIP: Use the tape measure to measure the garments you like best. This will help you determine the amount of ease you prefer in a finished garment. Write down all of the measurements in your notebook for future reference.

STEP: Don't worry about color. Try on garments for the style and design even if the color makes you look awful. Remember, the lighting in dressing rooms is generally poor. One of the benefits of sewing is that you can pick and choose fabric and style independently to get what is exactly right for you.

STEP 9: When a garment really feels and looks good, spend some time observing the construction and design details. Look at the collar, neckline, shoulder, yoke, sleeve, bodice front and back, waist, waistband, skirt, pant legs, and hems. Look at the closures, the buttons, the pockets, and other embellishments. What is it that you like about the style of the garment? Analyze the seams, shaping, ease, elastic, darts, or gathers—in other words, where are the opportunities for fit? Write down the answers to all of these questions in your notebook.

STEP 10: When you return home, pour yourself a refreshing beverage, and sit down at your kitchen table. Relax. Get your notebook and your croquis, and review all of your notations. If you want, use another piece of paper to organize your thoughts. Review the lists in the "Garment Style Checklist" on page 123. As you list your preferences and think about what types of clothing you like, be sure to check your perceptions by sketching your ideas on your croquis.

There is a careful balance between what is comfortable and what really is flattering. Sometimes we feel safer wearing the styles, colors, and designs we have always worn. Remember, you don't have to feel safe to look great!

If you find a garment that you like, use the three-way mirror in the dressing room to examine every side of your body thoroughly.

"Positive results can only come with positive action."

seams, and fitting devices—then check off the elements that you prefer in the garments that you enjoy wearing.)

You do not have to change your body to change how you look. Positive results can come only after you take positive action. Pay special attention to yourself and show the world that you are a valuable person.

Real Life

I know that you have worked through the process of seeing yourself in a leotard, creating your croquis, and accepting your body and its measurements, and I know that you have begun to develop some objectivity about your body and its shape.

Of course, you know you will not get a new body when you create new garments, but you can develop an individual look and style that makes you look your personal best. Size, weight, body shape, age—none of these should be a value judgment of who you are as a human being.

Regardless of what you think about who you are or what you look like at this moment, it is now time to develop and define your personal style and go forward. You need to make your life the best it can be.

Don't waste time focusing on what size you are, what size you used to be, or what size you want to be. See what styles, colors, and surface textures are out there now, and customize each of them to get your best look. (Use the "Garment Style Checklist" on the opposite page to help you to define your personal style. Read through the list of garment features—shapes, styles, pieces,

Cheryle has learned my fitting method and knows how to customize her patterns to get a garment that not only fits but also looks great.

Garment Style Checklist

Here is a checklist that you can use to help you determine your personal style. All of these terms describe garment shapes, styles, pieces, seams, and fitting mechanisms that you can combine to make a garment.

Check off the terms that describe what you like to see in a garment. (If you are unsure what a term means, consult the glossary on page 238.)

SHOULDERS AND ARMS

- [ ] *Neckline*
  - [ ] Cowl
  - [ ] Jewel
  - [ ] Scoop
  - [ ] Square
  - [ ] V-neck
- [ ] *Dropped shoulders*
- [ ] *Extended shoulders*
- [ ] *Yoke*
- [ ] *Sleeveless*
- [ ] *Sleeve*
  - [ ] Dolman
  - [ ] Raglan
  - [ ] Shaped raglan
  - [ ] Set-in
  - [ ] Short
  - [ ] Three-quarter
  - [ ] Long
  - [ ] One-piece
  - [ ] Two-piece
  - [ ] Full
  - [ ] Narrow
  - [ ] Push-up
  - [ ] Cuff
    - [ ] with button
    - [ ] without button
  - [ ] Ruffle at wrist
  - [ ] Fabric with stretch

BUST, CHEST, AND TORSO

- [ ] *No dart*
- [ ] *Standard dart*
- [ ] *Princess seam to armhole*
- [ ] *Princess seam to shoulder*
- [ ] *Yoke with tuck*
- [ ] *Dart under collar*
- [ ] *Open-ended dart*
- [ ] *Gathers*
- [ ] *Pleats*
- [ ] *Tucks*
- [ ] *Fabric with stretch*

WAIST

- [ ] *Waistband*
  - [ ] Interfaced
  - [ ] Elastic
  - [ ] Curved
  - [ ] Wide
  - [ ] Narrow
- [ ] *No waistband/facing only*
- [ ] *Fly front opening*
- [ ] *Skim over the waist (princess seam dress)*
- [ ] *Straight midriff (no indentation)*

HIPS

- [ ] *Smooth*
- [ ] *Full*
- [ ] *Yoke*

- [ ] *Gathers*
- [ ] *Darts*
- [ ] *Tucks*
- [ ] *Gores*

LEGS

- [ ] *Skirts*
  - [ ] A-line
  - [ ] Gathered
  - [ ] Gored
  - [ ] Pleated
  - [ ] Straight
  - [ ] Lined
  - [ ] Yoke
- [ ] *Pants*
  - [ ] Full
  - [ ] Tapered
  - [ ] Cropped
  - [ ] Flared
  - [ ] Yoke
  - [ ] Fly front
  - [ ] Elastic waist
  - [ ] Pleats
  - [ ] Cuffs
  - [ ] Fabric with stretch
- [ ] *Shorts*
  - [ ] Short
  - [ ] Midthigh length
  - [ ] Bermuda
  - [ ] Overall ease

Fit Is a Feeling, Not a Fact

Most women find it difficult to see themselves objectively. They are extremely critical. Unfortunately you will not get a new body with your new clothing that fits, but you can develop a style that makes you look your personal best.

Even when they look marvelous, most women will find fault with their appearance.

Have you ever been shopping with a friend who tried on something that really made her look great? Just as you were about to rave about the outfit, she tugged on it and said, "This is awful! It's just not right!" From your point of view, the garment made her look fabulous, but it somehow did not fit the preconceived way she saw herself.

There is a careful balance between what is comfortable and familiar and what is really flattering. Sometimes we get stuck in the safety of wearing what we have always worn.

Size, weight, age—none of these should be a value judgment of who you are as a human being. Regardless of what you look like at this very moment, accept yourself, and go forward. Make your life the best it can be today because today is the only day that counts. Don't focus on your size. See what is out there, and customize it to get your best look.

You do not have to change your body in order to change how you look. But you must pay special attention to yourself and show the world you are valuable.

How Are You Different?

If you haven't done it yet, sit down and develop a list of how you differ from the Wolf dress form, the pattern industry standard. Since everyone's body is different, everyone's list will be different.

Begin making a list of what does and doesn't fit you or what always seems to work. Jot down each thing as you think of it. For example:

Every time I try on a pair of pants, they:

☐ *Are too short/long in the crotch*

☐ *Have too much fabric below the fanny*

☐ *Are too big/small in the hips*

☐ *Are too big/small in the waist*

Every time I try on a skirt:

☐ *The waist is too big/small*

☐ *The waistband is too thick/narrow*

☐ *I find that I prefer an elastic or solid waistband*

Every time I try on a blouse, it:

☐ *Is too small/big across the tummy*

☐ *Pulls across the chest*

☐ *Is too tight/loose in the back*

☐ *Has sleeves that are too tight/loose*

☐ *Has sleeves that are too long/short*

☐ *Has cuffs that are too big/small*

Spend some time thinking about what garments you consistently have trouble finding in the stores and why.

If you think about things you consistently say to yourself, you will begin to

LOOK YOUR BEST

There is a common belief that a very full garment will make you look bigger. In reality, if the garment is made from a fabric that is thin, soft, and drapey, it will skim the body. The vertical lines of the folds will give an elongated look that can cover a multitude of sins. A woman with full hips or a full fanny is going to look much better in a soft gathered skirt than a stiff denim skirt.

Stiff denim fabric

Drapey rayon challis

If you have large hips or a large fanny, don't use a stiff denimlike fabric. Choose a gathered skirt pattern, and use a drapey rayon challis to give the illusion of a longer body.

"*Choose clothing with your personal style in mind.*"

understand what doesn't fit you. You will begin to understand how your body is different from "the standard," and you will also be able to define what styles work for you.

If jackets are always too tight for you, your body is probably deeper than the pattern industry standard.

Are your favorite clothes the most comfortable or the most flattering? If you are difficult to fit, you may have concentrated on comfort while ignoring how you look.

With a little insight and planning, you can achieve the fit and the comfort you want, while developing clothes that enhance your body shape.

Define Your Style

As you think about and develop your personal style, there are additional factors that you must consider. Think about your lifestyle. Do you need specific work clothes? Do you wear dressy clothes? Do you travel? What special clothes do you need? List all of the clothes you need in an average week.

Describe to yourself in detail the one garment that you own that makes you feel your best. It should be a garment that meets most of your lifestyle needs and is easy and comfortable to wear. It is the outfit you always grab when you suddenly have to go somewhere and make a good impression when you get there. This outfit should be the cornerstone of your wardrobe because it fits and flatters.

Now, write down and finish the following sentences:

I want to look _____.

I want people to see me as _____.

I like _____ clothes.

Be true to yourself! No one else will have the same answers that you do, and each of your answers will be correct.

Name Your Style

Finally, I want you to develop a phrase that defines your personal style. It will help you to focus your selection of patterns and fabrics so you can make gorgeous garments each time you sew.

To start, go to your local library and take out a variety of books that deal with personal image. As you read, remember that none of the explanations will describe you perfectly. Each of us is as unique as a snowflake. Just as you are not built exactly like a Wolf dress form, you cannot be categorized into one look.

STYLE DERIVED FROM FIT

Sometimes style decisions must be made because of fit decisions, and I am the perfect example. I happen to be deeper than I am wide. I have no side hip and not much of a fanny, but I have a very full tummy.

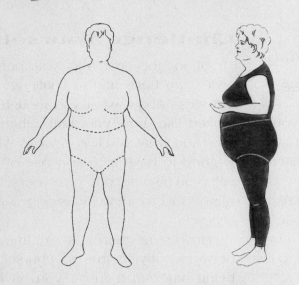

If you look at my croquis, you will see that my body is deeper than it is wide, and although I have no side hip and not much of a fanny, I do have a full tummy.

When I make a pair of pants, I must add 3 inches (7.6 cm) to the side of the front piece and 1 inch (2.5 cm) to the center, and then I redraw the straight of grain down the center to make the pants hang well.

If I were to follow the instructions on the pants pattern and fold the front down the middle and press the crease in place before I begin sewing, the crease would end up in the middle of my pant leg but off to the side of my body.

Instead, I use a standard pants pattern several sizes larger than my lower hip, thigh,

When I alter my front pants pattern, I have to add to the side and the center front, plus I redraw the straight of grain so the pants will hang better on my body.

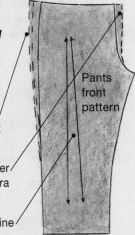

Add to front side seam

Add to center front for extra tummy

Move grainline

and calf measurements so that it will balance my full tummy. To add shape to the leg, I peg in the bottom at the hemline using a dart in the center front and back of each pant leg. I never make a crease down the front, which allows the pants to hang softly. This pants style does not accentuate my tummy.

If I don't move the grainline on my pants, the creases twist toward the sides of my body.

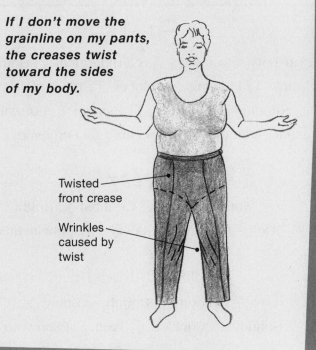

Twisted front crease

Wrinkles caused by twist

Sometimes we like certain clothes because they are soft and comfortable, but they may not be attractive. These garments are for days when we don't feel good, are doing messy work, or are just relaxing. I recommend that you limit the number of "ugly" outfits to three.

Humans are complex. Just as you do not fit in one body shape, you have a combination of styles for the different roles you fill in your life.

There is a small list of descriptive words for clothing styles below. Use the ones you want, add your own, or develop new ones: Do not limit yourself to just one view of your personal style.

Style

☐ Unusual ☐ Dramatic ☐ Asymmetrical ☐ Homespun
☐ Ethnic ☐ Flowing ☐ Eclectic ☐ Tailored ☐ Classic
☐ Structured ☐ Dressy ☐ Elegant ☐ Formal ☐
Casual ☐ Simple ☐ Serviceable ☐ Feminine ☐ Soft

Color

☐ Warm ☐ Cool ☐ Contrast ☐ Bright
☐ Dull ☐ Subtle ☐ Cheery ☐ Sophisticated

Surface Texture

☐ Smooth ☐ Rough ☐ Shiny
☐ Sparkly ☐ Crinkled ☐ Twill ☐ Plain weave

Make a list of the words that describe your style and then keep refining it until you can create a clear phrase describing yourself and how you want people to see you. Use what makes sense to you and discard the rest. You will find you will sew fewer wadders (see "Don't Sew Blindfolded" on page 7) if you have that clear vision of what style works for you.

Challenge Yourself

During this search for your personal style, you have had to challenge your old ideas about what you thought you looked like, how you think others see you, and what you like to wear. While it is good to have a clear sense of one's self, you also need to give yourself permission to try new ideas and garment styles.

However, there is a fine line between staying true to yourself and being stuck in a rut. If you have not changed your clothing style, hair, or makeup in ten years (or more!), it may be time for you to shake things up and take a fresh look at yourself. This may be difficult to do, but try it. Do it in baby steps so you don't get nervous and give up too easily.

I am not recommending that you make only perfect clothes. I want you to do your homework, make changes for comfort and drape, make the clothes, and wear them with pride.

Now you can choose clothing through realistic, kind, and accepting eyes with your personal style in mind.

Let's move on to the next chapter so you can learn how to alter your patterns to create clothing that you love and that defines your personal style.

Looking Good
My Personal Style Statement

I wear vests and T-shirts with pants or skirts as my uniform. I used to have difficulty finding T-shirts that didn't make me look boxy. But now I have a favorite pattern with a two-piece raglan sleeve that I have altered to fit me perfectly. Therefore, I buy knit fabric whenever I see a piece I like. That way I can whip up a new shirt whenever I need an instant lift to my wardrobe.

I have two vest patterns, one with princess seams and one that is a simple shape with fewer fitting opportunities. I can make these vests dressy, casual, simple, embellished, or wherever my imagination takes me.

I wear other garments for specific occasions, but this simple classic outfit makes daily dressing a snap for me. Because I've made most of my clothes in coordinating colors and patterns, they can interchange, which gives me more options, and I always look groomed and attractive.

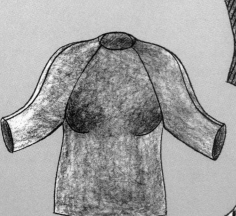

I love dressing comfortably but ready-to-wear T-shirts always make me look boxy. So I developed my own pattern for a knit shirt that has a two-piece raglan sleeve that flatters my body and is still comfortable to wear.

My two favorite vest patterns are so versatile that I can use them with a variety of techniques to create all of these vests, which range from simple to decorative styles.

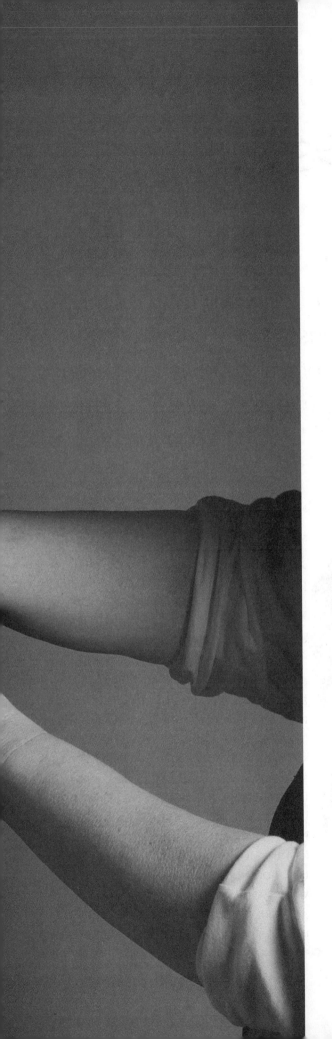

Making It Fit

ow it's time for you to learn how to make your garments fit your individual body. Test fitting a tissue pattern gave each woman profiled in this chapter additional insight into how an individual pattern fit her one-of-a-kind body. You may want to test fit your patterns as well. Read each woman's fitting process, find the similarities between these women and yourself, and then start sewing.

The Process of Fitting

In this chapter you will learn how women of various shapes and sizes with a variety of fitting challenges learned how to alter specific garments to fit themselves.

Women come in all shapes and sizes and thus have different fitting challenges. But you can learn how to alter garments to fit your body, no matter what your challenge may be.

I know that you were hoping for a universal explanation of how to alter your patterns for all of your fitting problems. But each one of us is so unique that it would be impossible to list all of the possible combinations of alterations.

You will see how a number of women evaluated their body shapes, and how and where they decided to add or subtract fabric to make their garments fit their bodies.

Although the process of fitting yourself may seem daunting at first, you'll find it gets easier the more you do it. If it is hard for you to find ready-to-wear that fits, keep working through the process of learning to fit your body. It may take some time, but the results will be well worth it when you have clothes that truly fit.

The wonderful thing to keep in mind is that once you get the process down and once you begin to understand what it

132

is you need to do to achieve a great fit and begin to do it, you should be able to build a repertoire of patterns that work for you every time.

Fitting each new pattern will become easier the more often you do it, and for basic dressing, you can use the same patterns repeatedly.

Soon you will find it much easier to fit and sew a garment than to search through department stores to find ready-to-wear that fits.

Always Test Fit Your Patterns

Test fitting a pattern is an essential and simple part of the fit process that a lot of sewers neglect.

I like to test fit a pattern by pin fitting it first. To pin fit a pattern, all you have to do is pin the pattern pieces together along the seamlines, keeping the seam allowances to the outside, as shown on this page, and try it on. Then you can see where you need to make adjustments.

TIP: You may want to have a friend help you pin fit your pattern. Have her pin it together as she assembles it on your body.

I am test fitting a princess seam vest on Karen in the photo on page 130. As you can see, this process helped me establish that Karen needs to remove excess fabric from the armscye of her vest. A woman with a bust larger than a B cup needs extra fabric to cover the bust, but usually she ends up with too much fabric between the bust point and the front of the arm. I removed the excess fabric in Karen's pattern by tak-

> *"Fitting patterns will become easier the more you do it."*

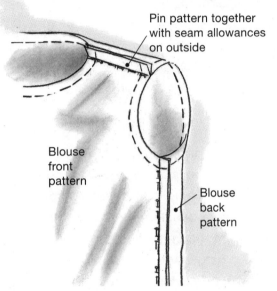

Pin pattern together with seam allowances on outside

Blouse front pattern

Blouse back pattern

To improve the fit of a garment, you should pin fit the pattern first. To do this, pin the pattern pieces together along the seamlines, keeping the seam allowances to the outside, and try the pattern on.

ing a small dart in each vest front pattern piece between the bust point and the armscye.

Pin fitting commercial pattern tissue can be challenging, however, and sometimes can be inaccurate. For additional tips on pin fitting, see "Perfect Pin Fitting" on page 134.

In some cases you will want to make a muslin test garment from your pattern. You'll want to do this if you are using a very expensive fabric or if you are working with an especially difficult or tight pattern. You'll also want to make a muslin test garment from your pattern if the garment you are making is very important to your wardrobe plans and you want to find out how comfortable it will be.

PERFECT PIN FITTING

Here are some tips for pin fitting patterns that will ease the process for you and will help to increase accuracy.

If the pattern paper tears easily or if you find it difficult to pin fit a pattern by yourself, I recommend you use Mönster Paper, a rayon pattern-drafting paper. (See "Resources" on page 241 for a source for Mönster Paper.) Before I pin fit Karen's vest pattern, as shown in the photo on page 130, she traced the front piece onto Mönster Paper and cut it out. Then I sewed the Mönster Paper pattern together on the sewing macine using long basting stitches along the seamlines, keeping the seam allowances to the outside, as shown on this page. That way, it was much easier to try on the pattern. If fabric must be added to or subtracted from a Mönster Paper pattern, small pieces of paper can be inserted and sewn into place. Plus darts can be stitched permanently, and the basting threads can be pulled out and readjusted as needed.

If the pattern tissue will not drape and the stiffness of the paper makes the garment stand away from your body, there is a danger that you might take out too much ease from the garment if you use the paper to fit the pattern. When the pattern recommends soft fabrics, use the paper-fitting process only to

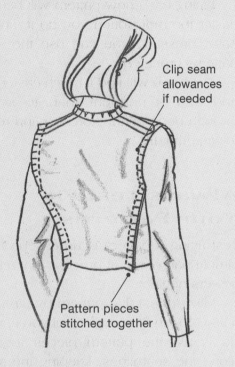

Clip seam allowances if needed

Pattern pieces stitched together

Trace your pattern pieces onto Mönster Paper, and sew the pieces together on the machine, using long basting stitches. Clip the seam allowances, and try on the pattern.

test the length of a garment. Otherwise, use your personal preference figures to calculate how much ease you want in the pattern.

If the curved areas of your pattern, such as necklines, armholes, and princess seams, are difficult to pin together, clip the pattern paper or tissue up to the stitching line around the curves to release the edges, as shown on the top left of the opposite page, and then pin the pieces together.

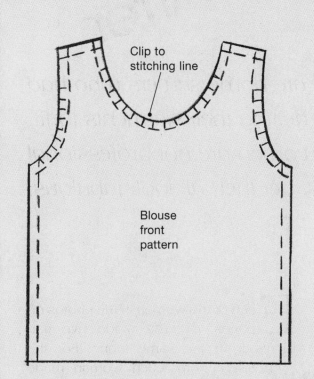

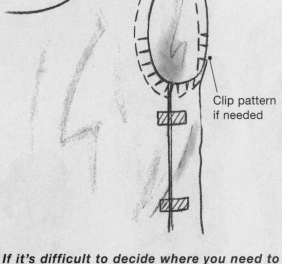

If the curved areas of your pattern are difficult to pin together, clip the pattern tissue to the stitching line around the curves, and then pin the pieces together.

If I am having a great deal of difficulty deciding where a pattern needs to be altered and I don't have flexible pattern paper, I use Scotch Removable Magic Tape to assemble the pattern. First, I cut the seam allowances off the pattern. Then I butt the edges of the pattern pieces together along the seamlines, and place 2-inch (5.1-cm) strips of tape across the seamlines every 3 to 4 inches (7.6 to 10.2 cm), as shown above right. By removing the seam allowances, I can assemble the garment in

If it's difficult to decide where you need to alter a pattern and you don't have flexible pattern paper, use Scotch Removable Magic Tape to assemble the pattern.

paper accurately without the excess paper getting in the way.

If you removed the seam allowances from the pattern, there are several ways to add them after the fitting is completed. I prefer to place tracing paper on the wrong side of the fabric and use a double tracing wheel to trace the stitching lines. A double tracing wheel has two wheels side by side, and on some versions the distance between the wheels is adjustable.

Before and After

These women are home sewers who had problems getting their garments to fit. These women are not professional models, yet they all look fabulous.

These women are not professional models, but they know how their bodies are shaped and have learned how to get a great fit.

Each of the women in the photos on pages 137–152 made two garments from the same fabric. For the "Before" photo, each woman made her garment and altered it according to the pattern instructions for her height and measurements. For the "After" photo, each woman altered the garment specifically to fit her body using my methods.

Examine each of the photos carefully. See the improvements in the "After" garments. These garments are comfortable and attractive on the women. The women's clothes reflect who they are and suit them to a T. These women have learned to see the positive in themselves, and it shows in their photos.

You, too, can alter patterns to fit your specific body shape. Instructions on how to make these alterations begin on page 153. Remember to use only your loving eyes while looking at these photos—and more important, at yourself.

▲ **BEFORE:** *Although Mary Ellen followed all of the fitting instructions on the pattern, her silk charmeuse blouse slides down her back and hikes up in the front of her neck.*

Mary Ellen

▶ **AFTER:** *By analyzing her croquis and her measurements worksheet, Mary Ellen realized her upper back uses up more fabric than the front of her body so she lengthened the upper back of her blouse (see page 155). The collar of the blouse now sits against her neck naturally, and there is plenty of fabric at the top of the blouse to cover her back.*

Beverly

▼ **BEFORE:** *Beverly's broad back and pronounced shoulder blades pull her silk camp shirt down her back, while the front of the shirt bulges and wrinkles between her shoulders and her bustline.*

▲ **AFTER:** *To accommodate her back and shoulder blades, Beverly widened the back of the blouse (see page 160). Because she has a small upper chest and her shoulder balls rotate forward, she rotated the shoulder seam forward slightly and decreased the front length of the garment. Now, the blouse hangs evenly on her body and is very comfortable to wear.*

▶ BEFORE: *The front of Carolalee's body is two sizes smaller than her back, causing her silk crepe de chine blouse to ride up in the front. The sleeves constrict her large upper arms.*

Carolalee

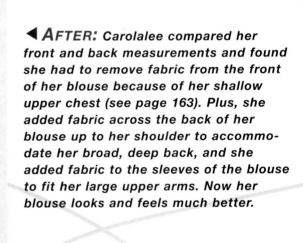

◀ AFTER: *Carolalee compared her front and back measurements and found she had to remove fabric from the front of her blouse because of her shallow upper chest (see page 163). Plus, she added fabric across the back of her blouse up to her shoulder to accommodate her broad, deep back, and she added fabric to the sleeves of the blouse to fit her large upper arms. Now her blouse looks and feels much better.*

▼ **BEFORE:** *Whenever Dorothy made a garment, she always ended up with too much fabric across her shallow bust and upper chest and in the sleeves, which left her feeling frumpy.*

Dorothy

▶ **AFTER:** *As soon as Dorothy removed the excess fabric from the front of the dress, the entire front of the garment sat firmly against her body. She also removed excess fabric from the sleeves, creating the smooth, lovely dress that you see here (see page 167). In fact, Dorothy was so excited to make a dress that fits that she planned to make two or three more.*

Shirley

▲ *BEFORE: Although full-figured, Shirley is less than 5 feet 2 inches tall. When Shirley made this blouse, she considered only her bust, waist, and hip measurements, ending up with a garment that is too big for her.*

▲ *AFTER: If Shirley had sketched the blouse on her croquis following the pattern company's length measurement, she would have seen that it was going to be too long and too big. To improve the fit, Shirley shortened the length of the blouse body and the sleeves (see page 169). Now when Shirley wears this blouse, she can tuck it in, blouse it slightly, or wear it open with a tank top underneath, as if it were a jacket.*

▲ *BEFORE:* *Cheryle, whose body is as deep as it is wide, made a big, boxy, unflattering blouse that did not allow for the depth of her body. The garment needs less fabric in the shoulders and more fullness in the torso.*

Cheryle

▶ *AFTER:* *To help the silk doupioni blouse fit better around the shoulders, Cheryle added darts under the collar (see page 174). Then she added contour to the garment by stitching small open box pleats at the waist on the front and the back of the blouse and by taking a tuck at the bottom of each sleeve. Now, Cheryle looks great in a blouse that not only fits but also flatters her body.*

▼ **AFTER:** *To allow her jacket to flow smoothly from her upper body to her lower body, Barbara chose a pattern with princess seams so she could make many small, gradual adjustments to the pieces (see page 176). The sleeves of her "Before" jacket were too tight and uncomfortable, so instead she used a two-piece sleeve pattern. Now Barbara has a jacket that allows her to move around comfortably.*

Barbara

▼ **BEFORE:** *Barbara is three sizes bigger in the hip area than she is in the bust and waist, which causes her jacket to get hung up on her fanny. By adding to the pattern only at the sides, the crosswise grain is forced off-kilter, causing wrinkles on the back.*

Cindy & Peggy

▼ **BEFORE:** Cindy, on the left, is full-busted, and this vest made to fit her bust measurement is too large everywhere else. Plus she is long-waisted, and the bone structure of her upper chest is small.

Because Peggy, on the right, has a shallow upper chest and small shoulders, her tank top gapes open in the front, causing long diagonal wrinkles on the sides of her body.

▲ **AFTER:** Cindy used a pattern two sizes smaller than her bust measurement and added only to the front of the pattern as needed (see page 181). She also lengthened the pattern. Instead of following the pattern guide and taking fabric out just at the side seams, she removed fabric from the area where her body is small. The end product sculpts and contours to her body—and she looks fabulous!

Peggy pared down the fabric in the upper body and shoulders on her tank top by adding what I call a "hookEdo," which forces a bubble of fabric at the front of the blouse so there is enough fabric for the garment to move smoothly over the bust and under the arm (see page 180). The garment lies firmly against her body with no gaping and no fabric sticking out under the arms, and it is very comfortable to wear.

▼ BEFORE: *Diane created her vest from a very simple pattern with no princess seams, no darts, nothing to help fit the garment to her body. The vest buckles along the front edge and sticks out along the side—what I call the "water wings" look.*

Diane

◄ AFTER: *Diane's vest is made from a fabric that has too much body for the simple loose-fitting pattern. The pattern recommended fabrics that are lightweight and drapey, while her fabric is thicker, crisper, and heavier and needs to be closer to her body. She made the garment smaller by removing fabric from the front of the vest and by adding a "hookEdo," which helps the vest to move smoothly over the bust and under the arm (see page 189).*

145

▶ **BEFORE:** *Although Millie chose the dress pattern according to her measurements, the garment shoulder is wider than her natural shoulder, and she cannot raise her arm easily. Her deep body also causes diagonal folds to form in the dress.*

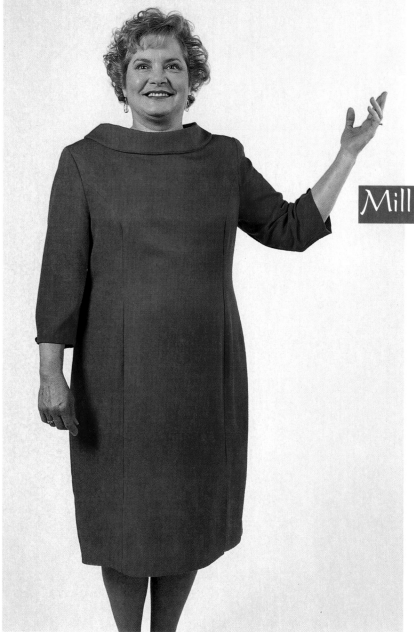

Millie

◀ **AFTER:** *Millie decided to use a pattern two sizes smaller than the pattern guide recommended. That way, the sides of the dress would be shorter, and her shoulder and neck area would be more proportioned to her body. She also used a two-piece sleeve pattern, narrowing the bottom of the pieced sleeve so it made her arm look longer and better proportioned (see page 194). In her "Before" garment, you can see the arm is binding when she tries to raise it. But if you look at her "After" photo, you can see that her arm can move more easily.*

Judy

▼ **BEFORE:** *Judy's rayon faille jacket pulls up in the back, and the hemline is much too short because of her long, round back and very shallow chest. Pronounced wrinkles extend from the center back to the side seam, and the sleeve hangs at an awkward angle.*

▲ **AFTER:** *To accommodate her very round back, Judy added 4 inches (10.2 cm) to the back of her pattern and removed 1 inch (2.5 cm) from the front (see page 198). This is a good example of establishing the horizon on a garment. It is important that the bottom of the garment be horizontal so it doesn't draw attention to the area of the body that is difficult to fit. Look at the difference in the back hemlines in Judy's jackets.*

▼ *BEFORE: Although Dale made the changes to the pattern pieces as the guide sheet recommended to accommodate her measurements, the shorts and top still aren't right for her. The sleeves are too long, the front opening is too deep, the front pulls apart at the bust, and the top is too long and hangs on her hip fluff.*

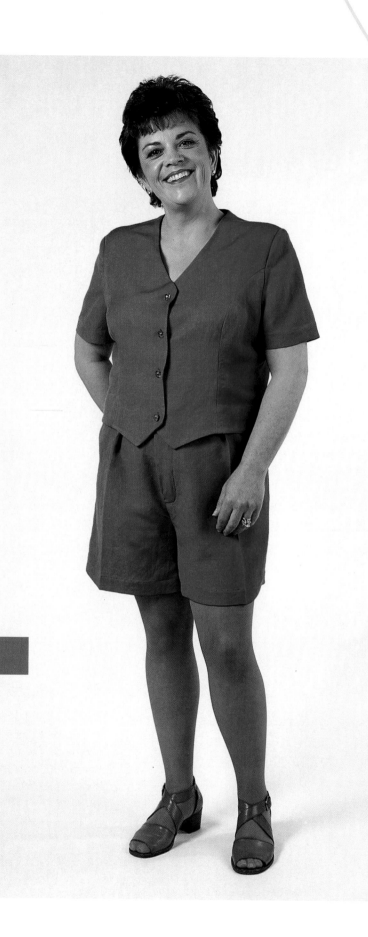

Dale

▶ *AFTER: By drawing on her croquis, Dale discovered that by removing the cuff and lengthening the shorts, she could get a longer legged look. She added to the front pattern to accommodate her little tummy (see page 200). Because the vestlike bottom on the blouse was too long for Dale on the "Before" garment, she chose a shorter length for the top. She also decided to shorten the sleeves.*

▲ BEFORE: *Dolores, on the left, does not have enough body mass to support the fabric between her waist and her fanny because she has a hollow back. And although her hips are small, she has a full fanny.*

Lynda, on the right, has hip fluff that forces her skirt to ride up and form a ridge just below her waist. The garment with its traditional darts doesn't have enough fabric to go around her body.

Dolores & Lynda

▲ AFTER: *Dolores trimmed the top of the pattern 1½ inches (3.8 cm) at the center back of the skirt, allowing it to hang correctly (see page 204). You can see how much smoother it looks in the back. Dolores also lengthened the hem on her linen/rayon skirt. This proportion works better with her overall wardrobe, and she prefers this length.*

To get more fabric in the skirt closer to the waistband to accommodate her hip fluff, Lynda eliminated the traditional darts at the waistline of the skirt and used curved darts, allowing more fabric in that area to go over her hip fluff (see page 208). That way, the skirt has enough fabric just below the waist so that it can hang from her upper hips and not ride up.

▲ BEFORE: *Jane's waist is 3 inches (7.6 cm) lower in the front than it is in the back. Therefore, the back of Jane's eight-gore cotton knit skirt hikes up and the front is too long.*

▼ AFTER: *Jane lowered the waistline 3 inches (7.6 cm) at the front of her skirt and added a separate waistband (see page 210). Jane knows that she must make this alteration on anything that hangs from her waist. Now, the gores on Jane's skirt hang straight and the fabric looks full and graceful.*

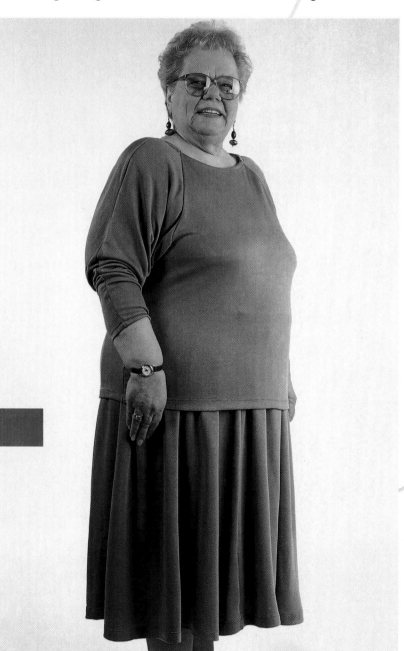

Jane

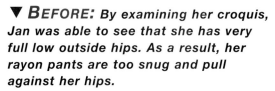

Jan

▼ **BEFORE:** *By examining her croquis, Jan was able to see that she has very full low outside hips. As a result, her rayon pants are too snug and pull against her hips.*

▲ **AFTER:** *To accommodate her wide hips, Jan lengthened the outside seam of the front and back pants patterns and made the overall pant leg wider (see page 214). She also changed the placement of the tucks to shape the waist.*

Karlene & Cynthia

▼ **BEFORE:** *Karlene, on the left, has a shallow and flat fanny and her rayon gabardine pants have way too much fabric hanging below her fanny. Plus, she is shorter than the height for which commercial patterns are designed.*

Since Cynthia, on the right, is 6 feet tall, she added to the length of the rayon twill pants according to what the pattern recommended for her height. But Cynthia is short-waisted and even longer legged than a 6-foot height requires. So, as you can see, the pants still aren't quite long enough.

▲ **AFTER:** *Karlene removed the excess fabric from the entire length of the pants inseam all the way to the hem cutting line (see page 218). She also removed 1 inch (2.5 cm) of length from the front and back patterns in the tummy area. These pants look great and don't overwhelm the shape of her body.*

Cynthia added to the length of her pattern pieces to go out and over her hips and fanny and to accommodate her height (see page 221). Cynthia also has a small waist, so she increased the number of darts on each side of the back from one to two. By creating her croquis and taking accurate measurements, Cynthia has been able to get a great-fitting pair of slacks.

Getting It Done

As you read the profiles of the women in this chapter, keep in mind the specific area of the body that you need to adjust every time you pick up a pattern.

To get additional insight into how to make adjustments for your own body, refer to the photos on pages 137–152 frequently. This information will help you create garments that fit time after time.

To accomplish any of my garment-fitting techniques, you will need a few important tools, including a commercial pattern, a see-through ruler, a hip curve, a pencil or marker, and pattern paper.

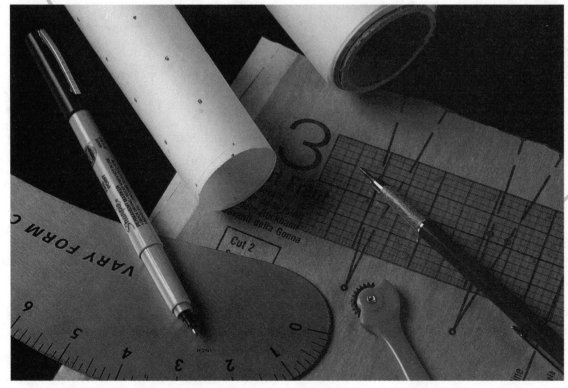

Tools for Altering Patterns

To accomplish any of my pattern adjustment techniques, you will need some, but not all, of the following tools:

✦ *Commercial pattern*

✦ *Pattern paper or Mönster Paper (see "Resources" on page 241 for a source for Mönster Paper)*

✦ *Tape measure, preferably 110 inches long*

✦ *Ruler or straightedge*

✦ *6-by-24-inch see-through ruler*

✦ *Flexible ruler (optional)*

✦ *Hip curve*

✦ *Rotary-cutting mat with 1-inch grid*

✦ *Scissors*

✦ *Pen, pencil, or marker*

✦ *Straight pins*

✦ *Transparent tape*

✦ *Fusible straight-of-grain tape*

Make a Full-Size Pattern

If the commercial pattern you are using includes pieces that are to be cut on the fold, you may want to create a full pattern piece. You will find it much easier to pin fit your patterns to your body if you use full pattern pieces. Follow these four steps.

STEP 1: Cut a large sheet of pattern paper.

STEP 2: Place the pattern onto the pattern paper right side up and trace the pattern.

STEP 3: Flip the pattern over and trace the other side. If your pattern paper is not wide enough, you'll have to tape two or more pieces together to accommodate the width of your pattern.

STEP 4: Cut out the new, full-size pattern.

ALTER YOUR PATTERNS TO FIT YOUR BODY

The alterations that the 19 women in this chapter made to their patterns were calculated for the specific individuals involved. Each woman made changes to her pattern pieces specifically to accommodate her individual body shape. Although you will follow the general guidelines I have provided for making additions and reductions to your pattern pieces, remember that you must always insert your unique, three-dimensional body shape and measurements into every pattern you choose to sew.

Although each of you wants specific information on your individual body shape, I couldn't make a book large enough to cover every variation. You need to understand the process, and then you need to take the time to do it. After that, with a little practice and patience, you will begin making clothes that fit you and that make you feel wonderful.

Mary Ellen
(see page 137)

LIFESTYLE

✦ **Loves to sew, do needlepoint, and read**

✦ **Travels**

✦ **Needs dressy clothing**

FITTING CHALLENGE

Upper torso that is longer in back than in front. *Whenever Mary Ellen makes a blouse, a top, or a dress, the garment slides down her back and hikes up in the front of her neck.*

GARMENT

Simple silk charmeuse blouse

REMEDY

STEP 1: Examine your body. Mary Ellen examined the side view of her croquis and her measurements worksheet. She found that she is longer in the back than in the front because her head sits forward on her shoulders, as shown in **Diagram 1.**

STEP 2: Determine where you need more fabric. Mary Ellen realized that her upper back uses up more fabric than the front of her body, so she decided to lengthen the upper back by adding enough fabric to come up and over the entire distance. This would allow the back of the blouse to hug her neck and would straighten the horizon of the garment at the hemline.

STEP 3: Alter the pattern. Mary Ellen compared the length of her back and the back-waist length on the pattern. She decided to add ¾ inch (2 cm) at the top of the back of the blouse pattern to get the back high enough so that the shoulder seam would lie along the top of her shoulder instead of sliding down her back. In other words, she did what I call "The Emily." (For detailed instructions, see "The Emily" on page 156.)

Diagram 1

By looking at her side croquis, Mary Ellen found that the back of her body is longer than the front of her body because her head sits forward on her shoulders.

Look at the "After" photo of Mary Ellen on page 137. You can see that the collar of the blouse is sitting against her neck naturally, and there is plenty of fabric at the top of the blouse to cover her back.

THE EMILY

Many years ago I had a client named Emily who constantly struggled to get her garments to fit. After analyzing her body visually and taking her measurements, I found that her upper back was longer and rounder than the industry standard, as shown below.

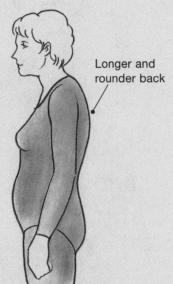

Longer and rounder back

I found that my client Emily had a very long and round back compared to the industry standard.

To accommodate her longer upper back, I had to lengthen the bodice back pattern. I wrote the instructions for this technique and used her name as the file name in my computer. Now I just refer to this easy-to-do alteration as "The Emily."

There are three reasons why I spend time teaching this alteration. First, this alteration is very common. From my experience measuring hundreds of women, I've found that more than 60 percent of women over the age of 40 need this alteration. The lengthening of the back is just part of what naturally happens to women's bodies as they get older. Second, it is almost impossible to get a clear, objective view of the back of your body. Third, once the garment sits evenly on the front and back shoulder area, it will hang correctly.

Perhaps you need this alteration. Must you continually pull your clothes down in the front? Does your collar refuse to sit against your neck? Do jewel necklines feel as if they are strangling you?

If you could stand behind yourself while you pulled down the front of a garment so that the collar would sit against your neck, you would see diagonal wrinkles along each side, pointing toward the top of your back, as shown below. These wrinkles indicate the fabric is off-grain on the crosswise grain.

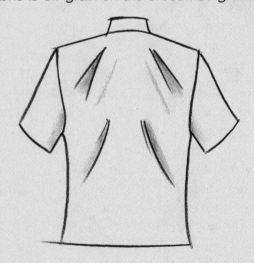

Diagonal wrinkles indicate the fabric is off-grain.

There is not enough fabric to get to the top of the back. The fabric keeps trying to force itself back into grain, and the result is that it pulls the garment to the back. In other words, the horizon of the garment is off.

To get a better-fitting blouse, you must compare your front length and your back length measurements using the measurements on the "Average Commercial Pattern Measurements" table on page 59.

Before you compare your front measurement, you must adjust that measurement for your cup size. Since commercial patterns are made for a B-cup body, you must increase your measurement by ½ inch for each size larger than a B, or you must decrease it for each size smaller. Then examine the horizon of your waist, as shown in Step 8 on page 53. If your waist rises in the front, you must deduct that amount from the front length, and if it is lower, you must add that amount. You may also have to adjust the overall length of the pattern to compensate for your shorter- or taller-than-average height. The front of your body is easy to see and fairly straightforward to alter. Therefore we can use it to begin solving our back-fitting puzzle.

After adjusting for the true front length, the front and back sizes should match. If the back length is longer than the comparable size, the difference needs to be added to the top back pattern piece at the neckline. With a little trial and error, you will find the

amount necessary for you. Patterns can vary slightly, but you will probably need to make this change in every pattern.

To do "The Emily," you need pattern paper, a pencil, transparent tape, and scissors.

STEP 1: *Place a piece of pattern paper on top of the blouse back pattern piece, as shown in* **Diagram 1.** *Make sure the pattern paper extends past the point that is the actual edge of the shoulder, which is about 4½ to 5½ inches (11.4 to 14 cm) from the neck edge. If the pattern has a dropped-shoulder sleeve, the pattern paper should not extend farther than your shoulder joint.*

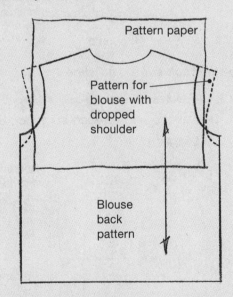

Diagram 1

Place a piece of pattern paper on top of the blouse back pattern, making sure the pattern paper extends past the point that is the actual edge of the shoulder.

(continued)

THE EMILY—CONTINUED

STEP 2: *Trace the neck edge of the pattern. Slide the pattern paper up by the amount you need to add to accommodate your longer back, raising the paper perpendicular to the straight-of-grain mark on the pattern. Tape the pattern paper to the pattern, as shown in* **Diagram 2.**

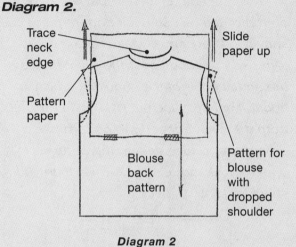

Diagram 2

Trace the neck edge, and slide the paper up.

STEP 3: *Redraw the shoulder line from the neck edge to the end of each shoulder, as shown in* **Diagram 3.**

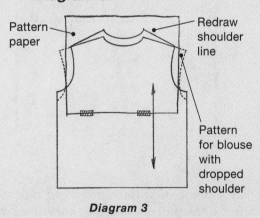

Diagram 3

Redraw the shoulder line of the pattern.

STEP 4: *Cut out the pattern. The back pattern will be longer at the shoulder than the front pattern. When you stitch the garment together at the shoulder seams, ease the back section onto the front, as shown in* **Diagram 4.** *The eased shoulder will create more room for your larger back.*

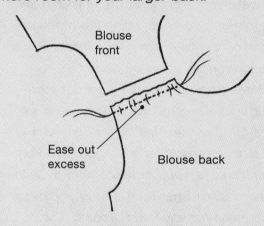

Diagram 4

Ease the back onto the front at the shoulder seams, creating more room for your larger back.

If your blouse or dress has a yoke, follow these instructions.

STEP 1: *Find the shoulder line on the yoke pattern, and cut off the front portions of the yoke, as shown in* **Diagram 5.**

STEP 2: *Place the yoke back pattern on a piece of pattern paper, and trace the neckline. Slide the back pattern piece down by the amount you need to add to accommodate your longer back, and tape the pattern to the pattern paper, as shown in* **Diagram 6.**

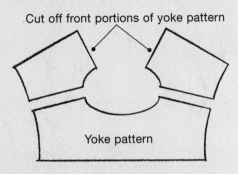

Cut off front portions of yoke pattern

Yoke pattern

Diagram 5

Find the shoulder line on the yoke pattern, and cut off the front portions of the yoke.

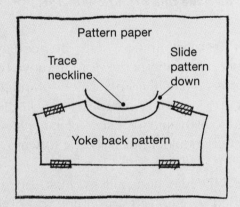

Pattern paper

Trace neckline

Slide pattern down

Yoke back pattern

Diagram 6

Place the yoke back pattern on a piece of pattern paper, trace the neckline, and slide the back pattern piece down.

STEP 3: *Tape the front pieces to the pattern paper, matching the new neckline cutting line and the shoulders, as shown in* **Diagram 7.**

If there is a gap at the shoulder edge, redraw the curve by marking a point halfway between the cutting lines on the top and bottom pieces, and blend the two lines together, starting and ending about 1 inch (2.5 cm) from the point, as shown in **Diagram 8.**

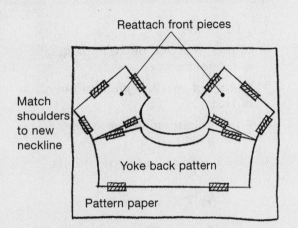

Reattach front pieces

Match shoulders to new neckline

Yoke back pattern

Pattern paper

Diagram 7

Match the new neckline cutting line and the shoulders, and tape the front patterns to the paper.

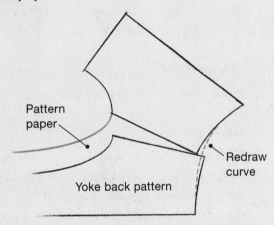

Pattern paper

Yoke back pattern

Redraw curve

Diagram 8

Redraw the curve, blending the two lines together.

STEP 4: *Cut out the pattern. The cross-grain of the fabric is now horizontal, while the garment is still long enough to reach the neck and to cover the back comfortably and attractively.*

Beverly
(see page 138)

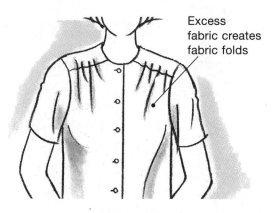

Excess fabric creates fabric folds

Diagram 1

LIFESTYLE

+ **Retired teacher, office manager, and bookkeeper**

+ **Mother of two and grandmother of two**

+ **Enjoys sharpening her garment sewing skills**

+ **Active runner and perfectionist**

FITTING CHALLENGE

Small upper chest; broad, deep back with pronounced shoulder blades. *Beverly's pronounced shoulder blades pull her garments down her back, restrict movement when she reaches forward, and pull the collars away from her body at the back of her neck.*

GARMENT

Silk camp shirt with front and back yokes

REMEDY

STEP 1: Examine your body. At 5 feet 1 inch tall, Beverly is petite and very trim. By examining her croquis and her measurements worksheet, Beverly discovered that although she has a small upper chest, she also has a very broad back. Her shoulder balls also rotate forward, causing her garments to bulge and develop wrinkles between her shoulders and her bust, as shown in **Diagram 1.**

STEP 2: Determine where you need more fabric. Beverly had to be able to get enough fabric across the back of her blouse without making the overall garment too loose and bulky.

Beverly's dresses and blouses bulge and wrinkle between her shoulders and her bust because her shoulder balls rotate forward. Check your side croquis to see if you have this fitting challenge.

STEP 3: Determine where you need less fabric. Beverly needed to remove the excess material from the front of the garment to accommodate her small chest and to eliminate the excess fabric caused by her shoulder balls rotating forward.

STEP 4: Alter the pattern. First, Beverly added ½ inch (1.3 cm) at the top of the blouse back pattern, using "The Emily." (For detailed instructions, see "The Emily" on page 156.)

TIP: Beverly's blouse not only has a yoke but also has a shoulder seam, which gives it additional opportunities for fit. If you need more curve in a garment that doesn't have a shoulder seam, you can add one. Cut apart the yoke pattern at the top of the shoulder. Tape the pattern pieces to pattern paper, and add seam allowances to the yoke front pattern and the yoke back pattern at the shoulder, as shown in **Diagram 2.**

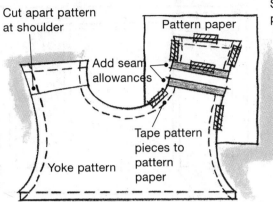

Cut apart pattern at shoulder

Add seam allowances

Pattern paper

Tape pattern pieces to pattern paper

Yoke pattern

Diagram 2

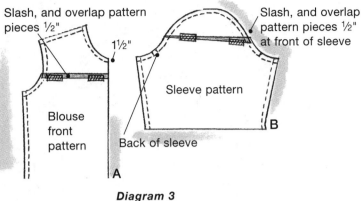

Slash, and overlap pattern pieces ½"

1½"

Slash, and overlap pattern pieces ½" at front of sleeve

Sleeve pattern

Blouse front pattern

Back of sleeve

A

B

Diagram 3

To add a shoulder seam to a garment that doesn't have one, cut apart the yoke pattern at the top of the shoulder, and tape the pattern pieces to pattern paper, adding seam allowances to both pattern pieces at the shoulder.

To fit her small upper chest, Beverly cut the blouse front pattern horizontally about 1½ inches (3.8 cm) from the neckline cutting line and removed ½ inch (1.3 cm) across the garment front by overlapping the pattern pieces, and taping them together, as shown in **Diagram 3A.** She also removed ½ inch (1.3 cm) in the same manner from the front of the sleeve, overlapping the pattern only at the front, as shown in **Diagram 3B.** This helped to shape the sleeve forward, making the blouse longer in the back and shorter in the front.

To allow for the forward thrust of the end of her shoulder, Beverly taped the back yoke pattern to pattern paper and added ½ inch (1.3 cm) to the armscye edge of each shoulder seam, as shown in **Diagram 4.** This caused the seams to curve forward. She also removed about ½ inch (1.3 cm) at the armscye edge of the shoulder area on each front yoke pattern piece to compensate for the addition to the back pattern.

To fit her chest, Beverly removed ½ inch (1.3 cm) across the blouse front pattern. She also removed ½ inch (1.3 cm) from the front of the sleeve pattern, which pulled the sleeve forward, making the blouse longer in the back.

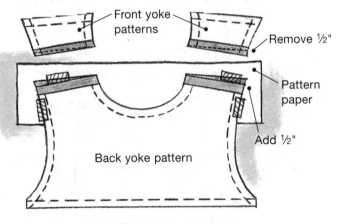

Front yoke patterns

Remove ½"

Pattern paper

Add ½"

Back yoke pattern

Diagram 4

To accommodate her forward-thrusting shoulders, Beverly added ½ inch (1.3 cm) to the armscye edge of each shoulder seam on the back yoke pattern and removed the same amount at the same seams on the front yoke patterns.

Beverly moved the top-of-the-shoulder mark on the sleeve forward ½ inch (1.0 cm), as shown in **Diagram 5** on page 162, to match the change made to the yoke.

To give her additional width across the bottom of the yoke, Beverly cut through the back yoke pattern from each shoulder seam, just outside the neck

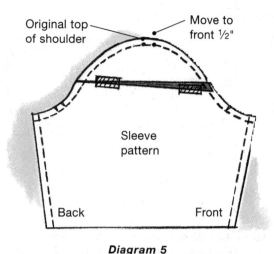

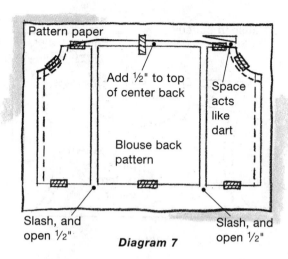

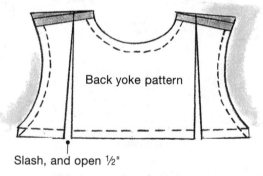

Diagram 5

Because Beverly moved the shoulder seam forward on the yoke of her blouse, she also had to move the top-of-the-shoulder mark on the sleeve forward.

edge, to the bottom of the pattern piece and opened each slash ½ inch (1.3 cm) at the bottom, as shown in **Diagram 6.**

Diagram 6

To help her blouse cover her broad back, Beverly cut through the back yoke pattern and opened each slash ½ inch (1.3 cm) at the bottom.

Beverly made a full back pattern and then added ½ inch (1.3 cm) to the width of the blouse back at each shoulder blade, as shown in **Diagram 7,** to allow for the extra inch (2.5 cm) she added to the bottom of the yoke.

Because Beverly's protruding shoulder blades pull down the back of the

Diagram 7

Because Beverly enlarged the bottom of the back yoke pattern, she had to enlarge the blouse back pattern, as well.

blouse, she added ½ inch (1.3 cm) to the top center of the blouse back pattern, blending to the edges of the pattern piece at the armscyes, as shown in **Diagram 7.**

TIP: If you have a long, broad back or pronounced shoulder blades like Beverly, choose a pattern with a center back seam, or add one to a garment. This will give you another place to increase the width of the back. If you add a center back seam, remember to add seam allowances after you increase the pattern to accommodate the fullness in your back.

If you look at the "After" photo of Beverly on page 138, you can see that her "After" blouse fits and flatters her. It's also very comfortable to wear. Beverly knows that she has to widen the back of each garment she makes, rotate the shoulder seams forward slightly, and decrease the front length so the garment will hang evenly.

Carolalee
(see page 139)

LIFESTYLE

✦ **Librarian for a large corporation**

✦ **Mother of five and grandmother of nine**

✦ **Enjoys sewing for herself**

✦ **Travels**

✦ **Loves to read mystery novels**

FITTING CHALLENGE

Very broad, deep back; shallow upper chest; very full upper arms. *The front of Carolalee's body is two sizes smaller than the back. This causes her blouses to ride up in the front. Sleeves are almost always tight on Carolalee.*

GARMENT

Silk crepe de chine blouse

REMEDY

STEP 1: Examine your body. Before Carolalee could decide how to alter her blouse pattern, she had to decide how she wanted the garment to look and, more important, to feel on her body. She examined the blouses that she owned and felt comfortable in, and she determined how much ease she preferred. She also examined her measurements worksheet and measured her pattern.

STEP 2: Determine where you need more fabric. Carolalee had to add fabric across the back of her blouse and up to her shoulders to accommodate her broad, deep back. She also had to add fabric to the sleeves of the blouse to fit her large upper arms.

STEP 3: Determine where you need less fabric. Carolalee compared her front and back measurements and decided she had to remove fabric from the front of her blouse because of her shallow upper chest. She also considered her bra size, but since she wears a B cup, no additional changes were needed in that area.

STEP 4: Alter the pattern. Carolalee widened the back of the blouse so that she could move her arms forward easily. She did this by slashing the back pattern piece about 2 inches (5.1 cm) from the neckline edge. She then laid the two pieces on a piece of pattern paper, spread them apart 1 inch (2.5 cm), and taped them to the paper, as shown in **Diagram 1.** She also created a short dart at the shoulder, inside the added section, so that the back would match the front when they were stitched together at the shoulder.

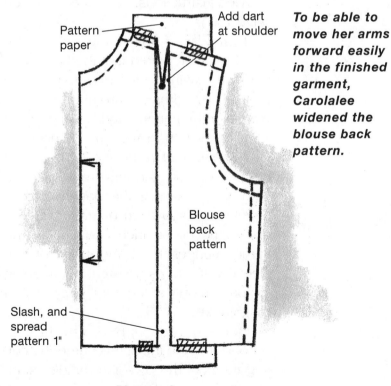

Pattern paper

Add dart at shoulder

Blouse back pattern

Slash, and spread pattern 1"

To be able to move her arms forward easily in the finished garment, Carolalee widened the blouse back pattern.

Diagram 1

Wit & Wisdom

Frequently, alterations affect how a garment "feels." If a jewel neckline feels as if it is strangling you, it's probably because you need extra length in the back of the garment. Once you know how to alter patterns, you won't have to restrict yourself to wearing V-necks and blouses with large openings.

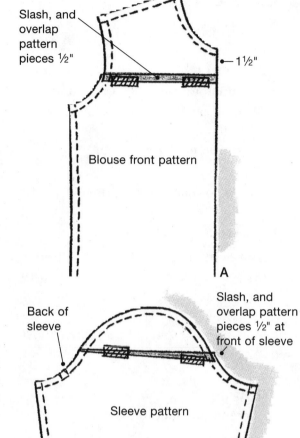

Diagram 2

To fit her shallow upper chest, Carolalee removed ½ inch (1.3 cm) across the front pattern piece. She also removed ½ inch (1.3 cm) from the front of the sleeve pattern.

Carolalee added a ¾-inch (1.9-cm) "Emily" to the top of the back of the blouse pattern to give her enough fabric to get up and over her shoulders. (For detailed instructions, see "The Emily" on page 156.)

During a pin fitting, however, Carolalee discovered that the bust point was too low in the front. To fit her shallow upper chest, Carolalee cut the blouse front pattern horizontally about 1½ inches (3.8 cm) from the neckline cutting line and removed ½ inch (1.3 cm) across the garment front by overlapping and taping the pattern pieces together, as shown in **Diagram 2A.** She also removed ½ inch (1.3 cm) in the same manner from the front of the sleeve in the armscye area, overlapping the pattern only at the front, as shown in **Diagram 2B.**

Because her upper arm is full, Carolalee made the sleeve larger by cutting the pattern down the middle, starting at the dot at the top of the shoulder.

She placed the sleeve pattern pieces on a piece of pattern paper, spread them 2 inches (5.1 cm) apart, and taped the pieces to the paper, as shown in **Diagram 3.**

To fit the altered sleeve into the original armscye on the blouse, Carolalee made a ½-inch (1.3-cm) box pleat at the center of the sleeve cap, as shown in **Diagram 4.**

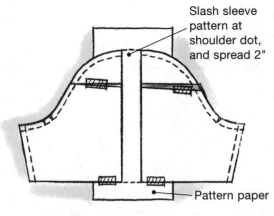

Slash sleeve pattern at shoulder dot, and spread 2"

Pattern paper

Diagram 3

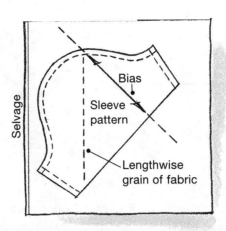

Selvage

Bias

Sleeve pattern

Lengthwise grain of fabric

Diagram 5

Carolalee has a full upper arm, so she made the sleeve larger by cutting the pattern down the middle and spreading the pieces 2 inches (5.1 cm) apart.

If you cut your sleeves on the bias, you will find that they will be much more comfortable.

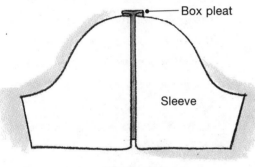

Box pleat

Sleeve

Diagram 4

Since Carolalee widened the sleeve, she had to make a ½-inch (1.3-cm) box pleat at the center of the sleeve cap so that the sleeve would fit into the original armscye of the blouse.

As a final touch, Carolalee added small shoulder pads to fill the ends of the shoulders on her completed blouse, as shown in **Diagram 6.** Carolalee's shoulders curve downward, and the shoulder pads give her added height, as shown in the "After" photo on page 139. I call shoulder pads "falsies for the shoulders." They improved the shape and the fit of Carolalee's blouse. They are not just a fashion item.

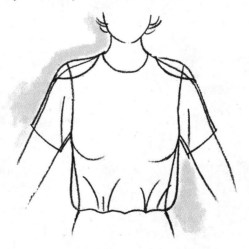

Diagram 6

TIP: To make your sleeves more comfortable, try cutting them on the bias, as shown in **Diagram 5.** However, if you decide to cut your sleeves on the bias, you will need approximately an extra ⅝ yard (0.6 m) of 45-inch-wide (114.3-cm) fabric for a long sleeve or an extra ¼ yard (0.2 m) for a short sleeve, depending on the pattern.

To give herself added height and to improve the shape and the fit of her blouse, Carolalee added small shoulder pads to fill the ends of the shoulders.

Looking Good
Enlarging a Sleeve

There are many ways to add room to your sleeves if you have full arms, and most of these alterations can be made to look like design details.

To do any of the following techniques, you must first enlarge the sleeve pattern in the center by cutting the pattern down the middle, starting at the dot at the top of the shoulder. Place the pieces on a sheet of pattern paper, spread the pieces 2 inches (5.1 cm) apart, and tape the pieces to the paper, as shown below. Then cut out the pattern.

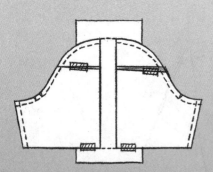

To enlarge the sleeve pattern, cut the pattern down the middle and spread the pieces 2 inches (5.1 cm) apart.

Once you have enlarged the pattern and cut your fashion fabric, you can do one of the following alterations:

✦ Gather the excess fabric to fit the armscye, as shown below.

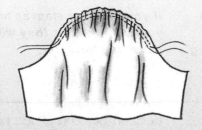

Gather an enlarged sleeve cap to fit the armscye.

✦ Take a series of tucks in the sleeve cap, as shown below.

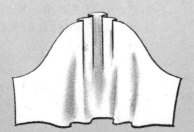

For a more elegant look, take a series of tucks in the sleeve cap.

✦ Add a dart to the sleeve cap, as shown below.

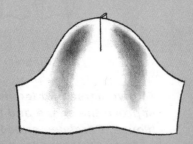

Darts can make an enlarged sleeve cap fit into a garment.

Another way you can widen a sleeve is to create a two-piece sleeve. To do this, split the pattern down the center of the sleeve, starting at the dot at the top of the shoulder. Tape the two pieces to a piece of pattern paper, and add a 1-inch (2.5 cm) seam allowance on each side of the split. Beginning 2 to 3 inches (5.1 to 7.6 cm) below the sleeve cap at the new extension, draw a line curving in to the original top, as shown below. This shaped sleeve fits into the armscye while still providing enough fabric to cover the full arm.

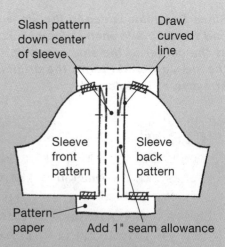

Slash pattern down center of sleeve

Draw curved line

Sleeve front pattern

Sleeve back pattern

Pattern paper

Add 1" seam allowance

You can also widen a sleeve by creating a two-piece sleeve. This shaped sleeve will fit into the armscye and will provide enough fabric to cover the full arm.

Dorothy
(see page 140)

LIFESTYLE

◆ **Edits monthly newsletter for the American Cancer Society**

◆ **Married with two grown children**

◆ **Loves to travel and read**

◆ **Attends theater and plays tennis regularly**

FITTING CHALLENGE

Small bust; small, shallow upper chest; very small arms. *Whenever Dorothy makes a garment, she ends up with too much fabric across the bust and the chest and sleeves that are too large. The bulk of the garment leaves Dorothy feeling frumpy.*

GARMENT

Silk matka dress

REMEDY

STEP 1: Examine your body. Dorothy is small and measures a size 6 in ready-to-wear, although she uses a size-8 pattern. By looking at her croquis and measurements worksheet, she determined that she has a small bust, a small upper chest, and small arms compared with the rest of her body.

STEP 2: Determine where you need less fabric. Dorothy's "Before" dress was very wide across the front and didn't fit her small upper body at all, as shown in the "Before" photo on page 140. Although the torso fit and the back length was correct, Dorothy needed to remove ¾ inch (1.9 cm) of length from the upper chest section of the garment and fabric from the sleeve.

STEP 3: Alter the pattern. To remove fabric from the front of the bodice, Dorothy slashed the pattern about 2 inches (5.1 cm) down from the shoulder, overlapped the pieces ¾ inch (1.9 cm), and taped them together, as shown in **Diagram 1**.

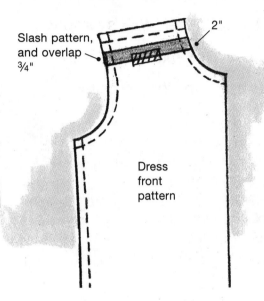

Slash pattern, and overlap ¾"

2"

Dress front pattern

Diagram 1

To accommodate her small upper body, Dorothy removed fabric from the front of the bodice by slashing the pattern about 2 inches (5.1 cm) down from the shoulder and overlapping the pattern pieces ¾ inch (1.9 cm).

She then created a full front and full back pattern from pattern paper. To eliminate the excess fabric across the sleeve, she slashed the front of the pattern and overlapped the pieces ¾ inch (1.9 cm), as shown in **Diagram 2**. She then taped the pieces together, taped the pattern to the pattern paper, and redrew the curve.

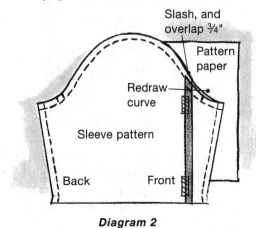

Slash, and overlap ¾"

Pattern paper

Redraw curve

Sleeve pattern

Back   Front

Diagram 2

To eliminate excess fabric from the sleeve, Dorothy slashed the front of the pattern and overlapped the pieces ¾ inch (1.9 cm).

Wit & Wisdom

I often hear full-figured women say, "You know, if I were skinny, I wouldn't have to alter things." Well, that's simply not true. Actually, it's much easier to make patterns larger than smaller.

TIP: If Dorothy were using a two-piece front pattern to accommodate her small upper chest, she would shorten the front pattern piece in two places and shorten the front side pattern to decrease the armscye, as shown in **Diagram 3.**

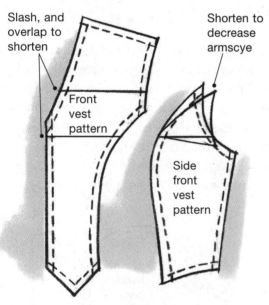

Diagram 3

If you have a small chest, use a pattern with princess seams. Shorten the front pattern piece in two places, and shorten the front side pattern to decrease the armscye.

When Dorothy test fit the partially altered pattern, she realized her bra straps were going to show at the neckline. She then taped the front and back patterns to a piece of pattern paper and added ½ inch (1.3 cm) to each neckline edge, as shown in **Diagram 4.**

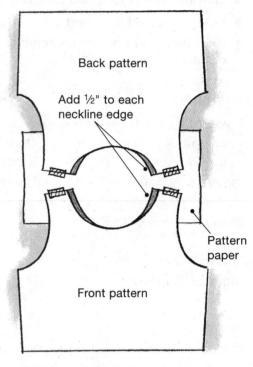

Diagram 4

When Dorothy test fit the partially altered pattern, she realized her bra straps were going to show at the neckline, so she added ½ inch (1.3 cm) to each neckline edge.

As soon as Dorothy removed the extra length from the bodice of the dress, the entire front of the garment sat firmly against her body.

By removing the excess fabric from the front of the dress and the sleeves, Dorothy created the smooth, lovely dress that you see in the "After" photo on page 140. In fact, Dorothy was so excited to make a dress that fits, that she planned to make two or three more.

Shirley
(see page 141)

LIFESTYLE

✦ Retired advisory nurse for a large medical group

✦ Loves to travel in her Airstream trailer and hopes to visit most of the United States

✦ Enjoys remodeling houses

✦ Loves to read mystery novels

FITTING CHALLENGE

Smaller in shoulder area than in other areas of body; depth of blouse front opening too low. *Shirley is less than 5 feet 2 inches tall. Although she is full-figured, her shoulders are small, and her garments are always too large.*

GARMENT

Microfiber-tissue faille camp shirt

REMEDY

STEP: Examine your body. When Shirley made her "Before" blouse, she considered only her bust, waist, and hip measurements, and her garment ended up too big, as shown in the photo on page 141.

The overall proportion of the garment was not right for Shirley. If she had sketched the blouse on her croquis following the pattern company's length measurement and compared that measurement to her own, she would have realized that this blouse was too big.

STEP: Determine where you need less fabric. To compensate for her small shoulder area, Shirley used a yoke two sizes smaller than her measurements called for. This pulled in the shoulder seam so that

While those of us who are full-figured believe we can hide our figures behind lots of fabric, too much fabric can actually overwhelm our bodies. More is not necessarily better.

the sleeve would sit on the end of her shoulder. If you look at the "Before" photo on page 141, you can see the neckline was too low, and she had to remove fabric from the front of the blouse.

STEP: Alter the pattern. Shirley raised the neckline by raising the point at which the collar folded back by 1½ inches (3.8 cm) and then raised the collar notch by half the distance of the front change, or ¾ inch (1.9 cm), as shown in **Diagram 1.** She adjusted the depth by following the instructions in "Ensure an Accurate Neck Opening" on page 170 and made the same changes to the facings.

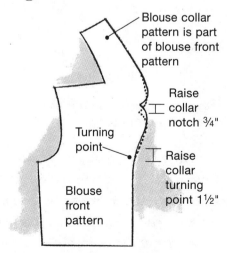

Blouse collar pattern is part of blouse front pattern

Raise collar notch ¾"

Turning point

Raise collar turning point 1½"

Blouse front pattern

Diagram 1

To raise the neckline of her blouse to fit her attractively, Shirley raised the point at which the collar folded back by 1½ inches (3.8 cm) and then raised the collar notch by half that distance.

(continued on page 173)

Ensure an Accurate Neck Opening

Have you ever nearly completed a garment and discovered that to wear it modestly, you will have to add a safety pin closure at the neckline or wear a dickey? Do you find neck openings too loose or too tight? Do your bra straps show on scoop-neck blouses? You can eliminate all of these problems by following this step-by-step method. Using a 6-by-24-inch see-through ruler, a water-soluble marker or pen, pattern paper, and these instructions, you will be able to determine how wide or how deep a neckline will be before you cut into your fabric.

STEP 1: *Sketch a diagram for recording your measurements, as shown in* **Diagram 1.**

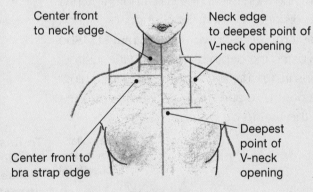

Center front to neck edge

Neck edge to deepest point of V-neck opening

Center front to bra strap edge

Deepest point of V-neck opening

Diagram 1

After measuring your neckline, note the measurements on this diagram.

STEP 2: *While wearing only a bra, look straight into a mirror and hold the 6-by-24-inch see-through ruler in front of your neck and shoulder area vertically. Place the long edge of the ruler at the center of your neck, and measure to the edge of your neck, as shown in* **Diagram 2.** *Record your center-front-to-neck-edge measurement.*

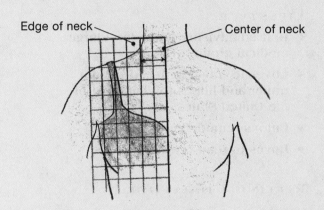

Edge of neck

Center of neck

Diagram 2

Hold the 6-by-24-inch see-through ruler in front of you vertically, and measure from the center to the edge of your neck.

STEP 3: *Measure from the center of your neck to the inside of your bra strap, as shown in* **Diagram 3,** *and record your center-front-to-bra-edge measurement. If you are broad from the neck to your shoulder, you may want to hold the ruler horizontally.*

STEP 4: *Look in the mirror and find the lowest point at which you want a neckline to end, whether it is a V-neck, a scoop neck, or the*

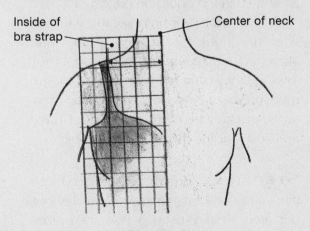

Inside of bra strap

Center of neck

Diagram 3

Then measure from the center of your neck to the inside of your bra strap.

top button on a garment with a front opening. Make a mark on the center front of your body with a water-soluble marker or pen.

STEP 5: *Place the short end of the ruler at the top of your shoulder with the long edge next to your neck (the ruler will be sticking out in front of your body), as shown in* **Diagram 4.**

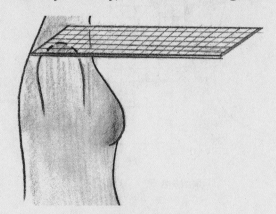

Diagram 4

Place the short end of the ruler at the top of your shoulder.

Then pivot the ruler downward so it lies vertically against the chest, as shown in **Diagram 5.** Note where the mark on your body aligns with the ruler, and record the neck-edge-to-V-opening measurement.

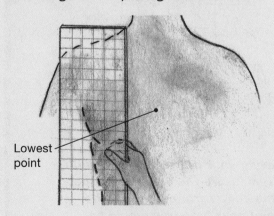

Lowest point

Diagram 5

Then pivot the ruler downward so it lies vertically against the chest, and see where the mark on your body falls under the ruler.

STEP 6: *Compare your measurements with the pattern piece, excluding the seam allowances.*

For a V-neck, tape the blouse front pattern to a piece of pattern paper, and measure the neck width on the front pattern piece, excluding the seam allowance, as shown in **Diagram 6.** Then use the see-through ruler to measure downward from the center of your neck to establish the actual depth of your preferred low point.

TIP: To get an accurate measurement of the neckline depth, you may want to extend the shoulder stitching line onto the pattern paper. To do this, align the see-through ruler with the extended stitching line, and measure to your preferred low point.

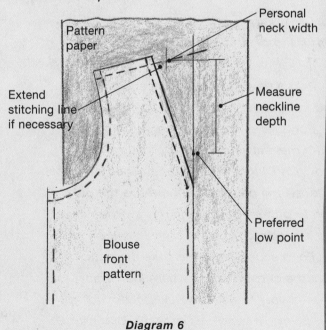

Pattern paper

Personal neck width

Extend stitching line if necessary

Measure neckline depth

Preferred low point

Blouse front pattern

Diagram 6

For a V-neck, measure the neck width, excluding the seam allowance, and then measure downward from the center of the neck to find the actual depth of your low point.

(continued)

Ensure an Accurate Neck Opening—Continued

*If necessary, redraw the neckline to the desired depth, as shown in **Diagram 7**.*

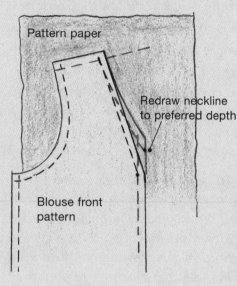

Pattern paper

Redraw neckline to preferred depth

Blouse front pattern

Diagram 7

Redraw the neckline on the blouse front pattern to the desired depth.

Add a new seam allowance if needed, and cut out the pattern.

*For a jewel neckline, compare your neck width measurement with the pattern, as shown in **Diagram 8,** to determine how tight or loose the neckline will be. Tape the pattern to pattern paper, and redraw the neckline if needed.*

*For a scoop neck, measure the pattern from the center front to where the inside edge of your bra strap would be, excluding the seam allowance, as shown in **Diagram 9.** Tape the pattern to pattern paper, and redraw the neckline if needed.*

Measure neck width of pattern

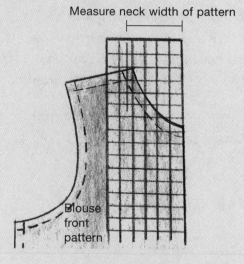

Blouse front pattern

Diagram 8

Compare your neck width measurement against the blouse front pattern to determine how tight or loose a jewel neckline will be.

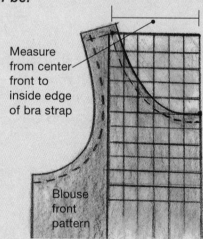

Measure from center front to inside edge of bra strap

Blouse front pattern

Diagram 9

To avoid having your bra straps show with a scoop neck, measure the blouse front pattern from the center front to where the inside edge of your bra strap would be, excluding the seam allowance.

Shirley made the rest of the garment the same size as her "Before" garment so that she had the same amount of fabric through the bust and through the back. But the upper bodice gathers, as shown in **Diagram 2A,** were too loose. So she tightened the gathered area at the top of the upper bodice to fit the larger size bodice on the smaller yoke, as shown in **Diagram 2B.** This gave her a more shapely bust by putting the fullness directly over it to give the blouse a more fitted look in that area.

To make this blouse look great, Shirley also shortened the length of the overall garment and shortened the sleeves.

TIP: Sleeve length is important. Short sleeves should be long enough to cover the upper arm but not so long or full that they look sloppy. Draw the garment on your croquis, adjusting the sleeve length until it is attractive and in proportion to your body. Measure your body to that point. Then adjust the pattern length if necessary.

Now when Shirley wears this blouse, she can tuck it in and blouse it slightly so that it shows her waist, or she can leave it open with a tank top underneath, as if it were a jacket, as shown in **Diagram 3.**

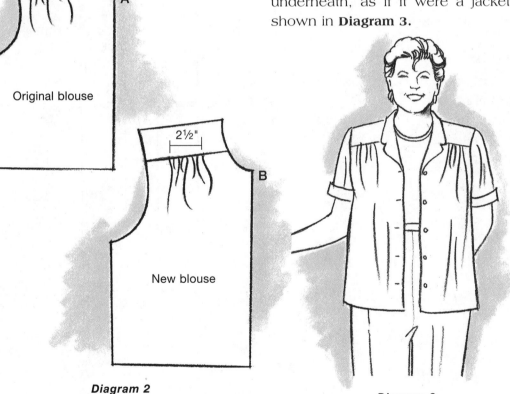

3"

A

Original blouse

2½"

B

New blouse

Diagram 2

Diagram 3

To give her blouse more shape over the bust, Shirley tightened the gathered area at the top of the upper bodice until it was only 2½ inches (6.4 cm) wide.

Shirley can now wear this blouse jacket-style with a tank top underneath or tucked in and bloused slightly so that it shows her waist.

Shirley can now make and wear clothes that celebrate, instead of simply cover, her body.

Cheryle
(see page 142)

LIFESTYLE

- ✦ **Computer specialist and consultant**
- ✦ **Owns business that helps people in the sewing industry with their publishing needs**
- ✦ **Loves animals and grows her own vegetables**

FITTING CHALLENGE

Torso that is as deep from front to back as it is wide. *Cheryle needs to get enough fabric around her body without overwhelming her silhouette.*

GARMENT

Silk doupioni blouse

REMEDY

1 STEP: Examine your body. Cheryle looked at her side and front croquis, as shown in **Diagram 1,** and found that her torso is as deep from the front to the back as it is wide.

By examining her side and front croquis, Cheryle found that her body is as deep as it is wide.

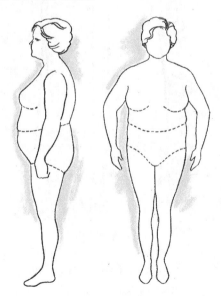

Diagram 1

2 STEP: Decide where you need more or less fabric. Cheryle's "Before" blouse was too loose and boxy, as shown in the photo on page 142. The pattern she used had side seams, no darts, and no opportunities for fit.

The pattern Cheryle chose went up only to a size 14, so she altered it to provide enough fabric to go around her body, as shown in **Diagram 2.** She slashed the front and back patterns vertically and horizontally, spread the pieces 1 inch (2.5 cm) apart, taped them to pattern paper, and added 1 inch (2.5 cm) each to the side seams and the front undercollar. She split the sleeve pattern horizontally and in two places vertically, as shown in **Diagram 2,** and spread the pieces 1 inch (2.5 cm) apart.

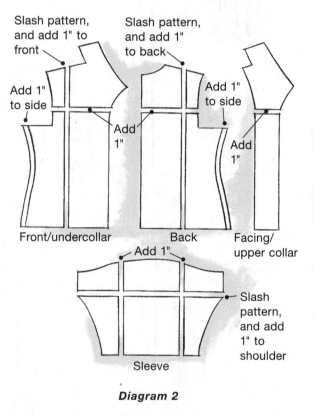

Slash pattern, and add 1" to front

Slash pattern, and add 1" to back

Add 1" to side

Add 1"

Add 1" to side

Add 1"

Front/undercollar

Back

Facing/upper collar

Add 1"

Slash pattern, and add 1" to shoulder

Sleeve

Diagram 2

To accommodate her deep body, Cheryle added to the front, back, facing, and sleeve patterns to provide enough fabric to go around her body.

But when the blouse was completed, Cheryle found that she couldn't move her arms easily. She had extended the shoulder out so far that the pivot point for the shoulder was far below the edge of her shoulder, constricting the movement of her arm, as shown in **Diagram 3.**

Diagram 3

Cheryle extended the shoulder pivot points too far, which hindered the movement of her arms.

If Cheryle had chosen a pattern with princess seams, she would have added fabric only in the front of the garment, accommodating her full abdomen and tummy, as shown in **Diagram 4.**

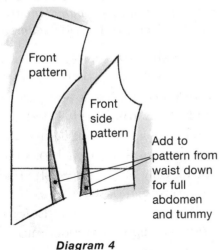

Front pattern

Front side pattern

Add to pattern from waist down for full abdomen and tummy

Diagram 4

If Cheryle uses a pattern with princess seams, she has to add fabric only to the front of the garment.

STEP: Alter the pattern. Cheryle created 1½-inch (3.8-cm) darts under the collar on the front and back, as shown in **Diagram 5.** This pulled up the shoulders so the blouse looked proportioned and fit better.

She added very small open box pleats at the waist on the front and the back, stitching a button in the center of each pleat to nip in the blouse slightly at the waist. This created a smooth, contoured line.

When Cheryle added the darts to the shoulders, the hemlines of the sleeves rose, so she lengthened the sleeve pattern.

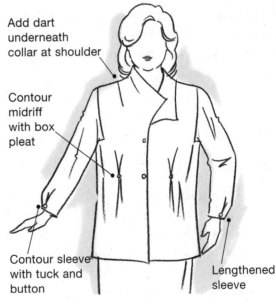

Add dart underneath collar at shoulder

Contour midriff with box pleat

Contour sleeve with tuck and button

Lengthened sleeve

Diagram 5

Cheryle eliminated the excess fabric in her blouse by adding darts at the shoulders and inverted box pleats at the waistline. She also lengthened each sleeve and took a tuck at the sleeve hem for a more contoured look.

TIP: If a garment seems too full or unshapely or if the fabric you have chosen is a little crisper than the pattern calls for, create a little contour by removing excess fabric. Cheryle took a tuck at the bottom of the sleeve and stitched on a button to hold it in place.

Now Cheryle looks great in her blouse that not only fits but also flatters.

Barbara
(see page 143)

LIFESTYLE

✦ **Marketing supervisor for a clinical laboratory**

✦ **Mother of two school-age children**

✦ **Enjoys variety of needle arts**

✦ **Very talented knitter**

FITTING CHALLENGE

Hips that are almost three sizes bigger than bust and waist; small, shallow shoulders. *Because Barbara's hips are much larger than her bust and waist, her jackets bunch up over her hips. Even though her arms are small, she finds sleeves binding.*

GARMENT

Wool jacket

REMEDY

STEP: Examine your body. Barbara wears a suit to work nearly every day, so she sews many jackets. She had great difficulty in fitting garments, however, until she looked at her croquis and her measurements worksheet and acknowledged that she is almost three sizes bigger in the hip area than she is in the bust and the waist. Many women have the same problem.

In addition, Barbara has small and shallow shoulders—from front to back, her shoulder ball is quite small. But even though her arms are small, many sleeves bind her while driving.

When Barbara sketched jacket styles on her croquis, she decided that a slightly shorter jacket looks better on her figure. If she were to make a long jacket, it would have to be very long, falling at least 6 inches (15.2 cm) below the fullest part of her hip.

STEP: Determine where you need more fabric. In the "Before" photo of Barbara on page 143, Barbara is wearing a simple jacket with midriff darts and a one-piece sleeve. She made the jacket according to her measurements, adding only to the side seams, as recommended in the pattern guide and as shown in **Diagram 1.**

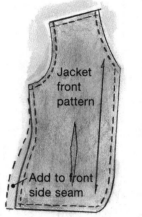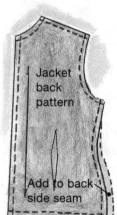

Jacket front pattern

Jacket back pattern

Add to front side seam

Add to back side seam

Diagram 1

Barbara made her "Before" jacket according to her measurements and followed the pattern company's recommendation by adding on only at the side seams.

Because her hips get full so fast, the jacket got hung up on her fanny, causing wrinkles on the back and pulling across the front. Barbara had added the correct number of inches, but by using a pattern with only front and back pieces and by adding only at the sides, she had forced the crossgrain off-kilter.

The sleeves of her "Before" jacket were too tight and uncomfortable, so she decided to add more fabric in that area, as well.

If Barbara had chosen a jacket with princess seams, it would have given her 12 areas where she could add or subtract fabric—that is, 12 opportunities for fit. If you add only ¼ inch (0.6 cm) at each of these areas, as shown in **Diagram 2,** you can add a total of 3 inches to the width of the garment. It is easy to see why adding more seams to a garment makes the change subtle and the garment flattering.

"Your body may be different sizes in different areas."

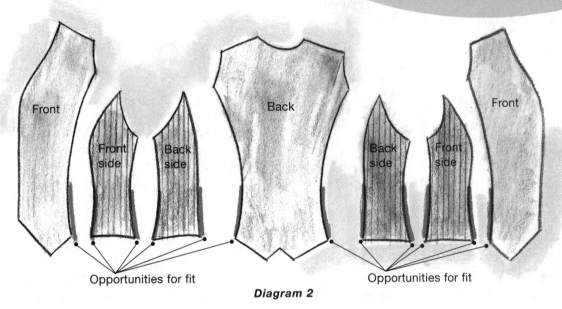

Opportunities for fit

Opportunities for fit

Diagram 2

A garment with princess seams has 12 opportunities for fit. If you add only ¼ inch (0.6 cm) at each of these areas, you can add a total of 3 inches (7.6 cm) to the width of the garment.

STEP: Alter the pattern. Barbara chose to make her "After" jacket from the same fabric but from a different pattern that had princess seams and the same V-neck but no collar, as shown in the "After" photo of Barbara on page 143.

To allow her jacket to flow smoothly from her small upper body to her larger lower body, she needed to have more pattern pieces so she could make many small, gradual adjustments.

Barbara added ¼ inch (0.6 cm) at the waist and gradually increased to between ½ and ¾ inch (1.3 and 1.9 cm) at the bottom of the jacket on each of the pattern pieces, as shown in **Diagram 3.** She added more to the back side pattern to allow for her full fanny.

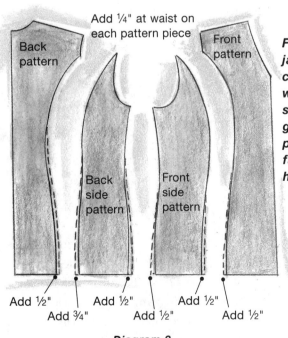

Add ¼" at waist on each pattern piece

Back pattern

Front pattern

Back side pattern

Front side pattern

Add ½" Add ¾" Add ½" Add ½" Add ½" Add ½"

Diagram 3

For her "After" jacket, Barbara chose a pattern with princess seams, which gave her more places to add fabric below her waist.

TIP: If your midriff is full, especially in the back, you must add fabric just where you need it—in the center of the body, as shown in **Diagram 4.**

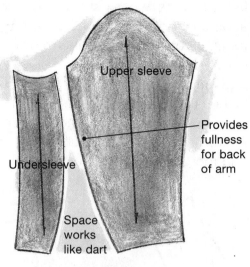

Diagram 6

If your midriff is full, you must add fabric just where you need it.

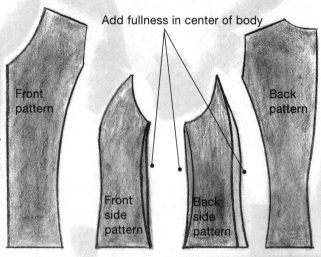

Add fullness in center of body

Diagram 4

Barbara chose a pattern with a two-piece sleeve that provided enough ease so that she could reach forward comfortably. It did not appear too full when hanging straight.

Barbara was careful to draw added width at the bottom of the jacket perpendicular to the hemline for at least 2 inches (5.1 cm), as shown in **Diagram 5,** rather than on an angle. This prevented what I call the "Judy Jetson look."

A two-piece sleeve allows enough ease so that you can reach forward comfortably but does not appear too full when it hangs straight. Your arms rarely hang perfectly straight. If you stand at attention with your arms absolutely straight and aimed slightly toward the back, a one-piece sleeve might appear straight on your body. But most of us do not stand that way, and a two-piece sleeve fits better and is more attractive.

To prevent what I call the "Judy Jetson look," Barbara added width at the bottom of the jacket pattern pieces.

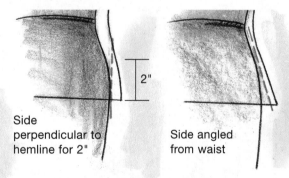

2"

Side perpendicular to hemline for 2"

Side angled from waist

Diagram 5

Barbara chose a pattern with a two-piece sleeve for her "After" jacket. Since the two-piece sleeve functions like a dart, as shown in **Diagram 6,** it provides sufficient fullness across the back of the arm and the elbow.

If you have a good two-piece sleeve pattern that fits you, you usually can insert it into a variety of jackets. If Barbara finds a jacket that has details she likes but that doesn't have a two-piece sleeve, she drags out her favorite two-piece sleeve pattern and uses it. Before Barbara cuts the sleeve from the fabric, she always measures the armscye stitching line on the jacket front and back pattern pieces, as shown in **Diagram 7.**

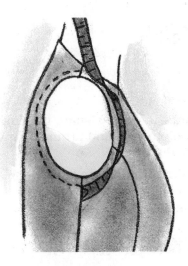

Diagram 7

To use a two-piece sleeve in a pattern that calls for a one-piece sleeve, Barbara must first measure the armscye stitching line on the jacket front and back pattern pieces.

TIP: If the length of the stitching line on the two-piece sleeve pattern is smaller than the length of the stitching line on the jacket body, she may have to raise the armscye in the jacket to fit the sleeve, as shown in **Diagram 8.** In rare cases, she may have to lower it.

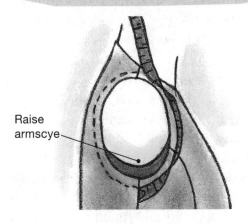

Raise armscye

Diagram 8

If the stitching line on the two-piece sleeve pattern is smaller than the stitching line on the jacket body, you may have to raise the armscye in the jacket.

Because Barbara's shoulders and upper chest are so small, she is very careful to beef up the shoulder areas of the jacket. Regardless of what a pattern recommends, Barbara adds a stay of plain weave poly/cotton sew-in interfacing, such as Armo Flex Soft, across the entire upper back of her jacket and at least one layer, and sometimes two, of fusible interfacing in the upper front of the jacket between the shoulders and the bust, as shown in **Diagram 9.** If she adds a second layer, she trims the seam allowances from the interfacing before fusing it to the jacket fabric.

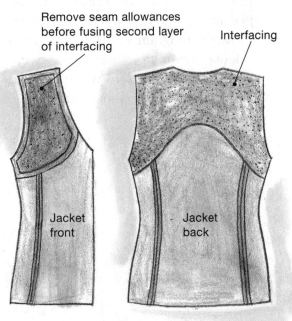

Remove seam allowances before fusing second layer of interfacing

Interfacing

Jacket front

Jacket back

Diagram 9

Barbara always adds layers of sew-in and fusible interfacing to the shoulders and upper chest area of her jackets to give that part of her body more volume.

The layers of interfacing lend structure to the jacket—like the framing on a house—so the front of the garment does not conform to the contours of her chest. This gives her the illusion of having a balanced upper body.

TIP: Your choices in the type of interfacing to use are dictated by the fashion fabric you are using. Barbara's favorite interfacing is a weft-insertion fusible called Armo Weft. She tests a piece of the interfacing on a scrap of her fabric, and if it still feels soft after two layers, she tries placing the second layer in the opposite direction. This creates a lot of structure without appearing stiff.

Finally, since Barbara has small shoulders, she added a nice, lightweight interfacing (Sof Knit, by Handler Textile Corporation) at the very top of the sleeve, as shown in **Diagram 10.** This prevented the sleeve head from becoming wrinkled—a common problem when the arm or shoulder can't fill up that area.

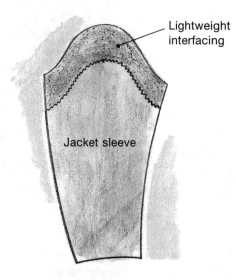

Lightweight interfacing

Jacket sleeve

Diagram 10

Barbara has small shoulders, so she added a lightweight interfacing to the top of the sleeve to prevent the sleeve head from becoming wrinkled.

Barbara now has a jacket that looks and feels great, and she can move around comfortably while wearing it.

Peggy
(see page 144)

LIFESTYLE

✦ **Works as my assistant, making appointments and arranging my schedule**

✦ **Mother of three, including one special-needs child**

✦ **Part-time nursing student**

FITTING CHALLENGE

Very shallow upper chest; small shoulders. *For someone as small as Peggy, it is difficult to fit tank tops. They either gape open in the front when she leans forward or are set away from the bust so much that there are big gaps at the armholes.*

GARMENT
Silk matka tank top

REMEDY

STEP 1: Examine your body. By looking at her croquis and her measurements worksheet, Peggy determined that her upper chest is very shallow.

STEP 2: Determine where you need less fabric. If you look at the "Before" photo of Peggy on page 144, you will see how the tank top gapes open in the front, causing long diagonal wrinkles on the side of her body. She decided she had to remove fabric from the front of the tank top but still retain an attractive contour.

STEP 3: Alter the pattern. Peggy followed the instructions in "Get a Great-Fitting Tank Top" on page 182.

Her new tank top fits her much better, as shown in the "After" photo on page 144, and she doesn't have to fear bending over in public.

> **TIP:** When Peggy makes a jacket or a vest using a two-piece front and back, she has to make changes to her pattern pieces to pare down the fabric at the upper body and shoulders. If you have the same problem, trim your pattern pieces to remove fabric, as shown in **Diagram 1.**

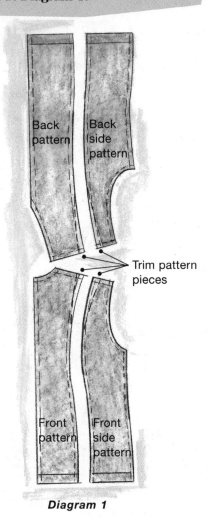

Diagram 1

When Peggy uses a pattern with a two-piece front and back, she has to pare down the pattern at the upper body and shoulders.

Cindy
(see page 144)

LIFESTYLE

✦ **Works part-time at my fabric store, The Sewing Place, chiefly as sample maker**

✦ **Mother of three**

✦ **Involved in Scouting and boating**

FITTING CHALLENGE

Small through torso but wears DD-cup bra; small across back and upper chest; long waisted. *Cindy's front bust measurement is larger than her back bust measurement, and her garments can be tight and pull across the front.*

GARMENT

Silk princess seam vest

REMEDY

STEP: Examine your body. Look at the "Before" photo of Cindy on page 144. You are probably thinking that you'd be very happy if you could get a vest to fit your body that closely. But Cindy has been fitting garments to her body for so long that she's become very particular about her fit.

You're looking at a woman who wears a DD-cup bra and yet is very small through the torso, although she is long-waisted.

By looking at her measurements worksheet, Cindy found that her front bust measurement is larger than her back bust measurement. She is not full all the way around her body, since the cup portion of her chest uses more inches than her small back. However, the bone structure of her upper chest is small.

(continued on page 186)

GET A GREAT-FITTING TANK TOP

When you make a tank top by following all of the pattern's instructions, you hang it on a hanger and it looks beautiful. But as soon as you put it on your body, it gapes and has all kinds of edges poking out here and there. Although a garment hangs nicely on a three-dimensional hanger, the drape will be distorted when you put it on a three-dimensional human form.

To get a great-fitting tank top will take time and effort, but I'm sure you will be very pleased with the results. You will need a tank top pattern, scissors, pattern paper, a pen or pencil, straight pins, a tape measure, transparent tape, a flexible ruler (optional)—and a sewing buddy.

STEP 1: Cut out the tank top pattern according to your bust and hip measurements. If it is not a full pattern, trace it on a piece of pattern paper, creating left and right sides. Trim away the seam allowances on the armscye and neck edges, but leave the seam allowances on the shoulder and side seams, as shown in **Diagram 1.**

TIP: If the front and back pattern pieces are to be placed on the fold of the fabric, trace a full pattern onto pattern paper for this fitting process, and mark the stitching lines on the pattern pieces.

STEP 2: Pin the front and back patterns together at the side seams.

Trim away the seam allowances on the armscye and neck edges of the front pattern pieces but leave the seam allowances on the shoulder and side seams.

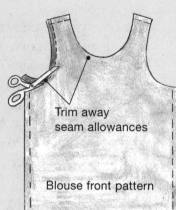

Trim away
seam allowances

Blouse front pattern

Diagram 1

STEP 3: Try on the pattern. As mentioned above, you will need another person to help you. Standing behind you, your sewing buddy lifts the back shoulder pieces of the pattern up over your shoulders, as shown in **Diagram 2.** Once she gets the back shoulder stitching line to the top of the shoulder, you can hold the pattern in place while she pins the pattern to the back of your bra to prevent it from falling off your body.

When you try on the pattern, your sewing buddy will lift the back shoulder pieces of the pattern up over your shoulder and will pin them to the back of your bra.

Diagram 2

STEP 4: *Your helper moves to the front of your body. Starting at the center of the pattern, she presses the front pattern piece against the center of your chest and brings it up to your shoulders. You will discover that the front shoulder pieces extend farther to the outside of your shoulders than the back pieces do, as shown in* **Diagram 3.** *Your helper will measure how far the pieces are offset.*

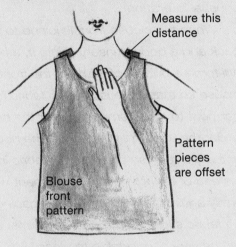

Measure this distance

Pattern pieces are offset

Blouse front pattern

Diagram 3

At the front of your body, your sewing buddy will press the front pattern piece against the center of your chest. The front shoulder pieces will extend farther to the outside of your shoulders than the back pieces.

This difference occurs because human beings are shallower and narrower on the fronts of their bodies than on their backs. A pattern that matches while lying flat will not fit when the human form is inserted.

STEP 5: *Unpin the sides of the blouse front pattern, and make the following alteration. Tape the blouse front pattern to a piece of pattern paper that has been placed on a* rotary-cutting mat with a 1-inch grid printed on it. The grid helps to keep the grain on track. Then lay a ruler or straightedge against the inside edges of the shoulders, as shown in **Diagram 4.** On the neckline side of the pattern, mark the paper at the right shoulder at the offset distance measured in Step 4. Repeat for the left shoulder. Then redraw the neck opening.

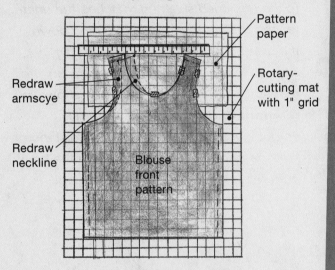

Pattern paper

Redraw armscye

Rotary-cutting mat with 1" grid

Redraw neckline

Blouse front pattern

Diagram 4

Redraw the neck opening on the blouse front pattern so that the shoulder seams will match the seams on the blouse back pattern.

TIP: *I like to use a flexible ruler when I redraw the neck opening. If you don't have a flexible ruler, a stiff tape measure set along its edge can also be used. Even a French curve might help you to get a nice, smooth line.*

STEP 6: *Mark the width of the strap on each shoulder, and redraw the armscye, as shown in* **Diagram 4.**

(continued)

Get a Great-Fitting Tank Top—Continued

Step 7: *Cut out the new pattern piece without adding the seam allowances at the neckline and the armscye.*

Step 8: *To find out how much excess fabric there is at the armscye, your sewing friend repins the altered front pattern to the back pattern on one side. Then she moves to the unpinned side and matches the unattached underarm seamlines, pulling down the side seam on the front pattern far enough to cause the side of the armhole to rest smoothly against the arm, as shown in* **Diagram 5.** *Once the front pattern is smooth, your friend measures the distance that the front pattern is offset from the back pattern and records the measurement.*

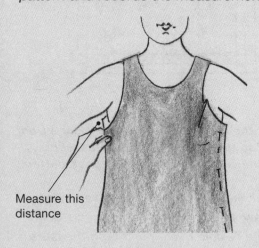

Measure this distance

Diagram 5

To find out how much excess fabric there is at the armscye, your sewing friend will measure the distance that the blouse front and back patterns are offset at the underarm in the same manner that she measured the patterns at the shoulder.

Step 9: *Your friend removes the pins from the pattern, including the pins holding the back pattern to your bra. Trim away the side seam allowances on the front and back patterns.*

Step 10: *Tape the front pattern to a piece of pattern paper. You are now going to create a "hookEdo" (my name for this unusual alteration).*

When the blouse front is joined to the back and a body is inserted into it, a hookEdo will force a bubble of fabric at the front of the blouse so that there is enough fabric for the garment to move smoothly over the bust and under the arm. In other words, the hookEdo is actually a reverse dart, putting fabric in instead of taking it out. The garment will lie firmly against your body with no gaping and no fabric sticking out under the arms, and it will be very comfortable to wear.

Mark a dot above the top of the right side seamline the same distance that the front pattern was offset from the back pattern. Connect the dot to the side seamline, as shown in **Diagram 6.** *Then draw a curved line from the dot to the armscye, creating the hookEdo. The bottom of the curve must be at least ½ inch (1.3 cm) below the dot. Repeat for the left side.*

Step 11: *You must remove an equal amount from the bottom of the blouse front pattern so the blouse front will match the blouse back when they are sewn together. At the side seams, measuring up from the hem cutting* line, mark a dot the same distance by which you increased the pattern at the bottom of the armscye. Draw a line from that point, gradually slanting toward the hemline to form a smooth arch, as shown in **Diagram 6.**

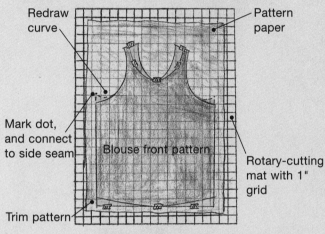

Redraw curve

Pattern paper

Mark dot, and connect to side seam

Blouse front pattern

Rotary-cutting mat with 1" grid

Trim pattern

Diagram 6

The "hookEdo," drawn at the underarm, will allow the blouse to lie firmly against your body with no gaping and no fabric sticking out under the arms.

STEP 12: Add ⅝-inch (1.6-cm) seam allowances on the sides, the neckline, and the armscyes, and cut out a new pattern, as shown in **Diagram 7.**

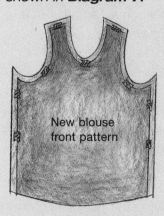

Add ⅝" (1.6-cm) seam allowances to your new blouse front pattern, and cut it out.

New blouse front pattern

Diagram 7

If you have an extremely large bust, you may have to add a dart to get a good fit. Cut the front pattern horizontally where the bust point occurs, lay the pieces on a piece of pattern paper, and spread them apart, lengthening the pattern. How far should you spread the pattern? The average is ½ inch (1.3 cm) for each bra-cup size over a B cup. So for a C cup, you would spread the pattern ½ inch (1.3 cm); for a D, 1 inch (2.5 cm); for a DD, 1½ inches (3.8 cm); and so on.

Tape the pattern pieces to the pattern paper. Draw a dart by marking a dot ½ inch (1.3 cm) outside the bust point on the pattern paper. Draw a line from the dot to one side of the split pattern and then from the bust point mark to the other side of the split, as shown in **Diagram 8.**

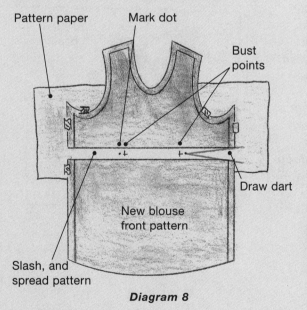

Pattern paper

Mark dot

Bust points

Draw dart

New blouse front pattern

Slash, and spread pattern

Diagram 8

If you have an extremely large bust, you may have to slash and spread the pattern and add a dart to get a good fit.

STEP 2: Determine where you need more or less fabric. Cindy determined that she needed more fabric on the front of her body. She decided to use a pattern two sizes smaller than her bust measurement and to add to the front of the pattern as necessary. She also had to remove fabric from the back pattern to accommodate her small back and from the front pattern to accommodate the small bone structure in her chest. Since Cindy is also long-waisted, she also needed to lengthen her pattern.

STEP 3: Alter the pattern. Cindy taped the pattern to a piece of pattern paper and added 1 inch (2.5 cm) to the front side princess seam at the deepest part of the bust, enough length to go out and over the depth of her bust, as shown in **Diagram 1.** Then she cut out the pattern.

Because Cindy has a full bust, she had to get more fabric onto the front of her body. So she added 1 inch (2.5 cm) to the front side princess seam at the deepest part of the bust.

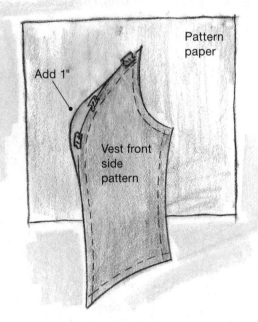

Diagram 1

Cindy measured the vest side pieces twice. First, she measured the original stitching line, and then she measured the new stitching line. The difference

between the two lines was added to the length of the vest front piece so that the two vest pieces would fit together. To do this, Cindy cut the pattern horizontally at the bust point, spread it ⅝ inch (1.6 cm), and taped the two pieces to a piece of pattern paper, as shown in **Diagram 2.** Then she cut out the new pattern.

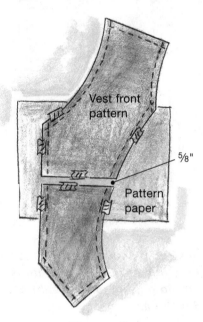

Diagram 2

Cindy slashed and spread the vest front pattern, enlarging it so that it would fit the enlarged front side pattern.

To accommodate her small back, Cindy made the curve on the back side pattern shallower so that it fit closer to her back. Again, she measured the old and new stitching lines and subtracted the difference from the vest back piece by slashing the pattern horizontally at the back bustline, overlapping the pattern pieces ½ inch (1.3 cm), and taping them in place, as shown in **Diagram 3** on page 188.

Instead of following the pattern guide instructions for taking fabric out only at the side seams, she removed the fabric from the area where her body is small.

ALTERING PRINCESS SEAMS

Many sewers are terrified of altering princess seams. Adding or deleting fabric at the armhole can be very complicated if you touch the seam itself.

Relax! Instead, wherever you want to add more fullness or delete fabric at the armscye, use the split-and-pivot method, and you'll never touch the actual arch of the seam. To do this, you will need the pattern, transparent tape, pattern paper, scissors, pencil, and a flexible ruler.

To add fullness to the armhole, slash the pattern above the curve toward the side, and spread the pattern at the armscye cutting line by the amount needed, as shown below.

If you have large upper arms or a full chest, you will want to slash and spread the front side pattern at the armscye cutting line.

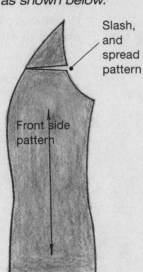

Slash, and spread pattern

Front side pattern

Tape the pattern to a piece of pattern paper, and cut it out. This alteration is most commonly made by someone who has large arms or a full chest. To delete excess fabric, slash the pattern at the same place, and overlap the pattern pieces at the armscye cutting line as needed, as shown above right.

Then tape the pattern pieces together, and tape them to a piece of pattern paper.

If you want to delete excess fabric, slash the pattern above the curve, and overlap the pattern pieces at the armscye cutting line as needed.

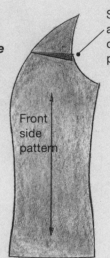

Slash, and overlap pattern

Front side pattern

When you overlap the pattern edges, the cutting line will be uneven, so you'll want to redraw the cutting line. Do this by marking a point halfway between the cutting line on the top piece and the cutting line on the bottom piece. Gradually blend the two lines together, starting and ending about 2 inches (5.1 cm) from the point, as shown below.

Redraw the cutting line, gradually blending the two lines together, starting and ending about 2 inches (5.1 cm) from the point.

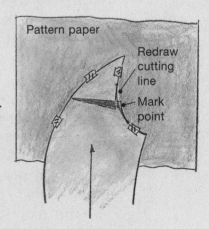

Pattern paper

Redraw cutting line

Mark point

These changes will also make the armscye diameter larger or smaller, so you must also alter your sleeve pattern. To do this, take the same amount out of the sleeve. (See "Adding and Removing Fabric" on page 40.)

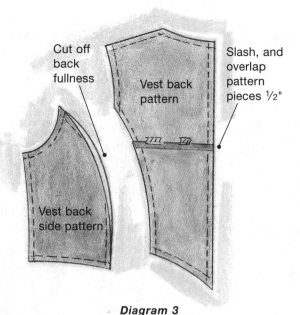

Diagram 3

Cindy made the curve on the back side pattern shallower so that it fit closer to her tiny back. To make the vest back pattern fit the altered back side pattern, she slashed the back pattern and over-lapped the pieces.

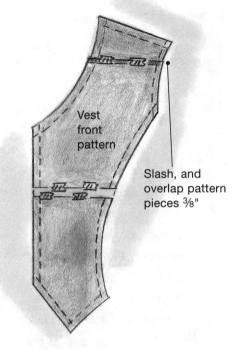

Diagram 4

Cindy has a small bone structure in her upper chest, so she slashed that area of the vest front pattern and overlapped the pieces to eliminate the excess fabric.

Next, to accommodate her small bone structure in her upper chest, Cindy short-ened that area of the front pattern by ⅜ inch (1 cm), as shown in **Diagram 4,** in the same manner as she shortened the back pattern piece.

Since Cindy is long-waisted, she lengthened the vest front pat-tern at a point 3 inches (7.6 cm) above her waist. She slashed each of the pattern pieces at the points shown in **Diagram 5,** placed them on pattern paper, spread them apart 1 inch (2.5 cm), taped them to the pattern paper, and cut out the new patterns.

This may seem like a lot of work, adding to one place and cutting off at another. But I think you will agree that the end product, as shown in the "After" photo of Cindy on page 144, sculpts and con-tours to her body—and she looks fabulous!

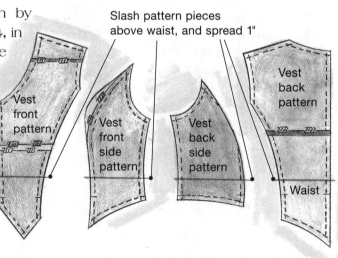

Diagram 5

To accommodate her long waist, Cindy slashed each of the vest pattern pieces 3 inches (7.6 cm) above the waist and lengthened them 1 inch (2.5 cm) to ensure that the vest would sit evenly at her waist.

Diane

(see page 145)

LIFESTYLE

+ **Assistant manager of
  The Sewing Place**
+ **Lifelong sewer**
+ **Lives near ocean and likes to sail**
+ **Avid gardener and great cook**

FITTING CHALLENGE

Deep and full across back; shallow upper chest; shorter than height for which commercial patterns are designed. *When Diane fits garments to her broad back, they end up being too large for her shallow upper chest.*

GARMENT

Silk/linen vest

REMEDY

STEP: Examine your body. By looking at her croquis and measurements worksheet, Diane determined that at 5 feet 3 inches, she is not as tall as commercial patterns expect her to be (5 feet 7 inches). She also has a deep, full back.

Diane's "Before" vest was a very simple pattern with no princess seams, no darts, nothing to help fit the garment to her body, as shown in the "Before" photo on page 145. The vest buckled along the front edge and stuck out along the sides—what I call the "water wings look." Unfortunately, this problem is common in vests, whether they are ready-to-wear or made from a pattern. Most sewers live with this problem, saying, "I just won't button it." Instead, try some of Diane's fitting techniques for a more flattering vest.

STEP: Determine where you need less fabric. Diane's "Before" vest was made from a fabric that combined silk and linen. The fabric had too much body for the simple, loose-fitting pattern that she chose. The vest pattern recommended fabrics that were lightweight and drapey. Also, the 10 inches (25.4 cm) of ease in the pattern exceeded what Diane needed for her silk/linen blend. Her fabric was thicker, crisper, and heavier and needed to be closer to her body. She needed to make the garment smaller.

STEP: Alter the pattern. To create a smooth fit across the upper body, Diane moved the front edge of the vest in the same manner that Peggy altered her tank top. (See "Get a Great-Fitting Tank Top" on page 182.) Diane made a full pattern piece from the vest back pattern, and trimmed the seam allowances on the armscye and the neck edges of the front and back pattern pieces. She pinned the vest front and back patterns together at the side seams and then tried on the pattern. I stood behind her and lifted the back shoulder pieces of the pattern up and over her shoulders, pinning the pattern to the back of her bra.

Then I moved to the front of Diane's body, and starting at the center of the pattern, I pressed the front pattern piece against the center of her chest and brought up the shoulder. The front shoulder piece lay farther to the outside of her shoulder than the back shoulder piece. I measured how far the pieces were offset, as shown in **Diagram 1** on page 190, and wrote down that measurement.

This difference occurs because human beings are shallower and narrower across the fronts of their bodies than on their

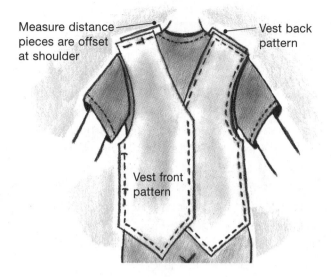

Diagram 1

When pin fitting the vest on Diane, I found that the front shoulder piece lay farther to the outside of her shoulder than the back shoulder piece. This occurs because human beings are shallower and narrower across the fronts of their bodies than on their backs.

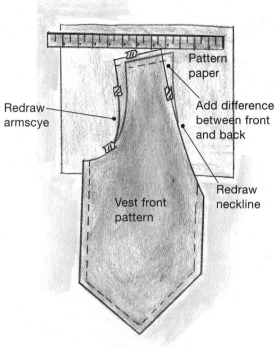

Diagram 2

To get the vest shoulders to match up, Diane redrew the neck opening and the armscye.

backs. A pattern that matches while lying flat will not fit when the human form is inserted.

Then I unpinned the sides of the vest front pattern, and Diane made the following alteration. She taped the vest front pattern to a piece of pattern paper and placed a straightedge against the inside edge of the shoulder, as shown in **Diagram 2.** On the neckline side of the pattern, she marked the paper at the distance I measured and redrew the neck opening. She then marked the width of the shoulder and redrew the armscye.

By changing the angle of the vest front piece, Diane kept the garment straight up and down. Even unbuttoned, this vest will hang straight and won't swoop to the side.

Next, Diane added a hookEdo at the underarm, just as Peggy did with her tank top. (See "Get a Great-Fitting Tank Top" on page 182.) Diane cut out the new front pattern piece without adding the seam allowances at the neckline and the armscye.

To eliminate the excess fabric at Diane's armhole, I repinned the altered front pattern to the back pattern at the shoulder and to the back of her bra. Then I matched the underarm seamlines. But the vest front armhole stuck out and looked boxy, so I pulled down the side seam on the front pattern far enough to cause the side of the armscye to rest smoothly against the arm, as shown in **Diagram 3.**

Once the front pattern was smooth, I measured the distance the front pattern was offset from the back pattern and wrote down the measurement.

I removed the pins, and Diane trimmed the side seam allowances on the vest front and back patterns. She taped the front pattern to a piece of pattern paper and created the hookEdo at the bottom of the armscye.

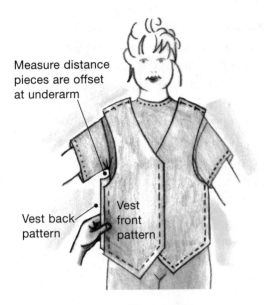

Measure distance pieces are offset at underarm

Vest back pattern

Vest front pattern

Diagram 3

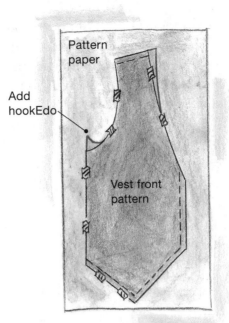

Pattern paper

Add hookEdo

Vest front pattern

Diagram 4

Using the measurements taken when we test fit the pattern at the side, Diane created what I call a "hookEdo," which will force the fabric in the vest to push out and over the bust.

When test fitting the altered pattern, I eliminated the excess fabric at Diane's armhole by pulling down the side seam on the front pattern far enough to cause the side of the armscye to rest smoothly against her arm. I then measured how far the pattern pieces were offset.

When the vest front is joined to the back and a body is inserted into it, the hookEdo will force a bubble of fabric at the front of the vest so that there is enough fabric for the garment to move smoothly over the bust and under the arm. The garment will lie firmly against her body with no gaping and no sticking out under the arms, and it will be very comfortable to wear.

Diane marked a dot above the top of the side stitching line the same distance that the front pattern was offset from the back pattern. She connected the dot to the stitching line, as shown in **Diagram 4,** and then drew a curved line from the dot to the armscye, creating the hookEdo. The bottom of the curve must be at least ½ inch (1.3 cm) below the dot.

Diane then removed an equal amount from the bottom of the vest front

pattern so the vest front would match the vest back when they were sewn together. At the side seam, Diane measured up from the hem cutting line, marked a dot the same distance by which she increased the pattern at the bottom of the armscye, and drew a line from that point, gradually slanting toward the hemline, as shown in **Diagram 5.**

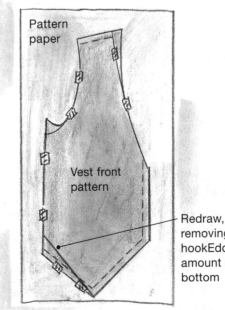

Pattern paper

Vest front pattern

Redraw, removing hookEdo amount at bottom

Diagram 5

Since she added to the top of the side seam on the vest front pattern, Diane removed an equal amount from the bottom so that the vest front would match the vest back when they were sewn together.

Diane then taped the front and back pattern pieces to a piece of pattern paper and added the seam allowances on the armscyes and the sides of both pattern pieces and to the neck edge of the front pattern piece, as shown in **Diagram 6.**

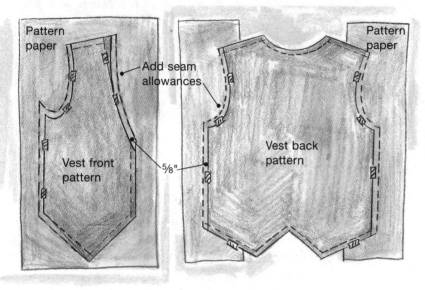

Diagram 6

Diane taped the vest front and back pattern pieces to pattern paper and added seam allowances as needed.

Diane cut out the vest pattern pieces and then her fashion fabric, but she still had a small problem at the armscye. She planned to pipe the edges of the vest as a design detail and wanted the vest to fit close to her body. When she pin fit the vest, she found that since the fabric was very crisp, the armscye didn't fit close to her body even with the hookEdo. There was still excess fabric at the center front of the armhole.

So Diane pinched out ⅜ inch (1 cm) of excess fabric and doubled that measurement for a total of ¾ inch (1.9 cm). To reduce the armscye, she pinned the shoulder of the vest front piece to the ironing

board about 2 inches (5.1 cm) from the shoulder stitching line and then pinned the bottom of the armscye to the ironing board, removing ¾ inch (1.9 cm) from the armhole of the vest front piece. She cut a piece of straight-of-grain tape ¾ inch (1.9 cm) shorter than the armscye stitching line, placed it on the armscye stitching line, and fused it in place, as shown in **Diagram 7,** using her fingers to ease in the excess fabric.

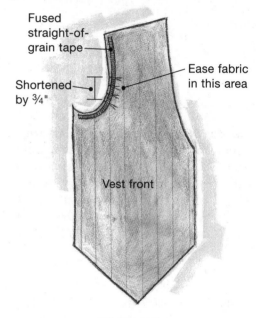

Diagram 7

Although Diane added a hookEdo, the fabric was very crisp and the armhole did not fit close to her body. So she fused a piece of straight-of-grain tape to the armscye of the vest, easing the fabric to fit the tape.

That way, she was able to get the vest to contour against the arm even using the crisp fabric.

TIP: The best way for you to decide how much to alter a vest front is to put on the fabric and pinch out the excess. The front curve is on the bias, so be very careful not to stretch it.

Diane also added fusible stay tape along the front of the vest neckline. Because she is a D cup, she removed fullness in the vest front so that the fabric would cup over the bust. To do this, she took out ¾ inch (1.9 cm) along the bottom of the vest front neckline, easing in the fabric with fusible straight-of-grain tape, as shown in **Diagram 8,** in the same manner as she did for the vest front armscye.

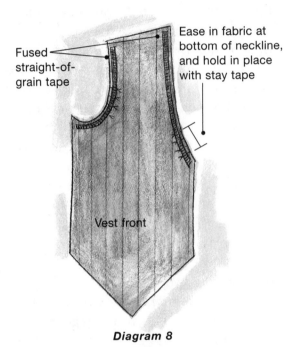

Diagram 8

Diane also added fusible straight-of-grain tape to the front of the vest neckline so that the fabric would cup over the bust.

TIP: To determine the length of the stay tape, measure the vest front pattern piece, not the garment. Even in a short amount of time, the front edge of the garment, which is cut on the bias, can stretch.

Since the front neck edges of the vest are cut on the bias, you can run the stay tape along the stitching line inch for inch if you are a B cup.

TIP: If your abdomen is full, you will want to add to the center front of the vest front pattern and redraw the front neck opening and the front bottom seam, as shown in **Diagram 9.**

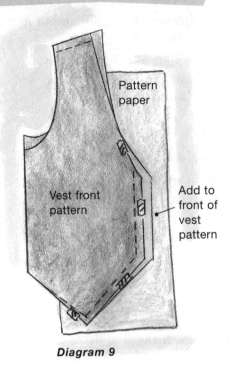

Diagram 9

To get a better-fitting vest if you have a full abdomen, add to the center front of the vest front pattern, and redraw the front neck opening and the front bottom seam.

With time and experience, Diane has learned that when fitting herself, she automatically has to remove ½ inch (1.3 cm) of the fabric horizontally across the front of a garment. Because she is deep and full across the back of her body, she knows she does not have to remove any fabric from the back of the vest to get an even horizon. The "After" photo of Diane on page 145 shows how beautifully a vest can fit her when she makes the right alterations to the garment.

Millie
(see page 146)

LIFESTYLE

✦ **Manages the large and varied pattern stock at The Sewing Place**

✦ **Mother of two and grandmother of one**

✦ **Enjoys sewing**

✦ **Sings at her church and with a choral group**

FITTING CHALLENGE

Deep body; full upper arms; shorter than height for which commercial patterns are designed. *Millie is 5 feet 1 inch tall, and the bust and waist areas on commercial patterns do not line up on her body. Her garments are usually too long and too tight.*

GARMENT

Rayon gabardine dress

REMEDY

STEP 1: Examine your body. After examining her croquis and her measurements worksheet, Millie determined that the inches that make up most of her torso measurements come from the depth of her body more so than from the width of her body. Millie also determined that she has full upper arms. In addition, at 5 feet 1 inch tall, Millie has found that commercial patterns are too long for her body.

STEP 2: Determine where you need less fabric. At first glance, Millie's "Before" dress looked as if it fit well, but the rayon gabardine dress had many problems, as shown in the "Before"

photo of Millie on page 146. Millie found she needed to eliminate some of the ease so that the dress didn't overwhelm her body.

Although Millie chose the dress pattern according to her bust, waist, hip, and back-waist measurements, the garment shoulder was much wider than her natural shoulder, so the sleeve cap fell off her shoulder. Millie shortened the dress pattern by following the pattern instructions, but the fullest part of the bust on her "Before" dress fell way below her bust. Because Millie's midriff runs straight up and down, she added extra room through the waist, but the dress still was not proportional for her body.

Since the inches that make up Millie's measurements come from the depth of her body more so than from the width, the depth takes fabric from the front and the back of the garment, as shown in **Diagram 1**.

This caused her "Before" dress to hang too long on the sides, resulting in diagonal folds running down the front of the garment, as shown in **Diagram 2**.

To improve the fit of her dress, Millie decided to use a pattern two sizes smaller than the pattern guide recommended for her measurements. That way, the sides of the dress would be shorter, and the shoulder and neck area would be more proportioned to her body.

STEP 3: Determine where you need more fabric. Since this dress was designed to fit close to the body, the straight sleeve that came with the pattern did not accommodate Millie's full upper arm, and the movement of her arm was restricted. Millie knew she had to get more fabric into the upper arm of the sleeve.

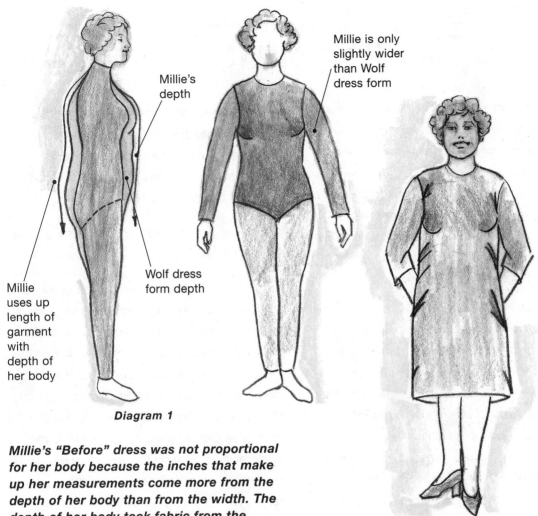

Millie's depth

Millie is only slightly wider than Wolf dress form

Wolf dress form depth

Millie uses up length of garment with depth of her body

Diagram 1

Millie's "Before" dress was not proportional for her body because the inches that make up her measurements come more from the depth of her body than from the width. The depth of her body took fabric from the front and the back of the garment.

Diagram 2

Because the depth of Millie's body took fabric from the front and the back of the dress, her "Before" dress hung too long on the sides, causing diagonal folds.

STEP 4: Alter the pattern. Millie first added onto the front side and back side pattern pieces in the same manner that Cindy added to her vest front side pattern. Then she lengthened the front and back pieces also in the same manner that Cindy lengthened her vest front. (For instructions, see Step 3 on page 186.)

To improve the fit of the sleeve at her upper arm, Millie decided to use a two-piece sleeve that she liked from another pattern. (See "Insert a Two-Piece Sleeve" on page 196.)

Millie also narrowed the bottom of the two-piece sleeve so that it made her arm

look longer and better proportioned. In the "Before" photo of Millie on page 146, you can see how the sleeve constricts the biceps area. But if you look at the "After" photo of Millie, you can see that her arm can move more easily.

To sew great-fitting garments for herself, Millie now knows that she must choose styles that have plenty of opportunities for fit, or her clothes will not flatter her body.

INSERT A TWO-PIECE SLEEVE

To insert a two-piece sleeve into a garment that calls for a one-piece sleeve, you will need the front and back pattern pieces of the garment with the one-piece sleeve and the front and back pattern pieces of the garment with the two-piece sleeve. You also will need a flexible ruler (optional), a tape measure, a pen or pencil, transparent tape, pattern paper, and scissors.

STEP 1: Using the flexible ruler, measure the armscye between the stitching lines on the front and back pattern pieces of the garment with the one-piece sleeve, as shown in **Diagram 1.** (If you do not have a flexible ruler, you can measure the armscye by standing a tape measure on its side.)

In the same manner, measure the armscye stitching lines on the front and back pattern pieces of the garment with the two-

piece sleeve. Write the measurement of the stitching line from the garment with the two-piece sleeve on one of the sleeve pattern pieces so you will have it handy the next time you use the sleeve pattern.

STEP 2: Find the difference between the two lengths.

STEP 3: If the armscye in the garment you are constructing is longer than the armscye in the two-piece sleeve source, raise the underarm on the new garment. To do this, tape a piece of pattern paper to the front pattern piece and a piece of pattern paper to the back pattern piece. Then tape the front and back pattern pieces together at the underarm, matching the stitching lines. Make a mark at 4 o'clock and at 8 o'clock on the armscye, as shown in **Diagram 2.**

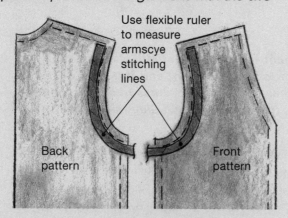

Diagram 1

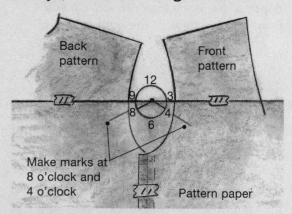

Diagram 2

To measure the armscye between the stitching lines on the front and back pattern pieces of the garment with the one-piece sleeve, use a flexible ruler.

Raise the underarm on the new garment by adding to the bottom of the armscye on the front and back pattern pieces.

STEP 4: *Using a flexible ruler (or a tape measure standing on edge), measure the original stitching line on the front and back pattern pieces between the marks made in Step 3, as shown in* **Diagram 3.**

STEP 5: *Subtract the amount calculated in Step 2, bring the flexible ruler (or tape measure) up to the new distance at the 4 o'clock mark, and redraw the bottom curve, as shown in* **Diagram 4.**

TIP: *Do not be afraid to raise the underarm on a pattern. A narrow sleeve always has to have a very high underarm, which acts as the pivot point. The pivot point on the sleeve should be approximately the same height as the pivot point on the arm, as shown in* **Diagram 5.**

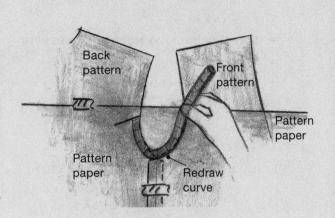

Diagram 4

Subtract the amount calculated in Step 2, move the flexible ruler up at the 4 o'clock mark, and redraw the armscye curve.

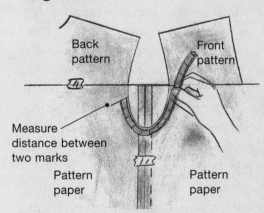

Diagram 3

Using the flexible ruler, measure the original stitching line on the front and back pattern pieces between the marks at 8 o'clock and 4 o'clock.

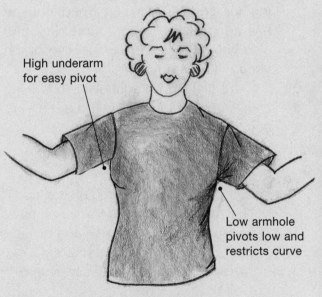

Diagram 5

Contrary to what most sewers believe, raising the armscye adds more flexibility to a garment, not less. The lower an armscye is, the lower the pivot point and the wider the sleeve must be to allow for movement.

Judy
(see page 147)

LIFESTYLE

+ **Travel agent who travels extensively**
+ **Mother of two**
+ **Active in her church**
+ **Loves to read**

FITTING CHALLENGE

Long, round back; very shallow chest.
Because of her body shape, most ready-to-wear garments don't fit Judy correctly.

GARMENT

Soft, flowing jacket made of rayon faille

REMEDY

STEP 1: Examine your body. By examining her croquis, Judy confirmed that she has an unusually long, round back and also gained a clearer perspective of the shape of her body.

As a first step in addressing her fitting challenge, I helped Judy choose a very soft, fluid fabric for her jacket.

TIP: If you are very difficult to fit, try using softer, drapier fabrics. That doesn't mean that everything you make has to be loose and over-size, but it does mean that soft fabric or knit fabric will easily shape itself over your body.

STEP 2: Determine where you need more fabric. Judy's "Before" jacket pulled up in the back, and the hemline was much too short, as shown in the "Before" photo of Judy on page 147. The jacket had very pronounced wrinkles coming from the center back area and extending to the side seams, and the sleeves hung at an awkward angle.

To accommodate her very round back, Judy needed to add 4 inches (10.2 cm) to the back of her pattern.

STEP 3: Determine where you need less fabric. Because Judy has an extremely shallow front, she determined she had to remove 1 inch (2.5 cm) from the front of the pattern.

TIP: This is a good example of establishing horizon on a garment. It is important that the bottom of the garment be horizontal so that it doesn't draw attention to the area of the body that is difficult to fit. Look at the difference in the back hemlines in the "Before" and "After" photos of Judy on page 147.

STEP 4: Alter the pattern. To get enough length in the back of her jacket, Judy decided to add a center back seam. First, she slashed through the jacket back pattern at three places from the center back to the armscye stitching line. She opened each slash 1 inch (2.5 cm) along the center back, pivoting at the armscye stitching line, and taped the pattern to a piece of pattern paper, as shown in **Diagram 1**.

Judy added a 1-inch (2.5-cm) "Emily" at the top of the jacket back pattern at the neckline and shoulder seam so that the seamline would rest on the top ridge of her shoulder. (For detailed instructions, see "The Emily" on page 156.) She also added a ⅝-inch (1.6-cm) seam allowance along the center back of the jacket back pattern, as shown in **Diagram 2**.

To increase the length of the back of her jacket, Judy slashed through the jacket back pattern at three places from the center back to the armscye stitching line and opened each slash 1 inch (2.5 cm).

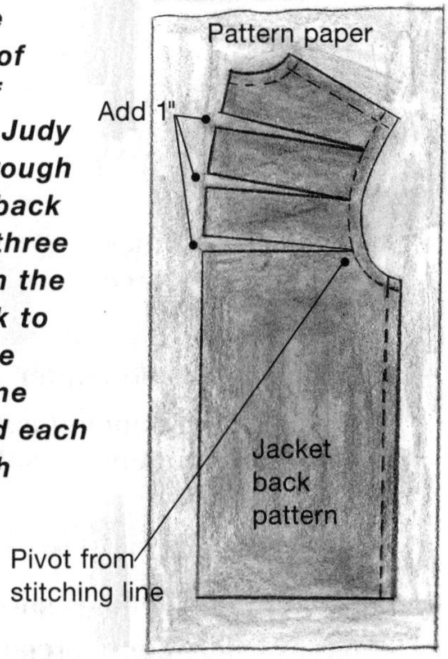

Pattern paper

Add 1"

Pivot from stitching line

Jacket back pattern

Diagram 1

Judy added a 1-inch (2.5-cm) "Emily" at the top of the jacket back pattern. She also added a ⅝-inch (1.6-cm) seam allowance along the center back of the jacket back pattern to create a center back seam.

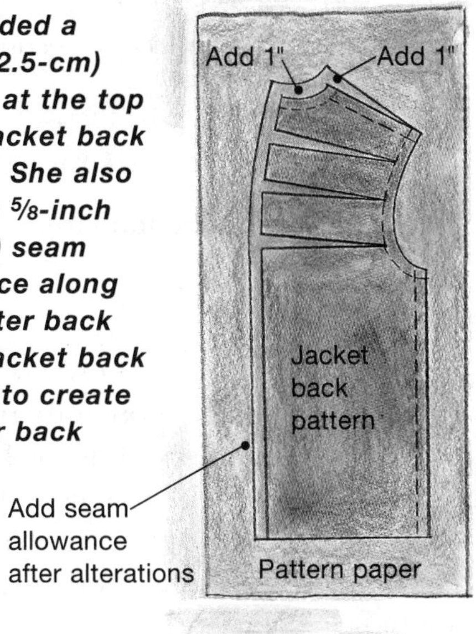

Add 1"   Add 1"

Jacket back pattern

Add seam allowance after alterations

Pattern paper

Diagram 2

Judy removed 1 inch (2.5 cm) from the upper front pattern piece at the armscye by slashing the pattern and overlapping the pieces, as shown in **Diagram 3.** She taped the lapel area to a piece of pattern paper, drew a new lapel cutting line, and trimmed the excess paper.

Judy then had to reshape the sleeve head completely. She had to remove fabric across the top of the sleeve head

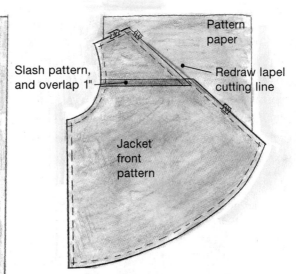

Pattern paper

Slash pattern, and overlap 1"

Redraw lapel cutting line

Jacket front pattern

Diagram 3

To reduce the fabric in the front of the jacket, Judy removed 1 inch (2.5 cm) from the upper front pattern piece by slashing the pattern and overlapping the pieces.

without reducing the height of the sleeve. She trimmed off the armscye seam allowance, slashed the sleeve pattern from the front to the back, overlapped it 1 inch (2.5 cm) along the front armscye edge, and taped it in place, as shown in **Diagram 4.**

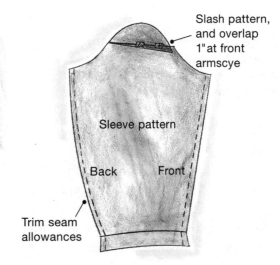

Slash pattern, and overlap 1" at front armscye

Sleeve pattern

Back   Front

Trim seam allowances

Diagram 4

Because Judy altered the armscye on the jacket pattern, she had to remove fabric across the top of the sleeve head by slashing the pattern and overlapping the pieces.

Since Judy changed the front pattern armscye stitching line, she had to alter the armscye stitching line on the sleeve to create a more acute curve. Judy taped the sleeve pattern to a piece of pattern paper, and using a flexible ruler, she reshaped and redrew the armscye curve, as shown in **Diagram 5,** making sure the height was the same as the original pattern. To do this, she measured the distance around the original sleeve cap, using the flexible ruler, and then squeezed the sides of the curve together so that it remained the same length but with a new curve.

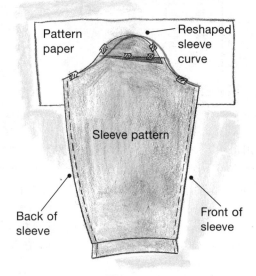

Pattern paper

Reshaped sleeve curve

Sleeve pattern

Back of sleeve

Front of sleeve

Diagram 5

Since Judy changed the front pattern armscye stitching line, she used a flexible curve to alter the armscye stitching line on the sleeve.

TIP: Always redraw the armscye at the stitching line, not the cutting line. As long as the length of the stitching line remains the same, the sleeve will fit into the garment. If you alter the curve of the cutting line, the stitching line will be lengthened.

Judy then added the seam allowance onto the sleeve. The adjusted sleeve fit Judy's arm and shoulder well, and it also fit into the new jacket back.

Judy loved her new jacket so much that she made another version of this soft, flowing coat to wear at her son's wedding.

Dale
(see page 148)

LIFESTYLE

✦ **My business partner in The Sewing Place**

✦ **Mother of two**

✦ **Lifelong sewer and crafter**

✦ **Takes ballroom dancing lessons with her husband and enjoys salsa dancing**

FITTING CHALLENGE

Small tummy; hip fluff; shorter than height for which commercial patterns are designed. *Dale's garments are usually too long, are too tight in the tummy, and pull just below the waist because she has hip fluff.*

GARMENT

Linen shorts and matching top

REMEDY

STEP: Examine your body. By examining her croquis and measurements worksheet, Dale determined that she has both a small tummy and hip fluff. Hip fluff occurs naturally on tiny women because the distance between their waists and their hips is short and the curve happens sooner than on taller women.

Dale is only 5 feet tall, so she chose a commercial pattern labeled "petite-able." She made the changes to the pattern pieces as the pattern guide recommended, as shown in **Diagram 1,** but the shorts and top still weren't right for her.

Drawing on her croquis, she discovered that removing the cuff helped because the cuff cut her across the leg and made her look even shorter. For a longer-legged look, she decided to lengthen the shorts.

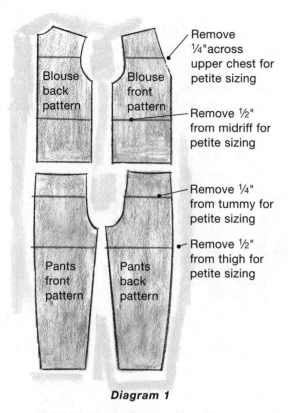

Remove ¼" across upper chest for petite sizing

Remove ½" from midriff for petite sizing

Remove ¼" from tummy for petite sizing

Remove ½" from thigh for petite sizing

Diagram 1

Dale followed the instructions on the pattern guide and made all of the changes to the "petite-able" pattern, but the garments still didn't fit correctly.

STEP: Determine where you need more or less fabric. When Dale made her "Before" garments, she said, "It's funny, a few years ago I would have been satisfied with this outfit. In fact, if I had tried it on in a store, I might even have purchased it because it probably was close enough." But as you can see in the "Before" and "After" photos of Dale on page 148, there is a big difference in the proportions of her "Before" and "After" garments.

The sleeve was too long and the front opening too deep on Dale's original top. The front pulled apart at the bust because the bust point was too low. The top was too long and hung on her hips. The shorts rode up along the hips because of her hip fluff, causing the hemlines to look uneven.

For the top and shorts, Dale chose a very crisp, medium-weight fabric of 100 percent linen, so the garment had to have many opportunities for fit. The top had princess seams on the front and the back to allow the fabric to contour to her small body. Dale knew she had to make her standard changes to the pants pattern, which included adding to the front pattern to accommodate her little tummy.

The vestlike bottom on Dale's "Before" top was too long for her. After drawing the garment on her croquis, she chose a shorter length for the top, which would be a better overall proportion for her petite body. She also decided to shorten the sleeves after sketching the top on her croquis.

STEP: Alter the pattern. To add fabric to cover her tummy, Dale slashed the pants front pattern from the side seam to the center front at the fullest part of the tummy, as shown in **Diagram 2.**

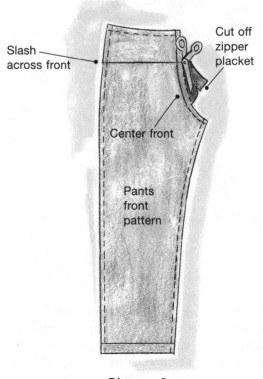

Slash across front

Cut off zipper placket

Center front

Pants front pattern

Diagram 2

Dale cut the zipper placket off the pants front pattern and slashed the pattern from the side seam to the center front at the fullest part of the tummy.

To accommodate her tummy, Dale then spread the center front edge of the pattern ½ inch (1.3 cm), as shown in **Diagram 3,** and taped the pattern to a piece of pattern paper. If you have a larger tummy, you can open up the slit to a maximum of 1 inch (2.5 cm). If you still need more room, make a nother slash and spread the pattern. You can make as many slashes as you need to allow the front of the pants to go up and over your tummy.

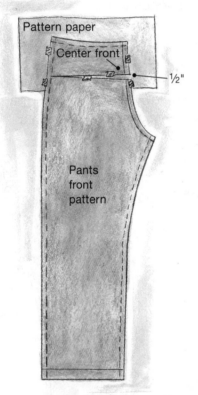

Diagram 3

To get enough fabric to cover her tummy, Dale spread the center front edge of the pattern ½ inch (1.3 cm) and taped the pattern to a piece of pattern paper.

By spreading the pattern open and adding a wedge, Dale added more than just height to the top of the pants. As she opened the slits, the center front seam widened and formed a dartlike shaping at the waistline, as shown in **Diagram 4,** which added shape across the tummy.

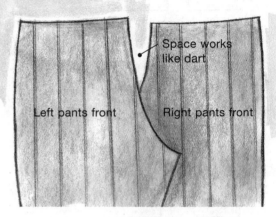

Diagram 4

By spreading the pants front pattern open, Dale widened the center front seam, which formed a dart at the waistline to add shaping across the tummy.

Dale then straightened the sides of the pants at the waistline, as shown in **Diagram 5,** providing extra fullness for her hip fluff.

In addition, Dale made the V-neck in the top much shallower, which was a better proportion for her body. (See "Ensure an Accurate Neck Opening" on page 170.)

She also narrowed the shoulder on the front and the back by removing 1

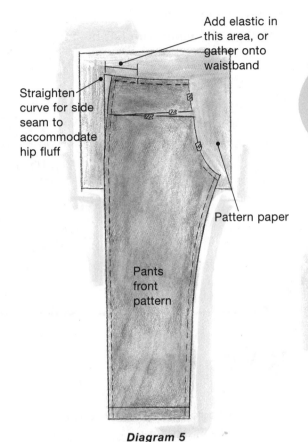

Diagram 5

By straightening the sides of the pants at the waistline, Dale added extra fullness for her hip fluff.

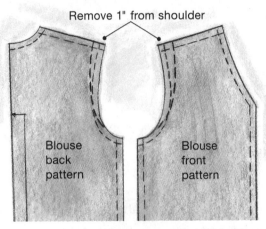

Diagram 6

To get a better fit in the shoulders, Dale narrowed the front and back patterns 1 inch (2.5 cm) each.

"Shoulder pads help to make a waistline appear smaller."

inch (2.5 cm) starting at the shoulder seam and tapering to nothing at the bottom of the armscye, as shown in **Diagram 6.**

Then Dale raised the height of the sleeve cap 1 inch (2.5 cm), as shown in **Diagram 7,** so that it would fit the altered armscye. (See "Looking Good: The Tailored Sleeve" on page 204.)

Dale regularly wears shoulder pads to widen her shoulders and make her waist appear smaller in comparison. The same shoulder pads were used in both her "Before" and "After" garments, but because the shoulders are narrower in the "After" garment, the pads are positioned better and look more in proportion with her body.

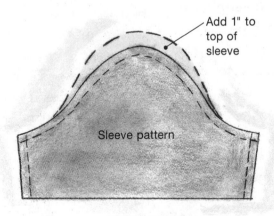

Diagram 7

To get the sleeve to fit into the altered armscye, Dale raised the height of the sleeve cap 1 inch (2.5 cm).

Dolores
(see page 149)

LIFESTYLE

✦ Works at The Sewing Place, keeping a large variety of thread ordered and in stock

✦ Mother of two

✦ Recently remodeled her home, adding a fantasy sewing room

✦ Loves playing golf

✦ Enjoys traveling with her husband

FITTING CHALLENGE

Tiny waist; hollow back below waist; small upper hips; full fanny. *Because Dolores has a concave back, her garments exaggerate the size of her hips and fanny.*

Looking Good

The Tailored Sleeve

If you prefer a tailored look to your sleeves, this is a technique that you will find very useful. Commercial patterns frequently feature dropped-shoulder sleeves because they can be sewn into the armscye flat. Then the underarm seam and the sleeve can be stitched in one pass under the needle. This is a great time-saver, but it leaves you with a full, loose sleeve and excess fabric at the underarm.

If you prefer a more fitted sleeve, follow these instructions. To do this, you will need a ruler, a 6-by-24-inch see-through ruler, shoulder pad (optional), transparent tape, pattern paper, flexible ruler, masking tape, pen or pencil, and scissors.

STEP 1: Check how tall the sleeve cap should be by measuring the distance from your shoulder to your underarm. Place a ruler under your arm horizontally, and ask a sewing buddy to place a 6-by-24-inch see-through ruler against your outer arm, aligning one long edge with the ruler, as shown in **Diagram 1.**

Note the distance between the bottom of the ruler and the top of the shoulder, and record it on the pattern guide sheet. If you are going to be using a shoulder pad in the garment, set the shoulder pad on your shoulder, and measure to the top of the shoulder pad, as shown in **Diagram 2.**

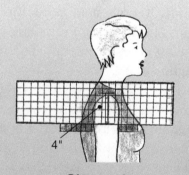

4"

Diagram 1

By measuring the distance from your shoulder to your underarm and comparing that measurement to the sleeve pattern, you can determine how tall a sleeve cap will be.

GARMENT
Linen/rayon straight skirt

REMEDY

STEP 1: Examine your body. By looking at her croquis, Dolores determined that her back is very hollow, as shown in **Diagram 1** on page 206. This shape is often referred to as a swayback.

She also noticed that she is unusually small in the upper hip area, which tends to exaggerate the fullness of her fanny because of her concave back.

STEP 2: Determine where you need less fabric. Dolores's "Before" skirt pressed against the backs of her legs and pushed out in the front of her body, as shown in the "Before" photo on page 149. This was a sign that the horizon of the garment was off. Dolores does not have enough body mass in the back of her body to support the fabric between her waist and her fanny because of the hollowness of her back. Dolores decided to remove excess fabric at the center back of her skirt.

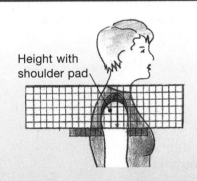

Height with shoulder pad

Diagram 2

If you are using shoulder pads in your garment, place the pad on your shoulder, and measure to the top of the pad.

STEP 2: Using the see-through ruler, measure the height of the sleeve pattern, as shown in **Diagram 3.**

STEP 3: If necessary, raise the top of the sleeve cap. Tape the sleeve pattern to a piece of pattern paper. Bend the flexible ruler so that it matches the cutting line on the armscye seam

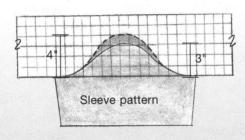

4"   3"

Sleeve pattern

Diagram 3

Measure the height of the sleeve pattern.

of the sleeve, placing one end of the ruler at one of the ends of the armscye cutting line. Place a small piece of masking tape on the ruler at the other end of the armscye cutting line. Bend the sides of the ruler together in the sleeve cap area to increase the height of the sleeve cap, as shown in **Diagram 4.** Mark the pattern at the end of the ruler and the taped mark, and then redraw the underarm cutting

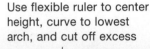

Use flexible ruler to center height, curve to lowest arch, and cut off excess

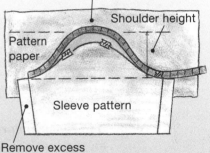

Shoulder height

Pattern paper

Sleeve pattern

Remove excess

Diagram 4

You may have to raise the top of the sleeve cap. Use a flexible ruler to set the new curve, and redraw the cutting line.

lines by tracing along the edge of the flex ruler. Cut off the excess pattern tissue.

The amount of height that you add to the top of the sleeve must also be removed from the armscye at the shoulder. (See "Adding and Removing Fabric" on page 40.)

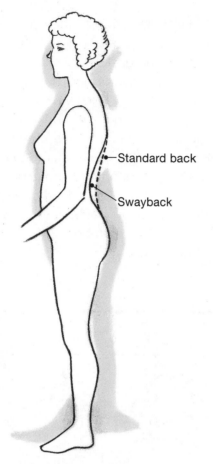

Diagram 1

Dolores examined her croquis and determined that she has a very hollow back—what is commonly called a swayback.

STEP: Alter the pattern. Depending on the depth of the swayback, there are several options for accommodating this shape. You can put a single dart on each side of the skirt back. But it may be difficult to get from the waist to the fullness of the fanny without exaggerating the problem. Anyone whose waist is two or more sizes smaller than her hips should put in at least two darts on each side in the back, as shown in **Diagram 2**. This will take in the fabric in small sections for a more subtle fit, without drawing attention to the larger fanny.

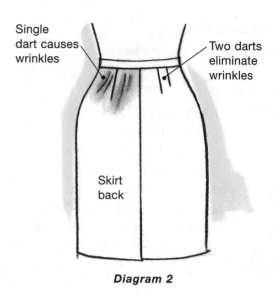

Diagram 2

By adding darts to the back of your skirt, you will take in the excess fabric in small sections, without drawing attention to your fanny.

Dolores chose to leave out the darts and instead to ease the fabric onto the waistband. This filled in the swayback area with teeny, tiny, soft gathers, creating a more uniform body shape, as shown in **Diagram 3.**

Diagram 3

Instead of using darts, Dolores decided to ease the back of the skirt onto the waistband, which gave her teeny, tiny, soft gathers.

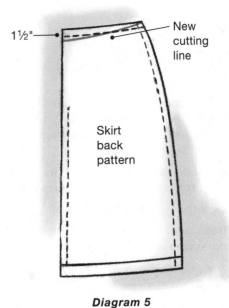

Diagram 5

To allow the back of the skirt to hang correctly, Dolores removed the excess fabric from the top of the skirt back pattern.

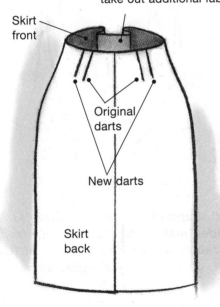

Diagram 4

If you have a small waist, you can take up the excess fabric by adding additional darts to the back of the skirt or by increasing the depth of the pleats on the front of the skirt.

Dolores lowered the top of the skirt back pattern 1½ inches (3.8 cm) at the center back, tapering to nothing at the side seam, as shown in **Diagram 5.** This removed excess fabric at the top of the skirt, allowing it to hang correctly. You can see how much smoother her skirt looks in the back in the "After" photo on page 149.

Dolores also has a small tummy, so in the front she actually raised the center front of the skirt at the fold by 1 inch (2.5 cm), as shown in **Diagram 6.** This added enough fabric to go up and over her tummy, allowing the skirt to hang correctly.

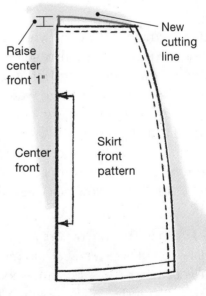

Diagram 6

To accommodate her small tummy, Dolores added to the skirt front pattern at the center front of the waist, tapering to the side seam.

Dolores's "After" skirt is a little bit longer than her "Before" skirt. This proportion works better with her overall wardrobe, and she prefers this length.

Lynda
(see page 149)

LIFESTYLE

✦ Graphic artist who does layout for all printing and publishing at The Sewing Place

✦ Develops patterns, books, and advertising for many experts in sewing field

✦ Sews most of her wardrobe

✦ Flies small planes, skydives, and scuba dives

FITTING CHALLENGE

Hip fluff; shorter than height for which commercial patterns are designed. *Lynda's garments tend to pull across her body just below the waist.*

GARMENT

Short skirt of wool crepe

REMEDY

STEP 1: Examine your body. Lynda examined her croquis and her measurements worksheet and determined that even though she has an average-size waist, she flares out immediately below her waist with hip fluff. Instead of her body gradually flaring out to the hip, she has already reached the fullest part of her hip about 2½ inches (6.4 cm) below her waist.

TIP: If the bottom of your rib cage and the top of your hip seem to meet and your body looks like a cylinder, you can camouflage the problem with a garment made from soft fabric with gathers that pull in at the waist. The gathering will give you a more curvaceous look, as shown in **Diagram 1.**

Diagram 1

If the shape of your body resembles a cylinder, make a skirt and blouse from soft fabric so that gathers form at the waist, giving your body more curves.

STEP 2: Determine where you need more fabric. Lynda's "Before" skirt rode up and formed a ridge just below her waist because of her hip fluff, as shown in the "Before" photo on page 149. The pattern didn't allow enough fabric to accommodate her upper hip measurement until about 7 inches (17.8 cm) below the waistline. Therefore, the garment, with its traditional darts, didn't have enough fabric to go around her body, and so it slid up until it had sufficient fabric to go around the high hip area. Lynda needed to get more fabric in the skirt closer to the waistband to accommodate her hip fluff.

STEP: 3 Alter the pattern. Lynda eliminated the traditional darts at the waistline of the skirt. Instead, she curved each dart toward the outside of the fold, as shown in **Diagram 2,** so that there was more fabric in that area to go over her hip fluff.

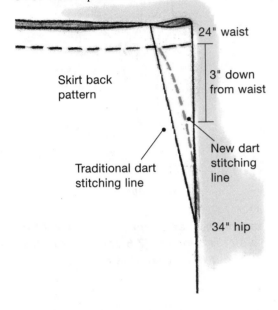

Diagram 2

To allow the skirt to fit smoothly over her hip fluff, Lynda curved the darts at the waistline of the skirt toward the outside of the fold.

That way, the skirt would have enough fabric just below the waist so that it would hang from her upper hip and not ride up.

Look at the "Before" and "After" photos of Lynda on page 149. Because it pulls up in the waist and does not hang to its full length, the original version of her skirt looks shorter than the new version. (So you can orient yourself, Lynda is 5 inches (12.7 cm) shorter than Dolores, and Lynda is standing on three pattern books so that you can see the two skirts clearly in the photographs.)

"To get a good fit, get more fabric where you need it."

TIP: If you have hip fluff and a swayback at the same time, you will want to add two darts on each side of the center back to contour the skirt to the body and to create a garment that hangs smoothly. One dart should curve out, as shown in **Diagram 2,** and the other should curve in, as shown in **Diagram 3,** removing excess fabric.

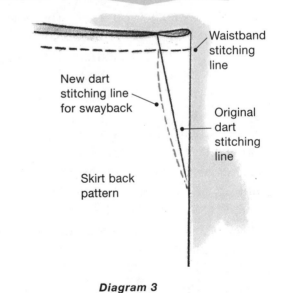

Diagram 3

If you have a swayback, your darts should curve in.

Lynda looks great in her new, simple business skirt that doesn't give a hint of her daredevil hobbies.

Jane
(see page 150)

LIFESTYLE

✦ **Handles mail orders for The Sewing Place; employee who has been with me longest**

✦ **Mother of six and grandmother of nine**

✦ **Sews much of her wardrobe**

✦ **Needlepoint and stitchery expert**

✦ **Enjoys all types of handicrafts**

FITTING CHALLENGE

Waist that is lower in front than in back.
The hemlines of Jane's skirts are longer in the front than in the back.

GARMENT

Cotton knit skirt

REMEDY

STEP 1: Examine your body. By looking at her croquis and her measurements worksheet, Jane determined that her waist is 3 inches (7.6 cm) lower in the front than it is in the back, as shown in **Diagram 1.**

The hem of Jane's "Before" garment, an eight-gore cotton knit skirt, was much longer in the front than in the back, as shown in the "Before" photo of Jane on page 150. The hemline is frequently uneven on full-figured women because their waistline is uneven.

STEP 2: Determine where you need more or less fabric. On Jane's "Before" skirt, the back hiked up and the front was too long. Plus, there were wrinkles angling back to front caused by the uneven crossgrain, as shown in **Diagram 2.**

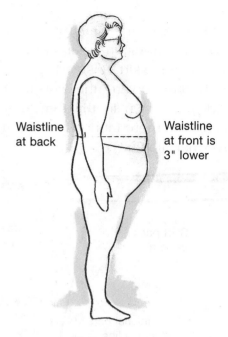

Waistline at back

Waistline at front is 3" lower

Diagram 1

By examining her croquis, Jane found that her waist is 3 inches (7.6 cm) lower in the front of her body than it is in the back.

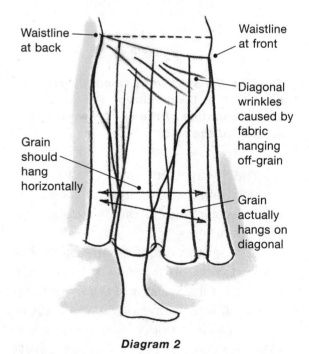

Waistline at back

Waistline at front

Diagonal wrinkles caused by fabric hanging off-grain

Grain should hang horizontally

Grain actually hangs on diagonal

Diagram 2

Because Jane's waist is lower in the front than in the back, the back of her "Before" skirt hiked up and the front was too long.

STEP 3: Alter the pattern. Jane traced the gore pattern onto pattern paper three times, cut out the patterns, and taped the four gore pattern pieces together. She drew a point 3 inches (7.6 cm) down from the top center of the pattern at the center of the gores and redrew the top of the pattern, starting at the center front and gradually moving upward to the side seams, as shown in **Diagram 3.**

By altering the top of the pattern, Jane was able to make a skirt that sat at her natural waist and still had an even horizon at the hemline.

Jane knows that she must make this alteration on anything that hangs from her waist. She also lowers pants 3 inches (7.6 cm) in the front to prevent a bulge of fabric from occurring at the front of the crotch, as shown in **Diagram 4.**

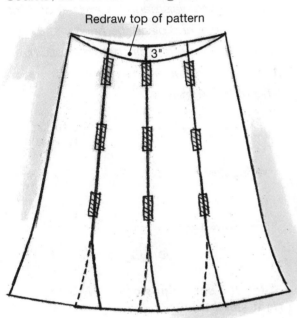

Redraw top of pattern

3"

Diagram 3

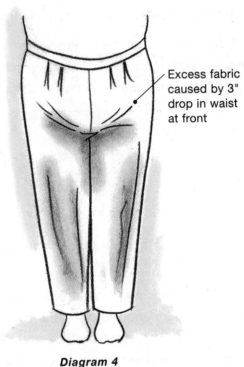

Excess fabric caused by 3" drop in waist at front

Diagram 4

After taping together the gore patterns, Jane redrew the top of the pattern, lowering the center front of the waist 3 inches (7.6 cm).

She then labeled the gores left, left front, right front, and right and removed the tape.

TIP: When altering patterns, you might want to keep a roll of removable transparent tape on hand. This tape peels off pattern paper and other surfaces easily.

Jane always alters any garment that hangs from her waist, including her pants. Otherwise, she gets a bulge of fabric at the front of the crotch.

On both skirts and pants, Jane adds a separate waistband rather than folding over the top of the skirt. (See "Stitch a Waistband Casing for an Uneven Waistline" on page 212.)

If you look at the "After" photo of Jane on page 150, you will see that the bottom of the gores hang horizontally. The skirt now looks straight and is flattering on Jane.

STITCH A WAISTBAND CASING FOR AN UNEVEN

I f you have an uneven waist horizon, you'll get better results if you add a separate waistband.

To do this, you will need a waistband pattern, scissors, a tape measure, nonroll elastic, your sewing machine, and thread.

STEP 1: Trim the casing portion from each of the skirt pattern pieces, leaving a ⅝-inch (1.6-cm) seam allowance, as shown in **Diagram 1.**

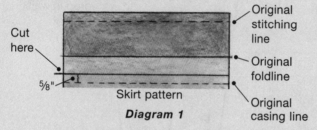

Diagram 1

Trim the casing portion from each of the skirt pattern pieces.

STEP 2: Measure the distance around the top of the garment, excluding the seam allowances. Cut out a waistband that is as long as the distance you measured plus 1¼ inches (3.2 cm) (for two seam allowances) and twice the width of the elastic plus 1½ inches (3.8 cm) (for two seam allowances plus ¼ inch [0.6 cm] for the turn of the cloth), as shown in **Diagram 2.**

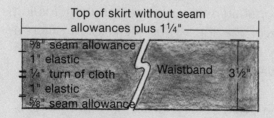

Diagram 2

Cut a separate waistband.

STEP 3: Place the two short ends of the waistband right sides together, and mark the center of the short side. Stitch a seam ⅝ inch (1.6 cm) long at the stitching line, as shown in **Diagram 3,** and backstitch. Lift the presser foot, slide the waistband toward the back of the machine, and place the needle at the center mark. Take a few stitches, backstitch, and then stitch the remainder of the seam, as shown in **Diagram 3.**

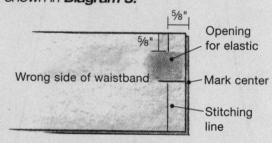

Diagram 3

Stitch the short ends of the waistband right sides together, leaving an opening for the elastic.

STEP 4: Press the seam allowances open and stitch them to the waistband to make it easier to insert the elastic, as shown in **Diagram 4.**

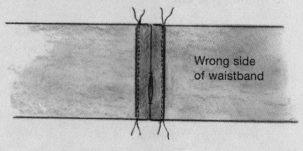

Diagram 4

Press the seam allowances open and stitch them to the waistband.

WAISTLINE

STEP 5: *Fold the waistband in half lengthwise, with the wrong sides together, and machine baste the two layers together at the stitching line, as shown in* **Diagram 5.** *Do not skip this step. It may seem like more work, but it will prevent the layers from slipping and forming a big pucker. Ripping takes more time than does sewing one extra seam.*

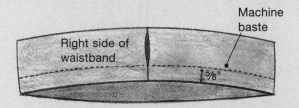

Right side of waistband

Machine baste

5/8"

Diagram 5

Machine baste the two layers of the waistband together at the stitching line.

STEP 6: *With right sides together, sew the waistband to the top of the skirt, as shown in* **Diagram 6.**

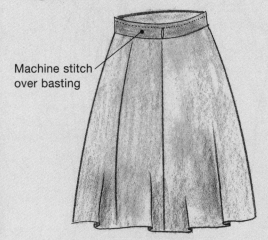

Machine stitch over basting

Diagram 6

With the right sides of the fabric together, sew the waistband to the top of the skirt.

STEP 7: *Measure the elastic by stretching it around your waist and testing it for comfort, as shown in* **Diagram 7.** *Each type and brand of elastic has a different amount of give. Always preshrink elastic, and test each piece on the body area where you are using it. This will ensure a comfortable and stable fit.*

To ensure a good fit, test the elastic by stretching it around your waist. When it feels comfortable, measure that length.

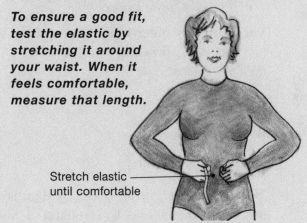

Stretch elastic until comfortable

Diagram 7

STEP 8: *Insert the elastic into the casing, overlap the ends, and stitch them together using a zigzag stitch, as shown in* **Diagram 8.** *Never place the sides of the elastic together and then stitch, creating a seam. It only adds bulk. Instead, overlap the pieces and sew them in place.*

Overlap, and sew

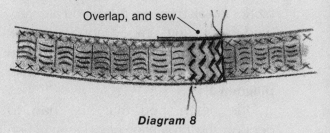

Diagram 8

Insert the elastic into the casing, overlap the ends, and stitch them together using a zigzag stitch.

Jan
(see page 151)

(see page 151)

LIFESTYLE

✦ **Runs a small farm with her husband, raising vegetables, herbs, and flowers**

✦ **Mother of six and grandmother of seven**

✦ **Sews most of her clothing**

✦ **World traveler**

FITTING CHALLENGE

Very full, low outer hips. *If Jan makes her slacks to fit her waistline, they are too tight in the hips.*

GARMENT
Rayon slacks

REMEDY

STEP 1: Examine your body. By examining her croquis and by creating a My Twin Bodyform of herself, Jan found that she has very full, low outside hips, as shown in **Diagram 1**.

Jan constantly has a problem getting garments to hang from her waist and go out and over her hips without drawing attention to the fullness at that area of her body. (See the "Before" photo of Jan on page 151.)

STEP 2: Determine where to add more fabric. Jan also knows that if you are very hard to fit, a soft, drapey fabric will work and look much better on your body than a thick, crisp fabric will, as shown in **Diagram 2**.

Jan determined that she had to deepen the crotch of her pants. Since she has such wide hips, she also needed to add extra fabric to both the width and the length of her pattern pieces so

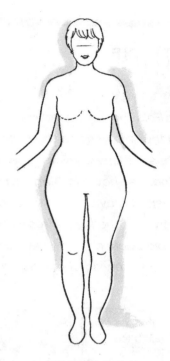

Diagram 1

By examining her croquis, Jan determined that she has a very full, low outside hip.

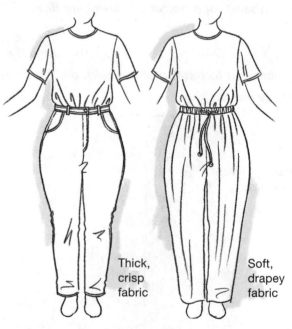

Thick, crisp fabric

Soft, drapey fabric

Diagram 2

Jan knows that a soft, drapey fabric will look better on her full hips than a thick, crisp fabric will.

that the pants can go out and over this area without pulling against the hips, as shown in **Diagram 3**.

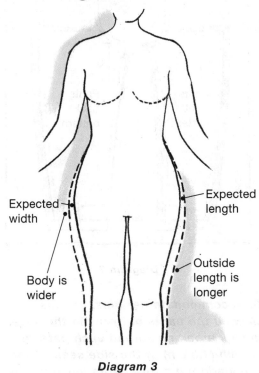

Diagram 3

Since Jan has such wide hips, she needs to add extra fabric to both the width and the length of her pattern pieces so that the pants can go out and over her hips.

STEP: Alter the pattern. Jan taped the pants front and back patterns to a piece of pattern paper. She drew the front crotch ½ inch (1.3 cm) deeper along the entire inseam, and she drew the back crotch 1¼ inches (3.2 cm) deeper, tapering to the inseam about 6 inches (15.2 cm) from the crotch point, as shown in **Diagram 4**. She made these alterations so that the fabric could reach the side seam and the inseam without having any pulls or wrinkles.

The addition to the back pattern made the back pattern longer than the section it had to match. Jan eased this back section onto the pants front, as shown in **Diagram 5**.

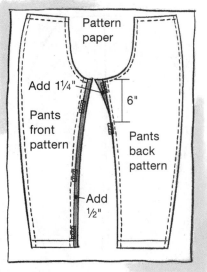

Diagram 4

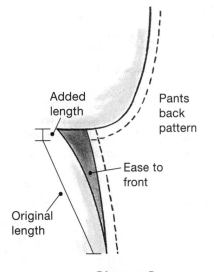

Diagram 5

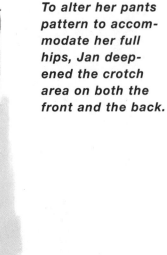

To alter her pants pattern to accommodate her full hips, Jan deepened the crotch area on both the front and the back.

Since the addition to the pants back pattern made it longer than the section it had to match, Jan eased the back section to the pants front when she stitched the pants together.

TIP: The only way anyone will see this easing is if Jan stands with one leg held up or sits with her legs spread wide apart. But the pants will fit much better with this alteration. If Jan added only to the outside seam, she would end up with a bulge at the outside of the hip area, as shown in **Diagram 6** on page 216, and the pants would resemble jodhpurs, which would be very unflattering.

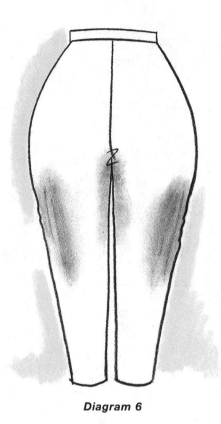

Diagram 6

If Jan had added only to the outside seam of the pants pattern, she would have ended up with a very unflattering bulge in the outside hip area.

To accommodate her wide hips, Jan lengthened the outside seams of the pants front and back patterns by slashing each pattern at her actual hip level and opening the slash ½ inch (1.3 cm) at the side seam only, pivoting from the stitching line at the center front and the center back, as shown in **Diagram 7**. Then she made the overall pants leg wider by adding 1 inch (2.5 cm) at the side seam cutting line along the length of each pattern.

Jan added a dart at the center front and the center back of the hemline of each pants leg, as shown in **Diagram 7**, to give the pants added contour.

Then she added two tucks to each pants front pattern to shape the waist, as shown in **Diagram 8**.

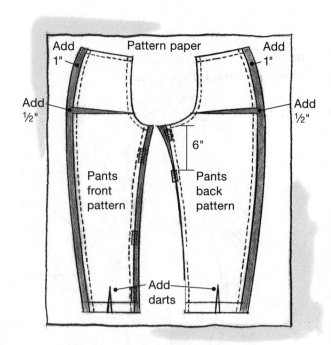

Diagram 7

To accommodate her hips, Jan also slashed the pants patterns in the lower tummy area and spread each pattern ½ inch (1.3 cm) at the side seam. Then she made the entire pants leg wider by adding 1 inch to each side seam.

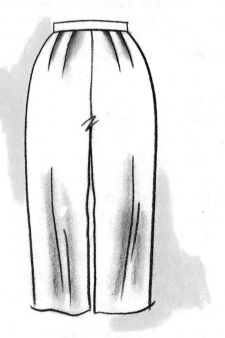

Diagram 8

Jan used four tucks to shape and contour the waistline of her pants.

After Jan assembled the pants, she pinned a length of elastic around her waist, catching the top of the pants under it. She folded the tucks at different positions across the front of the pants, analyzing how they worked, using straight pins to hold them in place, as shown in **Diagram 9.** It's best to decide the placement, number, and depth of the tucks at this stage because the different combinations of body shape, pattern, and fabric will give varied results. It is best to create a custom fit on each garment you sew.

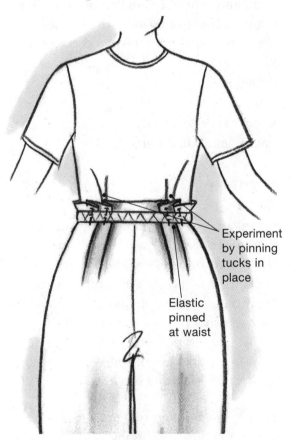

Diagram 9

Test the placement of the waistline tucks before you sew them in place on your pants. Put on the partially assembled pants, and experiment folding the tucks at different positions on the front of the pants.

Because her waist is so much smaller than her hips, Jan never uses diagonal slashed pockets. This pocket would point straight to the fullest part of her body. Jan knows that an inseam pocket is more flattering to her, and so she puts this pocket in all of her slacks and skirts. To do this, she tapes into place the pocket piece that fills in the slash space, matching the stitching lines and taping the pattern pieces together, as shown in **Diagram 10.**

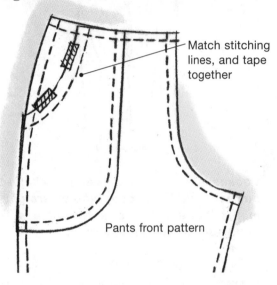

Diagram 10

Because diagonal slashed pockets would draw attention to the large difference between her waist and hip sizes, Jan always creates inseam pockets, taping into place the pocket piece that fills in the slash space.

Look at the "After" photo of Jan on page 151, and you will see the improved fit in her slacks. By examining her croquis and her measurements worksheet, Jan learned how important it is to balance out her lower body. Garments that add a lot of extra fullness and width to her shoulders are particularly flattering to Jan's body type, as shown in **Diagram 11** on page 218.

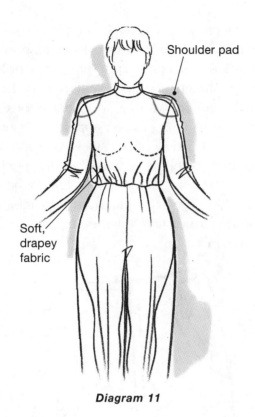

Shoulder pad

Soft, drapey fabric

Diagram 11

Because Jan knows she has to balance out her wide lower body, she wears garments that add a lot of extra fullness and width to her shoulders.

To have a pleasing outline, it is very important that the shoulders be wide enough to match, or at least complement, the hip area.

From season to season, fashion experts declare shoulder pads either in or out. Professional models have shoulders that stick out farther than the rest of their bodies, so clothes hang on them easily and attractively. If your body is less than ideally proportioned and your shoulders are narrow compared to your arms, waist, or hips, you should add width with shoulder pads—no matter whether the fashion experts have declared them "in" or "out." Shoulder pads will help your clothes hang better and will give you a more attractive appearance.

Karlene

(see page 152)

LIFESTYLE

+ **Mother of six and grandmother of three**
+ **Enjoys textile arts**
+ **Teaches special reading classes**
+ **Reads and enjoys listening to jazz**
+ **Likes to paint with watercolors and belongs to artists' group**

FITTING CHALLENGE

Flat fanny; shorter than height for which commercial patterns are designed. *Karlene's pants are always too baggy in the fanny, and she always has to adjust the length.*

GARMENT

Rayon gabardine pants

REMEDY

STEP: Examine your body. Karlene examined her croquis and her measurements worksheet and determined that she has a very shallow, flat fanny. Almost every pair of pants she has tried on or attempted to sew in the past has had way too much fabric hanging below her fanny, like the pair shown in the "Before" photo of Karlene on page 152. In addition, Karlene's pants are always too long.

STEP: Determine where you need less fabric. Because her fanny is shallow and flat, Karlene needed to remove the excess fabric in that area. The fanny is supposed to fill in the distance between the back seam and the inseam on the shelf of the pants, as shown in **Diagram 1** on page 220. When there is not enough flesh to support the fabric, the fabric collapses.

STEP 3: Alter the pattern. To get rid of the fullness in the fanny area, fabric must be removed the whole length of the inseam. To decide how much to remove from the pattern, I measure the front of the crotch and the back of the crotch separately so I can determine where the inseam should

hang. I've made my own tool to take this measurement. (See "Make a Crotch Tape Measure" below.)

With the crotch tape measure placed loosely against Karlene's body and her feet spread far enough apart to allow the tape to hang straight between the legs, I slid the tape from front to back until the tail

Make a Crotch Tape Measure

I like to measure the front of the crotch and the back of the crotch separately so that I can determine exactly where the pants inseam should hang. To make your own crotch tape measure, you will need three tape measures, each 60 inches (152.4 cm) or longer, scissors, and duct tape.

STEP 1: Cut two tape measures in half at the 30-inch (76.2-cm) mark, as shown in **Diagram 1.**

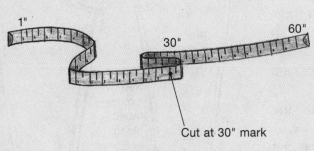

Cut at 30" mark

Diagram 1

Cut two tape measures in half at the 30-inch (76.2 cm) mark.

STEP 2: Join the zero ends of the two tapes that were cut in Step 1 in the center, facing you, and then tape them together on the back side with duct tape, as shown in **Diagram 2.**

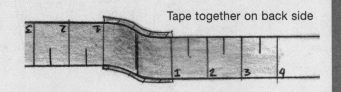

Tape together on back side

Diagram 2

To make the portion of the tape that measures from the crotch to the waist, join the zero ends of two tapes in the center, facing you, and then tape them together on the back side with duct tape.

STEP 3: Using a piece of duct tape on each side, attach the third tape measure so that its zero end is perpendicular to the zero marks on the front of the joined tapes, as shown in **Diagram 3.**

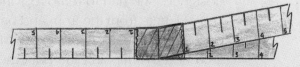

Diagram 3

Using duct tape, attach the third tape measure so that its zero end is perpendicular to the zero marks on the joined tapes.

Because her bottom is shallow and flat, Karlene needed to remove excess fabric from the back of her pants.

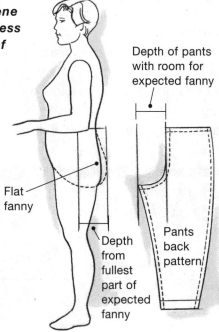

Diagram 1

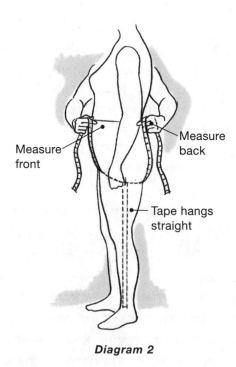

Diagram 2

By using the crotch tape measure, you can measure the front of the crotch and the back of the crotch separately to determine where the inseam should hang.

hung between her ankles, as shown in **Diagram 2.** Then I noted the length of the tape at the front and the back of the waist.

Next, Karlene measured along the center back stitching line on the pants back pattern. Her back measurement was much shorter than the pattern measured. In Karlene's case, she had to remove the excess fabric from the inseam all the way to the hem cutting line, as shown in **Diagram 3.**

Because she is shorter than the height for which the pattern was designed, she had to remove 1 inch (2.5 cm) of length from the front and back patterns by slashing them in the tummy area and overlapping the pattern pieces ½ inch (1.3 cm), as shown in **Diagram 3.**

Because Karlene is not very tall, she looks best in slacks made with a small amount of ease in a medium-weight fabric, like those shown in the "After" photo of her on page 152. That way, the pants don't overwhelm the shape of her body.

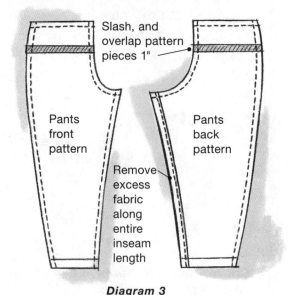

Diagram 3

To accommodate her small fanny, Karlene removed the excess fabric from the entire inseam length on the back pattern. Because she is not as tall as commercial patterns expect her to be, she also removed 1 inch (2.5 cm) of length from the front and back patterns.

Cynthia

(see page 152)

LIFESTYLE

✦ **Works in human resources department of large company**

✦ **Enjoys sewing for herself and her family**

✦ **Quiet soul who nevertheless has a penchant for Godzilla and other horror movies and has read every Stephen King and Dean Koontz novel**

FITTING CHALLENGE

Full fanny; short-waisted; taller than height for which commercial patterns are designed. *Cynthia is 6 feet tall, and her slacks are always too short. Her slacks frequently pull across her full fanny.*

GARMENT

Rayon twill pants

REMEDY

STEP 1: Examine your body. When Cynthia examined her croquis, she discovered that she is short-waisted and has a very full fanny. Plus, patterns are never long enough to fit Cynthia's 6-foot-tall body.

STEP 2: Determine where you need more fabric. Cynthia needed to add to the length of her pattern pieces so that her garments would go out and over her hips and fanny.

STEP 3: Alter the pattern. To make her "Before" garment, Cynthia added to the length of the pants according to what the pattern instructions recommended for her height. But Cynthia is short-waisted and even longer legged than most 6-foot-tall women, so the pants still weren't quite long enough, as shown in the "Before" photo of Cynthia on page 152.

Because Cynthia has a full fanny, the depth of the crotch from the fullest part of the bottom to the inseam was not deep enough in her pattern size. She taped the pants back pattern to a piece of pattern paper and added to the crotch depth at the inseam, as shown in **Diagram 1.**

Cynthia doesn't have much of a tummy, but she is full over the side hip. To get an even horizon, she slashed the pants back pattern 10 inches (25.4 cm) from the waistline seam (where her fanny is widest) and added 1½ inches (3.8 cm) at the center back and 1 inch (2.5 cm) at the side seam, retaping the pattern pieces to the pattern paper, as shown in **Diagram 1.** She then cut out the new pants back pattern.

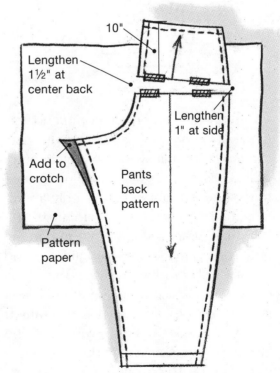

10"

Lengthen 1½" at center back

Lengthen 1" at side

Add to crotch

Pants back pattern

Pattern paper

Diagram 1

Although Cynthia doesn't have a tummy, she does have full hips. To get an even horizon, she slashed and added to the pants back pattern and also added to the crotch.

To get additional fabric to cover her hips, Cynthia also slashed the pants front pattern and spread it 1 inch (2.5 cm) at the side seam, tapering to nothing at the center front, as shown in **Diagram 2.** She taped the pattern to a piece of pattern paper and cut out the new pattern piece.

To get extra fabric to cover her hips, Cynthia also slashed the pants front pattern and spread it 1 inch (2.5 cm) at the side seam, tapering to nothing at the center front.

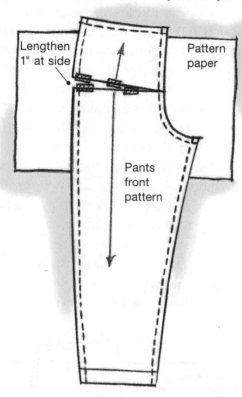

Diagram 2

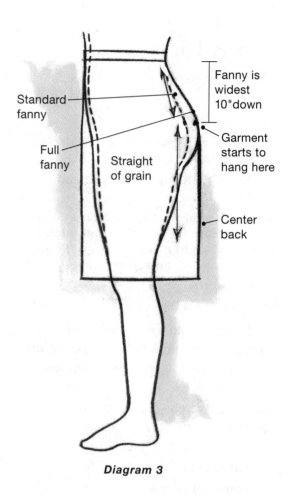

Diagram 3

Cynthia can make the changes to her skirt and pants patterns without concern about the fabric grain. The straight of grain is only important once the garment starts to hang.

Frequently, when I recommend this kind of alteration, sewers will ask, "Doesn't that throw off the straight of grain?" The straight of grain creates smooth, even drape, but it's only important once the garment starts to hang. The straight of grain is going to be true to the grain of the fabric, both lengthwise and crosswise, from the fanny and the hips downward, which is where the garment is hanging from, as shown in **Diagram 3.**

Cynthia has a small waist, so she increased the number of darts on each side of the back from one to two, as shown in the "After" photo of Cynthia on page 152.

TIP: If you have a small waist and take in a garment only at the side seams, the overall proportion of the garment will generally be off. Instead, I take it in in small increments all the way around the top of the garment by increasing the number of darts.

By creating her croquis and taking accurate measurements, Cynthia has gained a complete view of her individual body, and she now creates great-fitting garments.

Looking Good
Short-Waisted Solutions

If you are short-waisted, you are shorter from the base of the back of your neck to your waist than the length for which commercial patterns are designed. You must find ways to get the fabric of a blouse or top to extend below the waist, thereby lengthening the waist. You can drop the waistline on your blouse, top, or sweaters in order to give the illusion of having a longer waist, as shown below and at right.

Deepen a ribbed waistband and shorten the body of the garment.

You can also wear a vest or a blouse with a vest-shaped bottom, as shown below.

If you are making a pair of pants or a skirt that goes with a blouse, make the waistband for the pants or the skirt from the blouse fabric instead of the pants fabric, thereby lengthening the waist visually, as shown below.

Make a blouse that has a dropped waistline.

A short waist can be visually lengthened by changing the hemline on a blouse.

Make your waist appear longer by using the blouse fabric for the pants waistband.

Putting the Pieces in Place

Now is the time to put all the puzzle pieces together. Take your croquis and your measurements worksheet with you each and every time you go to the store to choose a pattern or fabric. Here, JoAnn has taken all of her tools with her and is trying to find just the right jacket pattern for her fabric and her body.

Seeing Is Believing

You cannot fit what you cannot see. If you've already made your croquis, taken complete and accurate measurements, and really looked at how you are built, please proceed. If you haven't, do it now!

To determine which garment styles are right for you, sketch the clothes on your croquis. When you use your croquis to plan your wardrobe, your clothes will be correctly proportioned.

I know by now you think I'm a nag, but working your way through the fitting process is exceedingly important if you want to achieve great results. I've given you all the parts of the fit puzzle. It's now your job to put these pieces together so you can begin to be happier and more successful in your sewing. You will find that the more you use the information you have collected, the easier it will be for you to make great-fitting garments.

Get Great Clothes from the Start

The photographs in the previous chapter show you different body shapes and the alterations that are necessary to make clothes to fit those bodies. You may have some of the same fitting challenges.

When you look through this book, notice all the women in leotards who are willing to let you observe their bodies. None of these women have bags over their heads or black lines through their eyes to hide their identities. They may not have "perfect" bodies according to Madison Avenue, but they are joyous about who and what they are.

Every one of these women has used my fitting process combined with her own sewing knowledge to make her garments. Each understands how important it is to know how her body differs from the shape of the Wolf dress form. It is important for you, too, to know the same things!

Every time you go to your favorite fabric store to browse through pattern books and fondle fabric, take along all of the new knowledge that you have gained. Most of you are aware of the kind of garments and the type of fit you don't

"Be joyous about who and what you are."

like. This book has focused on helping you to define clearly what it is you do like in your clothing before you pick a pattern and fabric and to understand that you have to make these decisions before you begin to create the garment.

So, when you look through the pattern books, do it with your eyes open. Keep in mind my three-dimensional fitting process as you take note of which patterns draw your attention. Be careful

(continued on page 230)

FOOLING THE EYE

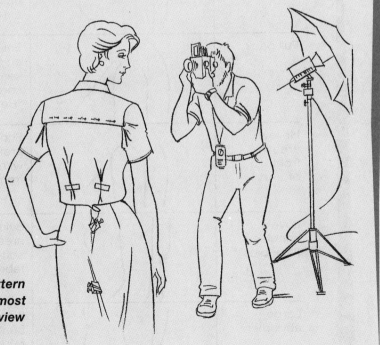

In the past, you may have fallen in love with a photograph in a pattern book because the professional model looked great. But what you didn't know is that the size 6 model may have been wearing a garment made from a size 14 pattern. You cannot see that behind her the clothes are taped, pinned, clipped, or stuffed so that they hang correctly.

Don't be fooled by all the gorgeous models with "perfect" bodies in magazines and pattern books. The clothes they are wearing are almost always manipulated in places hidden from view to give them that perfect look.

QUICK BODY REFERENCE

I have assembled some general guidelines for altering garments, and I've organized them by body part for easy reference. These are very broad recommendations.

You must consider your entire body, the fabric you've chosen, and your personal preferences. Use your croquis to verify which information will work best on your body.

FITTING CHALLENGE	BODY SHAPE	REMEDY
Small shoulders		Remove excess fabric from the shoulders without skimping on the rest of garment. Use a pattern with a yoke, shoulder alterations, princess seams, or darts. Check the width of the shoulder on the pattern piece. (See "Beverly" on page 160.)
Small bust		If your bust is smaller than a B cup, you must remove the excess fabric from the front of the garment or it will collapse and cause wrinkles in the chest area. Use a pattern without traditional darts. Princess seams can be adjusted. Knit fabrics are a good choice, and minimal ease is best. (See "Dorothy" on page 167.)
Large bust		Add ½ inch of fabric to the front pattern for each bust size larger than a B cup. Use a pattern with darts or princess seams and one that can be widened and lengthened to allow for the fuller bust depth. Single flat pieces cannot be contoured for a smooth fit. (See "Cindy" on page 181.)
Full back		Enlarge the pattern specifically in the back not just on the sides. Use a pattern with a yoke, princess seams from the shoulder or the armscye, or a center back seam. Create shoulder darts. (See "Beverly" on page 160.)
Hollow area in front of arm		Shorten the front of the garment in the upper chest area and narrow the area if necessary. Use a pattern with princess seams extending from the armscye or from a yoke. (See "Dorothy" on page 167.)
Love handles ("floobies")		Select garments that have fullness in the midriff area in the front and especially in the back. Use a soft fabric that has lots of ease, or use a crisp fabric with a pattern with princess seams. (See "Your Body's Clothes Hanger" on page 86.)
Large abdomen		If your abdomen is larger than or equal to your bust, you must find ways to keep the fabric from pulling against your body. Use a pattern with princess seams or a yoke with gathers or tucks below it for extra fabric. (See "Cheryle" on page 174.)

FITTING CHALLENGE	BODY SHAPE	REMEDY
Large tummy		You must add length and width to the front of pants and skirts. Use gentle sloping lines to insert fabric. (See "Cheryle" on page 174.)
Extra-small waist		You must reduce the amount of fabric around the waist in a number of areas. Add more and/or deeper fitting mechanisms like pleats, tucks, or darts. (See "Dolores" on page 204.)
Thick waist		Choose garments that look good hanging straight or from the shoulder, or choose patterns that have fullness directly above and below the waist to create curves. (See "Your Body's Clothes Hanger" on page 86.)
Short waist		Find ways to get the fabric of a blouse, top, or sweater to extend below the waist, thereby lengthening the waist. (See "Looking Good: Short-Waisted Solutions" on page 223.)
Long waist		Nip in outer garments above the waist. (See my vest on page 98.) Use a wide waistband to visually reduce the length of the torso. (See "Cindy" on page 181.)
Large fanny		You must have enough fabric to cover the fullest part of the fanny to the center of the inseam on pants. Also, check your body outline: If you want to camouflage your fanny, use drapey fabric with medium to full amount of ease. (See "Cynthia" on page 221.) For jackets, choose princess seams to move from the upper body to the fuller lower body smoothly. (See "Barbara" on page 176.)
Small waist and full hips		Don't make pattern adjustments at the side seams only; this will only exaggerate the width of your hips. Choose a design that will allow you to increase the garment overall and decrease the waist. Remember, many small reductions (darts) will make the garment fit without creating unattractive pulls and wrinkles. (See "Jan" on page 214.)
Small waist and full fanny		Choose a pattern with darts. Make the skirt or pants fit the fanny and increase the darts to take in the waist. The bigger the difference, the more opportunities for fit are needed to make a smooth transition. Do not do this only at the sides as it will cause a bubble at the side and the garment will not fit smoothly. (See "Cynthia" on page 221.)

not to fall back into your old way of thinking. Do not concentrate on covering up your least favorite body area, but consider your overall body proportions.

When you find a pattern that you like, sketch it onto your croquis, paying careful attention to how it changes the overall proportions of your individual body shape.

As JoAnn, the woman pictured on page 224, begins to plan a jacket project, she will look at the finished length measurement on the back of the pattern envelope. Because she has her finished jacket length measurement noted on her worksheet, JoAnn will be able to sketch onto her croquis a fairly close picture of what the garment will look like on her body.

TIP: Add garment measurements to your worksheet as needed. If you know you want a 24-inch (61-cm) sleeve, write that on the worksheet. The more information you have at the beginning of a project, the more likely you are to be successful at the end.

Always compare the garment length measurement on the pattern with where that length would happen on your body. For instance, if a jacket says the back length is 33 inches (83.8 cm) and your back length is 15 inches (38.1 cm), that would leave 18 inches (45.7 cm) below your waist. If your hip is 8 inches (20.3

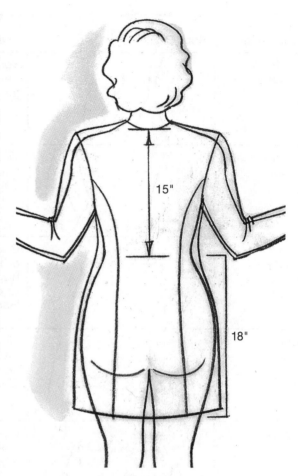

This sewer knows that her back measures 15 inches (38.1 cm). By using the length measurement provided on the jacket pattern, she sketched the garment on her croquis and found that it would fall 18 inches (45.7 cm) below her waist.

cm) below your waist, the jacket would end up at the middle of your thigh. Draw that on the croquis, too.

If you are planning to make other garments that will be worn with the jacket, such as a blouse and skirt, sketch them onto the croquis as well.

Build Your Wardrobe

*What each woman needs is a versatile wardrobe—
what I define as a related group of interchangeable garments
and coordinating accessories.*

Each woman's body is going to be enhanced by some garments and not as much by others. When you find a winning garment, use it more than once. As you sew garments that fit you as you had hoped, you will gradually develop a wardrobe of great interchangeable pieces that enhance your personal style. Mix and match the colors, textures, and prints, and suddenly you will have a group of clothes that intermix and make dressing a snap.

You don't need to be boring. You can change patterns as you go along. But remember no matter how well you alter and adjust certain patterns, some styles will never flatter your body. A woman with full hips will have a more pleasing silhouette if she wears a soft, flowing garment on the bottom. A full-busted woman needs opportunities for fit in the chest. Certain garments will be your favorites because they fit best.

You must use *all* of the tools I have given you, *and* you must use them correctly before you can begin to figure out the answers to your fitting problems.

As you sew garments that fit, you will develop a closet filled with great pieces that enhance your personal style.

Wit & Wisdom

If you want a new body to go with your new garment, stop now! Don't bother to strive for perfection because it doesn't exist. Be satisfied and happy with the comfortable and attractive clothes that enhance your individuality.

Successful Fabric Shopping

Now that you know why and how to alter your patterns to fit your body, you'll want to shop for fabric. To make every fabric shopping trip successful, follow these six simple steps:

STEP 1: After you record your measurements on a copy of the worksheet from page 52, make an extra copy to keep in your handbag.

STEP 2: Know what size pattern is recommended by the pattern companies for each area of your body. (See the charts at the back of each pattern manufacturer's catalog.)

STEP 3: Know how much wearing ease you prefer in your garments, including jackets, blouses, dresses, skirts, and pants. (See "Style, Fit, and Ease" on page 67.) Check the notes you took when you measured your favorite clothes for any ease information.

STEP 4: Check how your wearing ease preference compares to the ease that was designed into the pattern. Remove the pattern from the envelope, if needed, and measure between the stitching lines, as shown in **Diagram 1.**

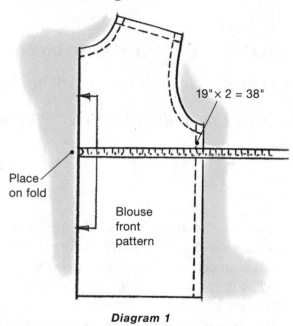

19" × 2 = 38"

Place on fold

Blouse front pattern

Diagram 1

To check how your wearing ease preference compares to the ease that was designed into a pattern, measure the pattern.

Also, check the "width at bottom edge" information on the pattern envelope for more insight into the design ease.

TIP: If the pattern is for a very loose-fitting garment, keep in mind that if you make it in a soft, drapey fabric, such as rayon challis, you should make the garment one size smaller than you normally would use.

STEP 5: Know what part or parts of your body are unlike the Wolf dress form, as shown in **Diagram 2.** This will show you

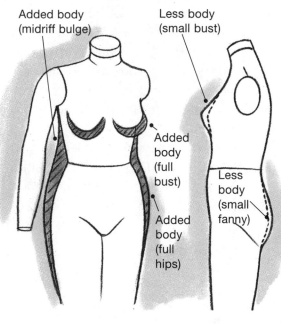

Added body
(midriff bulge)

Less body
(small bust)

Added
body
(full
bust)

Added
body
(full
hips)

Less
body
(small
fanny)

Diagram 2

"Follow the fabric guidelines on the pattern envelope."

Picture a Wolf dress form with your body shape. Would it have more or less of a bust? Larger or smaller fanny? Fuller hips? A tummy? It's important to know how you differ from this industry norm in order to buy patterns in the right size and alter them in the right places.

where you need more or less fabric. Where are your fitting challenges? Where are you uncomfortable about how the fabric hangs on your body?

STEP: Be sure the pattern you are considering has the correct opportunities for fit for your body. (See **Diagram 3**.) To do

Diagram 3

While the blouse on the left looks very attractive on the woman who has a very Norma Wolf–like figure, it does not have sufficient opportunities for fit for a woman with a very full bust and small shoulders.

this, look at the outline and the details of the pattern pieces. (For additional information, see the chapter "Opportunities for Fit" on page 74.)

Fabric and Fit

When I'm working in my store, I sometimes hear a customer say, "I just love this fabric." It is good to use great fabric, but you may like a fabric that won't work well in the garment you are planning.

You must *always* cross reference the garment design with fabric variables. For example, there are so many beautiful cotton fabrics in fabulous prints and yummy-colored solids on the market today. But most of them have been developed for quilting, so they have quite a lot of body in them. These quilting fabrics are so beautiful that garment sewers are tempted to make garments from them when, in fact, the recommendations on the pattern envelope call for

Wit & Wisdom

Instead of keeping a special piece of fabric for that day when you lose XX pounds, use it now. Dress the body you have in garments that make you look and feel your best.

rayon or a lighter, drapier fabric. Combining the wrong fabric with the wrong pattern can lead to a wadder.

There are some garment patterns made especially for quilting cottons, such as Rosemary Eichorn's collage vest, as shown at right. Use these pat-

terns if you can't live without the fabric. (See "Resources" on page 241.)

You must follow the fabric guidelines that are printed on the pattern envelope no matter how gorgeous the color, print, or texture of a fabric you find. If the pattern calls for a soft, drapey fabric, *use* a soft, drapey fabric.

You can't achieve great fit until you acknowledge the importance of fabric and take those differences into consideration in every project.

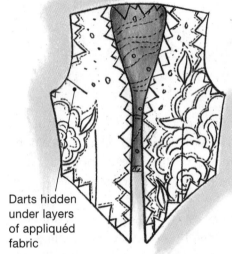

Darts hidden under layers of appliquéd fabric

If you can't live without the gorgeous quilting cottons that are available today, use a pattern made especially for those fabrics, such as Rosemary Eichorn's collage vest pattern.

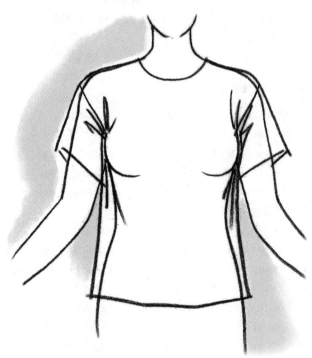

Sometimes you may like a fabric that just won't work in the garment you are planning. For example, dropped shoulder blouses just don't work well with crisp fabrics.

Design Ease versus Wearing Ease

For years, all garments were oversize. While it was part of a fashion trend, a sewer got into the habit of buying patterns smaller than the pattern would recommend for a person with her measurements. She used the full, oversize design ease as wearing ease. If a sewer did not like as much ease as the style dictated, she would just buy a smaller size pattern.

Looking Good
Choosing a Pattern

I am always amazed at how little attention sewers pay to the actual shape of garments they purchase. I know this is why they often choose a pattern that is so wrong for their bodies. I say, if sewers were as picky about the clothes they purchase as the ones they make, they would be naked most of the time.

I have a slender, petite client who has ample hips. Actually she insists on referring to that area of her body as "buffalo hips," and I constantly have to remind her that buffalo hips do not come in a size 6 dress pattern. She is very small above the waist, which exaggerates the lower half of her body.

One day she came into my fabric store and said she wanted to replace her favorite black linen jacket. She had found a pattern that she claimed was "just like the one I own and love." Since I knew her body and her style preferences, I knew the pattern she had chosen was

never going to work. I saw the pattern was a "fast and easy" jacket with one back piece and single piece for each side of the front. If the jacket fit the top of her body, the bottom would be too small. If she got the jacket to fit around her hips, the top would be huge.

But she insisted that the pattern was just like the jacket she owned. In order for her to truly see that these garment designs were very different, I made her bring the original jacket into the store. Lo and behold, the jacket she owned and loved had princess seams in the front and back, giving her great opportunities for fit. Needless to say, she immediately selected a new pattern—with princess seams.

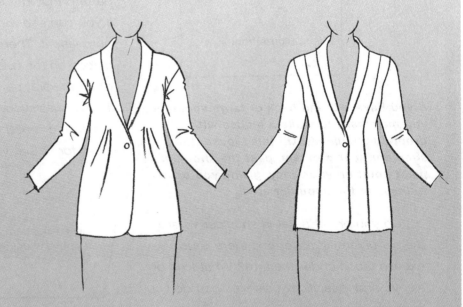

No matter how it looks in the pattern catalog, the "fast and easy" jacket on the left just won't look attractive on your body if your hips are a lot wider than your bust. You need a pattern with princess seams, like the jacket on the right, which has many more opportunities for fit.

Examine the Pattern Pieces

To get great-fitting garments, you must choose patterns that have opportunities for fit in the areas where you need to make changes. To help you recognize opportunities for fit, go back and look at the pieces of patterns you previously made. Start in the shoulder area, which is a prime area of dissatisfaction with patterns. What does a dropped shoulder look like?

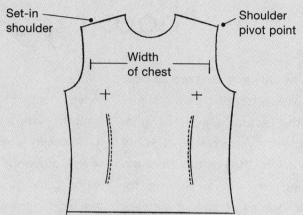

Set-in shoulder · Shoulder pivot point · Width of chest

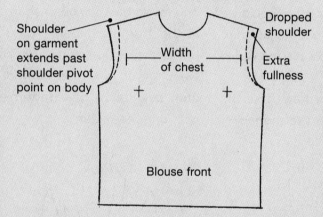

Shoulder on garment extends past shoulder pivot point on body · Dropped shoulder · Width of chest · Extra fullness

Blouse front

If you have a broad back or large shoulders, you may want to make a blouse with dropped shoulders. On this blouse, the shoulder seams extend past the shoulder pivot point on your body, giving you extra fullness in the shoulder area.

Do you prefer a set-in shoulder where the shoulders fit closer and there is no excess fabric under the arm? What kind of sleeve and, specifically, sleeve head do you prefer?

When choosing a pattern from a photograph or an illustration in a pattern catalog, it is often just about impossible to tell how the pattern pieces are shaped. When you see a

If you have small shoulders, you may prefer set-in shoulders where the shoulders fit closer and there is no excess fabric under the arms.

pattern that interests you, ask the salesclerk if you can see the actual pattern before you purchase it. There will be an outline of the pieces on the back of the pattern envelope or on the first page of the instruction sheet. These illustrations will give you insight into whether or not the pattern has the opportunities for fit that you need for your body.

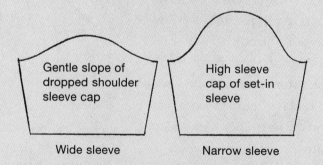

Gentle slope of dropped shoulder sleeve cap · High sleeve cap of set-in sleeve

Wide sleeve · Narrow sleeve

If you have full upper arms, you may prefer wide sleeves with dropped shoulders. If you have narrow upper arms, you may prefer high sleeve caps and narrow sleeves.

Clothes are now designed to be worn closer to the body. If you are still choosing a smaller pattern size, your garments are going to be too tight, and they won't fit you.

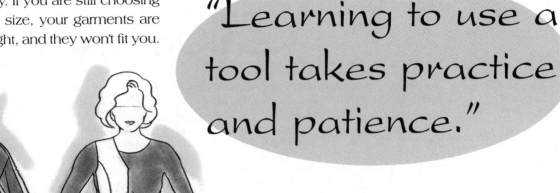

"Learning to use a tool takes practice and patience."

If you are a size 14, you may have been able to wear a size 10 in an oversize blouse, but you may find today's size 10 vest to be just too tight.

A few years ago I was working with a client who was very small-boned and did not like oversize clothing. At that time, most patterns were loose-fitting, and she had consistently purchased a size 10 pattern because she was using the design ease as wearing ease. When she chose a new, semifitted dress pattern that was designed to be worn closer to the body, she bought the same size 10 pattern.

As I looked at the pattern, I said, "You know, you'd better do some measuring and see how this close-cut style is going to fit." Unfortunately, she made the pattern according to the size she used in the past without allowing for the different ease factor, and guess what? After the dress was complete, she couldn't get into it.

Learning the Process

Before we can grasp new ideas, we must go through the learning process—even if we don't like it. The same is true with my fitting process. I know each of you wants absolute rules—a formula that will make everything come out fabulous. Well, I'm sorry, but there are no instant answers to getting a great fit. But I have given you the tools that will enable you to develop great fit.

You must follow all of the steps. You must find the correct combination of pattern, fabric, and ease. You must go through my entire process. Then you will find that each time you make a new garment, it will be easier to get a great fit. Soon it will become second nature.

Trust me. I know this process works.

Now you have to trust yourself and take time to experiment!

Glossary

Armscye (arms-eye): The opening in a garment for the arm and the sleeve; the armhole.

Basting: Large, loose stitches used to hold together two or more layers of fabric. Basting stitches, which can be sewn by hand or by machine, should be large enough to see and loose enough to be removed easily.

Bias: A 45-degree line that is diagonal to the selvage on a piece of woven fabric. Woven fabric has its greatest amount of stretch and flexibility along the bias.

Body form: A full-size representation of an individual's body that is created by wrapping the person with plaster casting, which is then removed, dried, and filled with foam. When smoothed and covered with fabric, a body form duplicates the person's body.

Box pleat: A pleat that is formed on the right side of the fabric by making two folds that face in opposite directions. The folds meet on the wrong side of the fabric.

Cap sleeve: A short sleeve that covers the top of the arm, ending approximately 3 inches (7.6 cm) from the shoulder.

Center back: The vertical line that runs the length of the garment in the middle of the back of the body.

Center front: The vertical line that runs the length of the garment in the middle of the front of the body.

Contour: To mimic the curves of the body.

Croquis (kro-key): The body outline used to design or illustrate fashions.

Crosswise grain: The threads that run from selvage to selvage in woven fabric.

Cuff: A separate band stitched to the end of a sleeve. The fabric above the cuff is usually pleated or gathered onto the band.

Dart: A fold of fabric that is stitched on the wrong side of the fabric to shape and contour a garment to the body. Darts are traditionally sewn from the raw edge of the fabric, tapering to a point at the interior of the garment.

Design ease: The amount of fabric in a garment in excess of the wearing ease that is needed to create the silhouette. *See also* **Ease** and **Wearing ease.**

Dickey: A piece of fabric that fills the neck opening of a garment.

Dress form: A full-size replication of an average human body. Some dress forms are made in the same sizes as ready-to-wear, and others can be adjusted to the same measurements as the sewer's body. *See also* **Gold dress form** and **Wolf dress form.**

Dropped-shoulder sleeve: A full, wide sleeve with a deep underarm that is stitched to the bodice of the garment past the actual shoulder joint on the body.

Ease: The amount of fabric in a garment in excess of the body measurements that allows room for movement or that is needed to create the silhouette. *See also* **Design ease** and **Wearing ease.**

Easing: Medium-to-long machine stitches that are pulled up slightly to allow the sewer to join two fabrics of slightly different lengths. Easing is used to contour flat pieces of fabric to fit a three-dimensional body.

Edgestitching: Machine stitching very close to the edge of a garment or a seamline for decoration and stabilization.

Elastic waistband: A waistband that is formed by stitching a casing and then threading elastic into the casing to pull up the excess fabric and hold the garment in place.

Extended shoulder: A garment shoulder that is 1 to 3 inches (2.5 to 7.6 cm) wider than the natural shoulder. Extended shoulders are usually supported by large, firm shoulder pads.

Fabric with stretch: Woven fabric with Lycra inserted to create stretch and recovery. Fabric with stretch improves comfort and allows garments to fit very close to the body.

Facing: A narrow piece of fabric that is stitched to the edge of a garment, right sides together; clipped; and then turned to cover the raw edges of the fabric.

Firm waistband: A waistband that has non-stretch interfacing and no give.

Full sleeve: A sleeve with more than 5 inches (12.7 cm) of ease. The fabric is gathered, tucked, or pleated to fit into the armscye.

Gathering: Long hand or machine stitches that are pulled up, creating gathers and eliminating excess fabric.

Give: Garment or fabric flexibility

Gold dress form: The full-size dress form that was designed to duplicate the average body of a woman age 55. *See also* **Dress form.**

Gore: A piece of fabric cut narrow at the top and full at the bottom. Several gores are sewn together to create a skirt.

Grain: The crosswise or lengthwise threads in woven fabric. *See also* **Crosswise grain** and **Lengthwise grain.**

Grainline: The line on a pattern piece that must be parallel to the lengthwise threads in woven fabric. *See also* **Lengthwise grain.**

Hemline: The line at the bottom of a garment where the fabric is turned to the wrong side to create a finished edge.

Hip fluff: The flesh that protrudes just below the waist and above the hip area.

Horizon: The garment hemline that should lie horizontally on the body so it doesn't draw attention to the area that is difficult to fit.

Interfacing: An additional layer of fabric that is added to a garment to provide extra support or stiffness.

In-the-ditch stitching: Machine stitching in the well of a seam or between two pieces of fabric to catch the bottom layer.

Inverted box pleat: A pleat that is formed on the wrong side of the fabric by making two folds that meet on the right side of the fabric.

Knit fabric: Fabric created by intertwining thread or yarn in a series of connected loops. Knit fabric has varying degrees of stretchiness.

Lengthwise grain: The threads that extend from one cut edge to the other in woven fabric. *See also* **Grainline.**

Lining: Fabric added to the inside of a garment to protect the fashion fabric from wear or to make the garment more comfortable to wear.

Narrow sleeve: A sleeve that fits very close to the skin and has very little ease.

One-piece sleeve: A sleeve constructed from a single pattern piece.

Open-ended dart: A line of stitching parallel to a fold that begins and ends perpendicular to the edge of the fabric.

Opportunity for fit: Any of various mechanisms that allow the sewer to fit clothes to the three-dimensional human body. These mechanisms include darts, pleats, princess seams, seams, tucks, yokes, and any other methods of helping the fabric shape to the body.

Pleat: A fold in the fabric made by doubling the material upon itself. A pleat is pressed or stitched to hold the fold in place.

Princess seam to armhole: A curved lengthwise seam that extends from the armscye to the hip. It is used to fit fabric smoothly to the human form and is an especially good fitting device for a person with a full bust.

Princess seam to shoulder: A curved lengthwise seam that extends from the middle of the shoulder to the hip. It is used to fit fabric smoothly to the body and is a good fitting device for a person whose shoulders, upper chest, or back are particularly small or large.

Push-up sleeve: A medium-to-long sleeve that has a larger than normal hemline opening so it can be pushed up and will stay in place.

Raglan sleeve: A one- or two-piece sleeve that joins to the bodice in a diagonal seam between the underarm and the neck on the front and the back of a garment. It may or may not have an additional seam on the shoulder and down the outside of the arm.

Seam: A line of stitches that holds two or more pieces of fabric together.

Seam allowance: The area between the stitching line and the raw edge of the fabric.

Seamline: The line on which the pieces of a garment are stitched together. Sometimes the seamline is marked on the pattern pieces. Also called stitching line.

Selvage: The finished lengthwise edge on a piece of woven fabric; each piece of fabric has two selvages.

Shaped raglan sleeve: A two-piece raglan sleeve that curves away from the front of the arm and away from the top center seam to take out excess fabric and create a flattering garment. *See also* **Raglan sleeve.**

Skim the waist: To create loose fit at the waist.

Sloper: A fitting shell made from muslin with minimum ease that fits the standard body for which a pattern company designs.

Stay stitching: Slightly shorter than normal stitches and sewn just inside the normal stitching line. This stitching is used to stabilize the area.

Stitching line: *See* **Seamline.**

Straight of grain: *See* **Grainline.**

Tuck: A flattened pleat. *See also* **Pleat.**

Two-piece sleeve: A sleeve with two lengthwise pieces. The curves and the angles of the pieces give shape and ease to the sleeve.

Wearing ease: The minimum amount of fabric allowed in a pattern so that a person can move about in the garment comfortably. *See also* **Design ease** and **Ease.**

Wolf dress form: A full-size, standardized and idealized human form for which designs are created by ready-to-wear and pattern companies. The shape has no lump or bumps and is very unrealistic. *See* **Dress form.**

Woven fabric: Cloth made by interlacing the crosswise and lengthwise threads on a loom. *See also* **Crosswise grain** and **Lengthwise grain.**

Yoke: A separate piece of fabric that closely fits the area it covers. It shapes the shoulder or the hip area. If the fabric that attaches to the yoke is wider than the yoke, the excess fabric can be tucked to give extra ease below the yoke.

Acknowledgments

I want to thank everyone who helped me make my vision for this book become a reality.

I extend my heartfelt thanks to all of the fabulous women from The Sewing Place, my fabric store in California. Employees, customers, students, and friends read, suggested, made samples, showed up just when I needed them, and generally encouraged me as I went through the painful process of birthing this book. I extend a special thanks to my partner, Dale Cunningham, who picked up the slack at the store when I was too busy to do my part.

I want to thank the models: Cara Alvernaz, Gena Alvernaz, Jane Arnold, Barbara Auer, Rosemary Berwald, JoAnn Bowser, Lynda Braden, Eileen Chang, Shirley Creitz, Dale Cunningham, Cheryle Custer, Cynthia Eckhart, Diane Emigh, Diane Ericson, Janet Hyland, Millie Kingham, Dorothy Klavins, Karlene Koketsu, Karen Kurtz, Mary Ellen Nixon, Ruth Paquet, Peggy Perruccio, Dolores Roseveare, Beverly Silva, Judith Van der Kooi, Cynthia Wakefield, Carolalee Winter, and Maureen Wormley. I can't thank them enough. They demonstrated their confidence and faith in themselves and me by sharing the clothes they made and, more important, their bodies with you. They worked diligently on their garments and put up with an incredible amount of pushing, prodding, and pos-ing for the photographs. All I can say is, "Bravo!"

To photographer John Hamel and assistant photographer John Grivas, thank you for seeing these women as beautiful and capturing that beauty and their radiant spirits in all of the photographs. I'd also like to thank Marta Strait for making the photos and the entire book look fabulous.

I want to thank my editor, Marya Kissinger Amig, who, with great humor and wisdom, guided me through writing and finishing this book even when I felt overwhelmed and discouraged. She kept the meaning intact while making my words flow more easily, and she polished the explanations to make them clear and concise.

To Cheryle Custer, who kept me from throwing my computer through the window by making it behave in spite of my lack of knowledge and enthusiasm for its idiosyncrasies—thank you. Thanks also to Cheryle, Dale, Eileen Chang, and several others for helping me to stay on the right track by reading many drafts.

From the bottom of my heart, I want to thank my husband, Dennis, and my daughters, Gena and Cara, who put up with take-out meals, microwave food, a permanent mess in the family room as well as my constant whining. Without their understanding, support, and love, this book would never have happened.

Resources

CSZ Enterprises

1288 W. 11th Street

Suite 200

Tracy, CA 95376

(209) 832-4324

Kits used to create the My Twin Bodyform

LH Enterprises

14403 Janal Way

San Diego, CA 92129

(619) 672-2122

Measuring Made Easy and Two Easy Tape™ set

Power Sewing

185 Fifth Avenue

San Francisco. CA 94118

(415) 386–0440

http://www.sandrabetzina.com

Books and videos by Sandra Betzina, which include Fitting Solutions *and* Fearless Serging

The Sewing Place

18476 Prospect Road

Saratoga, CA 95070

(408) 252-8444

(800) 587-3937 (for free catalog)

fax: (408) 252-8445

http://www.thesewingplace.com

Quality fashion fabrics; a wide range of unique patterns, including Gale Grigg Hazen's Patterns for EveryBODY, the Torii Collection from ReVision, and Rosemary Eichorn's vest patterns; Mönster pattern paper; interfacing, including Armo Weft and Sof Knit; shoulder pads; notions; and buttons; sewing classes by Gale Grigg Hazen, including special intensive courses for out-of-town students

Index

Note: Page references in *italic* indicate tables. **Boldface** references indicate photographs.

*Look for these and other Rodale Sewing books
wherever books are sold.*

High-Fashion Sewing Secrets from the World's Best Designers

A Step-by-Step Guide to Sewing Stylish Seams, Buttonholes, Pockets, Collars, Hems, and More

by Claire Shaeffer

Nationally known sewing expert Claire Shaeffer reveals the sewing secrets of fashion industry legends from Ralph Lauren to Yves Saint Laurent. You'll also discover that high-fashion sewing does not have to be difficult!

Hardcover ISBN 0-87596-717-5

Secrets for Successful Sewing

Techniques for Mastering Your Sewing Machine and Serger

by Barbara Weiland

The ultimate owner's manual, full of tips and techniques for mastering a machine—regardless of brand. Includes a comprehensive look at machines and their accessories, plus step-by-step instructions for the most popular and unique serger and sewing machine techniques. Barbara Weiland is the former editor of *Sew News*.

Hardcover ISBN 0-87596-776-0

The Experts' Book of Sewing Tips & Techniques

From the Sewing Stars of America— Hundreds of Ways to Sew Better, Faster, and Easier

edited by Marya Kissinger Amig, Barbara Fimbel, Stacey L. Klaman, Karen Kunkel, and Susan Weaver

Learn the trade secrets of the top sewing experts in this easy-to-use guide. Hints and tips, from appliqué to zippers, are covered in alphabetical order.

Hardcover ISBN 0-87596-682-9

No Time to Sew

Fast & Fabulous Patterns & Techniques for Sewing a Figure-Flattering Wardrobe

by Sandra Betzina

Sandra Betzina, star of the television series "Sew Perfect," helps you to sew in record time, offering stylish patterns, step-by-step instructions, timesaving tips, and wardrobe advice. A complete set of multisize patterns is included with the book.

Hardcover ISBN 0-87596-744-2

Sewing Secrets from the Fashion Industry

Proven Methods to Help You Sew Like the Pros

edited by Susan Huxley

Learn the same tips and techniques that the industry professionals use in their sample rooms and production factories. Over 800 full-color photographs accompany the step-by-step instructions.

Hardcover ISBN 0-87596-719-1

Serger Secrets

High-Fashion Techniques for Creating Great-Looking Clothes

by Mary Griffin, Pam Hastings, Agnes Mercik, Linda Lee Vivian, and Barbara Weiland

Get the most from your serger, regardless of brand! More than 500 color photographs guide you, step-by-step, through making beautiful serger details for your garments. Choose from more than 80 classy techniques. Learn to select the best threads, needles, and stitches. Master tension settings once and for all.

Hardcover ISBN 0-87596-794-9

Available September 1998